EX AUDITU

An International Journal for the Theological Interpretation of Scripture

VOL. 26   **2010**

Ex Auditu is published annually by Pickwick Publications, an imprint of
Wipf and Stock Publishers, 199 West 8th Avenue, Suite 3, Eugene, Oregon 97401, USA

SUBSCRIPTIONS

Individuals:
U.S.A. and all other countries (in U.S. funds): $20.00
Students: $12.00

Institutions:
U.S.A. and all other countries (in U.S. funds): $30.00

This periodical is indexed in the ATLA Religion Database, published by the American Theological Library Association, 300 S. Wacker Dr., Suite 2100, Chicago, IL 60606, Email: atla@atla.com, www: http://www.atla.com/; *Internationale Zeitschriftenshau für Bibelwissenschaft; Religious and Theological Abstracts;* and *Old Testament Abstracts.*

Please address all subscription correspondence
and change of address information to Wipf and Stock Publishers.

©2011 by Wipf and Stock Publishers
ISSN: 0883-0053
ISBN: 978-1-61097-482-0

EX AUDITU

An International Journal for the Theological Interpretation of Scripture

Klyne R. Snodgrass, Editor
Stephen J. Chester, Associate Editor
D. Christopher Spinks, Associate Editor

North Park Theological Seminary
3225 West Foster Avenue
Chicago, Illinois 60625-4987
USA

Tel: (773) 244-6243
Fax: (773) 244-6244
email: ksnodgrass@northpark.edu
Web site: http://wipfandstock.com/journals/ex_auditu

EDITORIAL BOARD

Terence E. Fretheim, Luther Seminary, St. Paul, MN
Richard B. Hays, The Divinity School, Duke University, Durham, NC
Jon R. Stock, Wipf & Stock Publishers, Eugene, OR
Miroslav Volf, Yale Divinity School, New Haven, CT
John Wipf, Wipf & Stock Publishers, Eugene, OR

THE EDITORIAL BOARD MEMBERS AND CONSULTANTS represent various disciplines and denominations. Theological interpretation of Scripture is a task to be taken seriously by scholars who are committed to the Christian faith and tradition. However, as one editorial consultant stated: "Let people gradually get used to the idea that a sane hermeneutics is both oriented in advance toward agreement/consent and is simultaneously exigent, discriminating, critical."

EDITORIAL CONSULTANTS

Richard Bauckham
University of St. Andrews, Emeritus
St. Andrews, Scotland

M. Daniel Carroll R.
Denver Seminary
Denver, Colorado

Jan Du Rand
Emeritus, University of Johannesburg
and Extraordinary Professor, North West University

Willie Jennings
The Divinity School
Duke University
Durham, N. Carolina

Robert Johnston
Fuller Theological Seminary
Pasadena, California

R. Walter L. Moberly
University of Durham
Durham, England

Kathleen M. O'Connor
Columbia Theological Seminary
Decatur, Georgia

Iain Provan
Regent College
Vancouver, B.C.

Anthony Thiselton
University of Nottingham
Nottingham, England

Augustine Thompson
University of Virginia
Charlottesville, Virginia

Marianne Meye Thompson
Fuller Theological Seminary
Pasadena, California

Kevin J. Vanhoozer
Wheaton College
Wheaton, Illinois

Geoffrey Wainwright
The Divinity School
Duke University
Durham, N. Carolina

Sondra Wheeler
Wesley Theological Seminary
Washington, D.C.

William H. Willimon
Bishop of the North Alabama Conference
The United Methodist Church
Birmingham, Alabama

N. T. Wright
St Mary's College,
University of St Andrews, Scotland

CONTENTS

Announcement of the 2011 Symposium	v
Abbreviations	vi
Introduction Klyne Snodgrass	vii
"In Him All Things Hold Together": An Ecology of Atonement William P. Brown	1
Response to Brown Michael LeFebvre	21
Effecting the Covenant: A (Not So) New, New Testament Model for the Atonement Michael J. Gorman	26
Response to Gorman Troy Martin	60
Response to Martin Michael J. Gorman	67
"Anyone Hung on a Tree Is Under God's Curse" (Deuteronomy 21:23): Jesus' Crucifixion and Interreligious Exegetical Debate in Late Antiquity Peter W. Martens	69
"Happily Ever After?" Paul Peter Waldenström: Be Ye Reconciled to God Michelle A. Clifton-Soderstrom	91
Response to Clifton-Soderstrom Timothy L. Johnson	107
The Social Dimension of Atonement in the Torah Viktor Ber	110

Contents

Response to Ber *Jeremy J. Wynne*	125
"To Those Who Were Distant and Those Who Were Near": Atonement, Identity, and Identification *Brian Bantum*	128
An Evangelical Feminist Perspective on Traditional Atonement Models *Linda D. Peacore*	145
Response to Peacore *Jo Ann Deasy*	164
Saving Bodies: Anagogical Transposition in St. Gregory of Nyssa's Commentary on the Song of Songs *Hans Boersma*	168
Ransomed, Healed, Restored, Forgiven (John 5:1–16) *Carol Norén*	201
Annotated Bibliography on Atonement	205
Presenters and Respondents	221
Ex Auditu – Volumes Available	223

ANNOUNCEMENT OF THE 2011 SYMPOSIUM

North Park Theological Seminary in Chicago, Illinois, is pleased to announce that the twenty-seventh Symposium on the Theological Interpretation of Scripture will take place September 29–October 1, 2011. The symposium will start at 7:00 p.m. on September 29 in Nyvall Hall and will extend through a Saturday afternoon worship service on October 1. The theme in 2011 will be a Christian view of Wealth and Possessions. The following persons have agreed to make presentations:

>   Jonathan Bonk, Overseas Ministry Studies Center, New Haven, CT, Missions
>   Javier Comboni, Wheaton College, Economics
>   Gary Hoag, Trinity College, Bristol, UK, New Testament
>   Mark Husbands, Hope College, Holland, MI, Theology
>   Kelly Johnson, University of Dayton, Theology
>   Bruce Longenecker, Baylor University, New Testament
>   Helen Rhee, Westmont College, Patristics
>   Hugh Williamson, University of Oxford, Old Testament
>   William Willimon, North Alabama Conference of the UMC, Preaching.

Persons interested in attending the sessions should write before September 1 to:

>   Ms. Guylla Brown
>   North Park Theological Seminary
>   3225 W. Foster Avenue
>   Chicago, Illinois 60625

Meals may be taken at North Park and assistance can be provided in finding nearby lodging.

ABBREVIATIONS

AnBib	Analecta Biblica
BibInt	*Biblical Interpretation*
ESV	English Standard Version
ET	English Translation
GNO	*Gregorii Nysseni Opera*
HTR	*Harvard Theological Review*
ICC	International Critical Commentary
Int	*Interpretation*
JECS	*Journal of Early Christian Studies*
JSOT	*Journal for the Study of the Old Testament*
JSOTSup	*Journal for the Study of the Old Testament: Supplement Series*
JTS	*Journal of Theological Studies*
LHB/OTS	Library of Hebrew Bible/Old Testament Studies
LXX	Septuagint
LW	*Luther's Works*, ed. Jaroslav Pelikan
MT	Masoretic Text
NAB	New American Bible
NAC	New American Commentary
NICOT	New International Commentary on the Old Testament
NIV	New International Version
NRSV	New Revised Standard Version
NTS	*New Testament Studies*
OTL	Old Testament Library
PG	Patrologiae cursus completus: series Graeca
R & T	*Religion and Theology*
RSV	Revised Standard Version
SP	Sacra pagina
StPatr	*Studia Patristica*
TDOT	*Theological Dictionary of the Old Testament*
TNIV	Today's New International Version
TS	*Theological Studies*
VC	*Vigiliae christianae*
ZNW	*Zeitschrift für die neutestamentliche Wissenschaft und die Kunde der älteren Kirche*

INTRODUCTION

Discussion of "atonement," no doubt, causes the eyes of some in the church to glaze over. Some might think atonement is a topic belonging to esoteric theological discourse, not something actually of much relevance for the life of the church. Admittedly, sometimes discussions of the atonement have generated more heat than light because of rather narrow conceptions of the subject. Obviously though for anyone who is reflective at all, atonement is what the Christian faith is about. It is not a narrow subject at all; it involves a comprehensive treatment of the way God brings people into relation with himself and how life is to be lived in that relation.

None of the presenters at the symposium was content to embrace one of the standard models of the atonement as sufficient. In fact, even the use of the word "models" was problematic for some. Traditional views were valued to one degree or another, but all, or nearly all, of the presenters recognized the inadequacy of any single explanation and sought some broader understanding. Obviously a theory of the atonement carries with it assumptions about God, Christology, and sin, and the inadequacy of our explanations of atonement often are rooted in inadequate views of God, Christ, sin, and other aspects of theology. In particular, the failure of our "models" stems from an inadequate Christology, one that separates the Father from the Son so that the latter is punished, rather than seeing God demonstrating love and identifying with the suffering of humanity—on the cross. Further, the role of the Holy Spirit in atonement is too frequently neglected.

Perhaps the central focus in discussions of atonement should be on participationist language, a theme that is emphasized in several papers, especially in Michael Gorman's focus on covenant as a model for understanding the atonement. Contrary to what some might think, participationist language is not something that emerged with the new perspective on Paul. Both Martin Luther and John Calvin emphasized these ideas, as many before them, not the least of which was Gregory of Nyssa, as Hans Boersma's paper shows, even though many will not be happy about Gregory's allegorical exegesis. Participationist language is related to ideas concerning theosis, which does not have to be understood in some extreme fashion. Regardless, the failure of the church to understand the gospel in participationist terms is surely one of the biggest errors possible, one that leaves individuals and the church inept both theologically and practically.

Introduction

Is the problem in our understandings of atonement that we are wrongly focused more on the human side of the equation and are not sufficiently focused on God and on Christ and *participation* with them? Focused on the human side, even when we tip our hats to divine initiative, we will never work out the atonement.

At the symposium twice as much time is given to discussion of the papers as to their delivery, and as always, the discussions on atonement were lively and engaging. The journal cannot reproduce the character of those discussions. Michael Gorman had a family emergency and was not able to attend the symposium. His paper was summarized and discussed in his absence, and that is why there is both a response to his paper and a response from him to his respondent.

Appreciation is expressed once again to all the presenters and respondents who made a significant investment in the life of North Park. The friendship of these people is a privilege. The authors of papers were given a chance to edit their contributions after the symposium, but the responses are essentially as they were presented. As is obvious, the views expressed are those of the authors and not necessarily those of the journal or of North Park. We also thank all those in attendance for their interest and contribution to the discussions. Special gratitude is expressed to Jenna Brand and Joel Johnson, students at North Park, for their work on the bibliography and especially to Guylla Brown from North Park's staff, without whom the symposium would be impossible.

Klyne Snodgrass
The Editor

"IN HIM ALL THINGS HOLD TOGETHER":
An Ecology of Atonement

William P. Brown

Any theology of atonement worth its blood should elicit astonishment, a sense of wonder at the unbridled extent and transforming power of God's love. Even Anselm speaks effusively of an "indescribable beauty" that is evoked by the atonement's logical elegance.[1] For many Christians today, however, a strictly rational explanation based on seemingly feudal notions of honor and economic valuation, specifically of debt and credit, penalty and satisfaction, does not inspire much wonder. Repulsion is more like it.[2] To be sure, a distinctly economic understanding of the atonement has its share of biblical support.[3] But with today's global markets ever vulnerable to disarray, operating under the grand but deadly illusion of growth at any cost,[4] a predominantly commercial view of the atonement smacks of a "business as usual" approach that may easily lead to theological bankruptcy, or worse. The satisfaction model, as with any "model" or "theory" of the atonement, whether objective

---

1. St. Anselm, *Cur deus homo* ("Why God Became Man") (I.3) in *Anselm of Canterbury: The Major Works* (ed. Brian Davies and G. R. Evans; Oxford World's Classics; Oxford: Oxford University Press, 1998) 269.

2. A wide range of charges have been leveled against Anselm's theory of the atonement, from divine child abuse to death fixation. See, e.g., the trenchant critiques in Delores S. Williams, *Sisters in the Wilderness: The Challenge of Womanist God-Talk* (Maryknoll, NY: Orbis, 1993) esp. 161–67; Rita Nakashima Brock, "And a Little Child Will Lead Us: Christology and Child Abuse," in *Christianity, Patriarchy, and Abuse: A Feminist Critique* (ed. Joannne Carlson Brown and Carole Bohn; New York: Pilgrim, 1989) 42–61; idem, "Paradise and Desire: Deconstructing the Eros of Suffering," in *Saving Desire: The Seduction of Christian Theology* (ed. F. LeRon Shults and Jan-Olav Henriksen; Grand Rapids: Eerdmans, 2011) 55–72; J. Denny Weaver, *The Nonviolent Atonement* (Grand Rapids: Eerdmans, 2001).

3. See Gary A. Anderson, *Sin: A History* (New Haven: Yale University Press, 2009) esp. 189–202, who focuses primarily, if not exclusively, on the commercial background of the atonement. It should also be noted that St. Anselm's satisfaction or penal understanding of the atonement is not uniquely medieval (contra Gustav Aulén). A comparable understanding is reflected in the work of Theodore Abu Qurrah (c. 750–c. 823). See the essay by Peter Martens in this volume.

4. See, e.g., Bill McKibben, *Deep Economy: The Wealth of Communities and the Durable Future* (New York: Henry Holt, 2007) 5–45.

or subjective, penal or moral, simply pales before the gloriously harrowing scene in Revelation that depicts the slaughtered Lamb worshipped by angels, elders, and animals.[5] Regardless of how it is to be interpreted for today, the atonement cannot be dismissed or ignored. It constitutes, no less, the centerpiece of the canonical drama of God's salvific work,[6] the greatest of the *magnalia dei*. Just ask the author of Hebrews.

In this essay, I seek a broader biblical understanding that captures something of the astonishing, transformative power of the atonement for contemporary readers of Scripture. I hope to do so by examining two interrelated issues: the significance of Christ's atoning work within the larger creational context of the biblical drama and the special significance of sacrifice, which is biblically central to the notion of atonement yet remains problematic in much contemporary reflection.[7] Exploring these issues takes us through a variety of texts and themes, from creation to sin to new creation.

Creation and Christ

The cosmic or creational context of the atonement is perhaps no better encapsulated than in the early hymn featured in Col 1:15–20, which declares Christ as the "goal and glue" of creation.[8]

> [15]He is the image of the invisible God,
>   the firstborn of all creation;
> [16]for in him all things in heaven and on earth were created,
>   things visible and invisible, whether thrones or dominions or rulers or powers
>   —all things have been created through him and for him.

---

5. See especially Rev 5:6–14, in which "every creature in heaven and on earth and under the earth and in the sea and all that is in them" is singing praises to the Lamb (v. 13). Specifically identified in this climactic worship scene are all-seeing "four living creatures" (vv. 8, 14; cf. 4:6–8). See also 7:9–12.

6. I prefer "drama" over "history" and "narrative" in referring to the canonical sweep from creation to new creation. Drama conveys a more active, participatory significance than most other categories that take account of the Bible as a whole. See the wide-ranging discussion in Kevin J. Vanhoozer, *The Drama of Doctrine* (Louisville: Westminster John Knox, 2005).

7. See, e.g., Ernst Käsemann's plea: "If we have any concern for the clarity of the Gospel and its intelligibility to the present generation, theological responsibility compels us to abandon the ecclesiastical and biblical tradition which interprets Jesus' death as sacrificial" (*Jesus Means Freedom: A Polemical Survey of the New Testament* [trans. Frank Clarke Philadelphia: Fortress, 1970] 114). There is a way, however, to incorporate the language of sacrifice that is theologically responsible, as I hope to show.

8. Thanks to my colleague Stanley Saunders (personal communication).

> ¹⁷He himself is before all things,
>   and in him all things hold together.
> ¹⁸He is the head of the body, the church;
>   he is the beginning, the firstborn from the dead,
>   so that he might come to have first place in everything.
> ¹⁹For in him all the fullness (of God) took delight to dwell,
> ²⁰and through him to reconcile all things to himself,
>   by making peace through the blood of his cross,
>   whether on earth or in heaven.

Specific reference to the atonement is found at the climactic position in the hymn in the final two verses. Far from being an afterthought, the atonement marks the culmination of a series of themes featured in this ancient hymn: creation, providence, authority, and incarnation. The hymn, moreover, explicitly identifies the consequence of Christ's atonement as reconciliation. The expressed purpose of the cross is found in peacemaking, whose scope is nothing short of cosmic. Note the poetic parallels: "*all things* have been created *through him*" (v. 16); "*through him* to reconcile *all things* to himself" (v. 20). Creation and atonement, thus, are cosmically co-extensive. Also of note, "to dwell" and "to reconcile"—hymnic references to the incarnation and the atonement—are both matters of divine delight (vv. 19–20).

The background to this hymn is found in Wisdom's aretalogy in Prov 8:22–31. As Wisdom declares herself to be prior to all creation (vv. 23–27a), so Christ is declared "before all things" (Col 1:17a). Both Wisdom and Christ, moreover, are intimately related to God's "delight" (Prov 8:30 [LXX *proschairō*]; Col 1:19 [*eudokeō*]): Wisdom delights in both God and creation; Christ is the locus of God's delight to indwell and reconcile the world. Such reconciliation, according to the hymn, has all to do with the earlier affirmation of "all things hold[ing] together (*sunestēken*)" in Christ (v. 17). Conceptually, this recalls the Septuagint of Prov 8:30: "I was beside him binding together (*harmozousa*)."⁹ Early in the interpretive history of this most enigmatic verse, regardless of its original Hebraic nuance, the Septuagint translators adopted a distinctly cosmological outlook in defining Wisdom's relationship to creation. Wisdom in LXX Proverbs is the binding, dynamic force behind creation. So also is Christ in Colossians. How, then, does creation inform, if not define, Christ's atoning work on the cross? How does the atonement transform creation? So begins our journey of texts, beginning "in the beginning."

---

9. Or "joining together in harmony."

The Relational World of Genesis

To state the obvious, the Bible does not begin with *Heilsgeschichte*, "salvation history," but opens with *Schöpfungsgeschichte*, cosmic history. Creation is the quintessentially first of the *magnalia dei*. In Gen 1 God establishes the cosmic infrastructure necessary for promoting and sustaining life in abundance. This primordial act, however, is by no means an instantaneous event. Creation involves a series of acts, both verbal and hands-on, all within an extended yet highly structured period of time. God's act of creation is more a process than an event. Genesis 1 is silent about God's alleged "need" to create. Such silence suggests that God acts freely[10] to create something finite and material yet powerfully fecund and dynamic, something that is itself creative and self-sustaining: a differentiated, living cosmos.

God's creation in Gen 1, and elsewhere in the Hebrew Scriptures,[11] involves the sharing or investing of power to human and nonhuman creation. For some interpreters this presupposes a concomitant act of self-limitation or withdrawal on the part of the divine. Terence Fretheim, for example, sees in God's act of creation "constraint and restraint in the exercise of [divine] power in the world."[12] God, in other words, must relinquish power in order to create, or to use a more spatial metaphor, God retracts to make room for creation so that creation can develop outside of God. I do not see this, however, at least not in Genesis. There is sharing of power, yes, but not relinquishing of it. "In the beginning God retracted . . ." is not how Genesis opens. Rather, the curtain rises on God ready to reach out and work with a cosmic mishmash, with "chaos" (*tōhû wābōhû*; 1:2).[13] Throughout Gen 1 God is found actively summoning, enlisting, collaborating, and generating. Divine subtraction is

---

10. See Terence E. Fretheim, *God and World in the Old Testament: A Relational Theology of Creation* (Nashville: Abingdon, 2005) 17–22.

11. See, particularly, Gen 2:4b–25; Pss 33, 104; Prov 8:22–31.

12. Fretheim, *God and World*, 21. See also Terence E. Fretheim, *The Suffering of God: An Old Testament Perspective* (Overtures to Biblical Theology; Minneapolis: Augsburg Fortress, 1984) 71–78. From a more systematic standpoint, see Jürgen Moltmann, *God in Creation: A New Theology of Creation and the Spirit of God* (trans. Margaret Kohl; The Gifford Lectures, 1984–85; Minneapolis: Fortress, 1985) 86–89. For critique of the notion of divine withdrawal, see Christopher Southgate, *The Groaning of Creation: God, Evolution, and the Problem of Evil* (Louisville: Westminster John Knox, 2008) 58–59, 157–58, n. 21; Celia Deane-Drummond, *Christ and Evolution: Wonder and Wisdom* (Theology and the Sciences; Minneapolis: Fortress, 2009) 172–74.

13. This is not to deny *creatio ex nihilo* (which itself may suggest divine withdrawal). There are other biblical texts that could be cited to support such a doctrine (e.g., Isa 45:7; 2 Macc 7:28), but Gen 1:1–2 is not one of them. Paramount for the Priestly writer was God's resolve to create differentiated order and life *from* lifeless, amorphous "chaos."

neither referenced nor implied. Far from being passive, God remains the primary active agent, initiating steps in the creative process that are then taken up by other elements in creation, those of earth and water (e.g., 1:11–12, 20–22, 24).

In creation the God of Genesis begins by reaching out, literally breathing out, as limned in the evocative image of God's breath (*rûaḥ*) suspended ("hovering" [*mĕraḥepet*]) over the dark waters, ready to be exhaled as uttered word to bring forth light (1:2-3) and thereafter usher creation into being (see also Ps 33:6). Far from espousing the doctrine of *creatio ex nihilo*, Gen 1 begins with God poised to work with what is already there.[14] In creation God *extends* power. If there is any hint of God setting the divine self apart from creation, it is not at creation's beginning but at its completion on the seventh day, a distinctly "holy" day. God's holiness ($\sqrt{qdš}$), however, is more a uniqueness of character than a matter of metaphysical withdrawal.[15] Perhaps God's cessation of activity on the seventh day requires restraint, but in the larger canonical drama it is only momentary. God continues to be involved, reaching out to creation in a variety of ways (see below).

God's power to create invests creation itself with the power to create, and therein lies creation's "goodness" (1:4, 10, 12, 18, 21, 25, 31). Seeds and sex are the means by which creation not only sustains itself but also advances itself to ensure the flourishing of all life. God, consequently, does not micromanage the direction and processes of life but allows life to proceed within established domains. But for every boundary established and domain created (as in the first three "days"), creation develops its differentiated, interrelational character to accommodate life in all its fullness and diversity. Psalm 104 sets creation's interrelatedness in sharpest relief: all living kind in its "manifold" nature depends upon God's gracious provision *and* upon itself. Each species has its designated habitation and habit, its rhythm and character in relation to other species. The overall picture of creation in the Bible is one of a relational God reaching out to create and sustain a relational world.

Though creation is established as a domain set apart from God, creation is also a domain in which God freely and ultimately enters. As is often noted, Gen 1:1—2:3 depicts the structure of creation, both chronologically and thematically, according to the layout of a typical Syro-Palestinian temple.[16] Its symmetric structure of cor-

---

14. Specifically, with empty, formless waters and an amorphous "earth" (vv. 2, 9).

15. As Kathryn Tanner pointedly observes, "What makes God different from creatures is also what enables God to be with what God is not, rather than shut up in self-enclosed isolation" (*Jesus, Humanity and the Trinity: A Brief Systematic Theology* [Edinburgh: T. & T. Clark, 2001] 14).

16. See William P. Brown, *The Seven Pillars of Creation: The Bible, Science, and the Ecology of Wonder*

responding days parallels that of the tripartite division of sacred space, culminating with the holy of holies, the innermost sanctum, whose literary parallel is found in the seventh day of creation, a day set apart for God's holy rest to mark creation's completion (Gen 2:1–3; cf. Exod 20:11; 31:17). The Genesis account, however, nowhere indicates God's formal entrance into creation, the cosmic temple. That is reserved for a later time in the Priestly narrative, namely, when God's presence fills the wilderness tabernacle in the last chapter of Exodus, marking the tabernacle's completion (Exod 40:33–35). God's glorious entrance is geared specifically toward Israel's world. But the canonical trajectory extends much further in view of John's rewriting of Gen 1: the preexistent Word made flesh marks God's *full* entrance into *all* creation (John 1:1–18), the *kosmos* no less (see 3:16). The same thought is found in Colossians: "in [Christ] all the fullness (of God) took delight to dwell" (1:19). The incarnation marks the full extent of God's outward-reaching, all-embracing, self-giving, in-dwelling love for creation. It is in such love, a cosmic love, that any theology of atonement must find its footing.

A "Falling" Out

While Gen 1 provides a creational context for the atonement, the *need* for atonement is not found until the following account. There is nothing in Gen 1 that portends a realignment or restoration of relationship. The *imago dei* establishes a formal and functional correspondence between Creator and human creature that is seemingly inviolable (vv. 26–28). Genesis 2:4b—3:24 proves otherwise.

It is possible to view the garden story as a "recapitulation" of Gen 1, specifically of the sixth day, but not without problems, as even Augustine noted.[17] It is more accurate to view the Yahwist account as the sequenced counterpoint or dialectic partner to the cosmic Priestly narrative. The Yahwist's curtain rises to reveal, for example, a dry land, not a watery muddle. God exchanges the royal decree for a garden

---

(New York: Oxford University Press, 2010) 37–41; John H. Walton, *The Lost World of Genesis One: Ancient Cosmology and the Origins Debate* (Downers Grove, IL: InterVarsity, 2009); S. Dean McBride Jr., "Divine Protocol: Genesis 1:1–2:3 as Prologue to the Pentateuch," in *God Who Creates: Essays in Honor of W. Sibley Towner* (ed. William P. Brown and S. Dean McBride Jr.; Grand Rapids: Eerdmans, 2000) 12–15.

17. Augustine, *De Genesi ad litteram,* VI.1, 1–2. See the translation by Edmund Hill in Augustine, *On Genesis* (ed. John E. Rotelle; The Works of Saint Augustine 1.13; Hyde Park, NY: New York City) 301–2. The discrepancies between Gen 1:26–28 (a "simultaneous" creation) and 2:7 (and elsewhere) led Augustine to conclude that the day referenced in Gen 2:4b was a "spiritual day," one that continues into the present (3, 4 [p. 303]).

spade. The God from on high becomes the God on the ground, a down-and-dirty deity who grubs about in the soil and enjoys a morning stroll in the cool breeze. Humanity is fashioned from the dirt rather than cast in God's magisterial image. Compared to the lofty liturgical cadences of its canonical predecessor, the garden account reads more like a Greek tragedy. While the Priestly account teeters on the edge of abstraction, the Yahwist story revels in messy drama, the drama of dirt. On the canonical level at least, even opposites attract.

It is within the fruitful setting of a garden that the tragic tale of estrangement unfolds. The creation of man and woman (the ʾādām from the ʾădāmâ, the ʾiššâ from the ʾîš) vividly evinces their creaturely status as well as highlights their linkage to all created life. The primordial couple is granted freedom in the garden with, of course, one restriction: a creational command that preserves a part of the garden, merely one tree, from human consumption. The serpent, who for Dietrich Bonhoeffer qualifies as the Bible's first theologian,[18] promises that they will "be like gods knowing good and bad (ṭôb wārāʿ)" (3:5).

On the serpent's promise, the couple grasps the fruit in order to achieve divine status, committing an ecological violation to attain a theological apotheosis. They succeed, but only halfway. It is a partial success that leads immediately to tragic consequences. Instead of gaining divine power, they gain sufficient (in)sight to discern their naked vulnerability and, consequently, suffer shame. Nevertheless, the serpent was correct in its wily promise. They did become like gods, as God readily admits in 3:22. Hence, the way to the tree of life is barred to prevent the couple from attaining immortality, the culminating mark of divinity. Contra Augustine and the weight of Western Christian thought, the primordial couple did not *lose* their immortality, because they never had it to begin with.[19] Created from dust, they remained bound to the ground, even within the garden and even as *their* ground became radically altered from fruitful to frictional. What they did lose was the opportunity for immortality as well as their symbiotic peace with the land, with each other, and within their own bodies. In this tale of two trees, grasping for God, for divine status, leads only to failure. By contrast, the Christ hymn in Phil 2:6–11 depicts the kenotic way

---

18. Dietrich Bonhoeffer, *Creation and Fall: A Theological Interpretation of Genesis 1–3: Temptation* (trans. John C. Fletcher; London: SCM, 1959) 69.

19. See Jon D. Levenson, *Resurrection and the Restoration of Israel: The Ultimate Victory of the God of Life* (New Haven: Yale University Press, 2006) 32; James Barr, *The Garden of Eden and the Hope of Immortality* (London: SCM, 1992) 5–6.

of Jesus as one who regarded divinity not as "something to be grasped" (*harpagmos*), let alone consumed!

The couple hoped for exaltation (cf. Phil 2:9) but instead found expulsion. Estranged from God, the land, and each other, they found themselves thrown into a world of hardship and conflict (3:14–19). Harmony in the fertile land-based community is shattered. Yet amid the dis-ease and disharmony, the primal couple must still contend with God, the land, and each other. They gain a new identity in the newly acquired capacity for discernment and moral agency. The episode of disobedience and curse is, to be sure, negatively portrayed. It is not a "fall upward," as some would claim,[20] but it is in some tragic sense a "fall forward," a falling flat that forces a painful crawl toward full human identity, an anthropological identity marred by the proclivity for sin as much as it is enhanced by the capacity for good. Humanity's "fall" has both its gain and its loss. The grasping for divinity is at once a willful violation and a critical, necessary step in the evolvement of humanity, the humanity that is much too familiar. Humanity becomes an embodied agency for committing remarkable good, rare that it is, and radical evil, common as it is.

The First Sin

Because the "fall" in Christian tradition forms the background to any understanding of the atonement, it is necessary to probe the nature and import of sin within the drama that unfolds outside of Eden. The "fall" reaches forward to shape the episodes that follow in the Genesis narrative, from fratricide to the floodwaters. Violation inside the garden leads to violence outside it. Before Cain murders Abel, God issues him a challenge: "YHWH said to Cain, 'Why are you angry, and why has your face fallen? If you do good, will you not be accepted? And if you do not do good, sin (*ḥaṭṭāʾt*) is crouching at the door; its desire is for you, but you must master it'" (Gen 4:6–7).

This is the first time "sin" is actually registered in the Bible, and it is likened to a predator, such as a lion stretched out in its lair.[21] The term is never used in reference to the couple's disobedience in the garden. The couple's violation of God's command, one could say, lays the groundwork for sin, for sin to rise up and attack. Violation

---

20. E.g., Gregory Peterson, "Falling Up: Evolution and Original Sin," in *Evolution and Ethics: Human Morality in Biological and Religious Perspective* (ed. Philip Clayton and Jeffrey Schloss; Grand Rapids: Eerdmans, 2004) 273–86. Such an interpretation does not do justice to the degree of evil that humanity is capable of committing.

21. See Gen 49:9; Ps 104:22, in which the same verb is used (√*rbṣ*).

leads to violence. God challenges Cain to "master" the sin that is crouched within him and, in so doing, to choose life instead of death, kinship over fratricide. But Cain succumbs. His sin, the *first* sin, sheds blood.

God consigns Cain to a life of aimless wandering, cursed as he is "from the ground," which had received the blood of his brother (4:11). Cain reacts with consternation: "My sin is too great to bear" (*gādôl ʿăwōnî minněśōʿ*). Gary Anderson, drawing from the work of Baruch Schwarz, argues that "sin" (*ʿāwōn*) is the preferable translation instead of "punishment," contra most translations.[22] After denying responsibility and God's curse, Cain now feels the full weight of his crime and thus "owns up to his culpability."[23] Perhaps. What is more certain is the metaphor behind Cain's lament: weight. Whether as punishment or guilt—to make the distinction here is perhaps too fine—Cain cannot bear the weight of it, including the danger it poses. So God takes steps to protect him from blood avengers.

This episode sheds dramatic light on a common formula for sin in biblical Hebrew. *Nāśāʾ ʿāwōn* conveys the sense of either "bearing sin" (i.e., suffering its consequences like a weight placed upon one's shoulders) or "bearing away sin" (i.e., removing sin to make forgiveness possible).[24] Sin is a burden either to be borne or to be removed. According to Anderson's survey, the metaphor of sin as weight dominates in the Hebrew Bible, surpassing even that of stain.[25] As Lev 5:1 stipulates: "When any of you sin (*teḥĕṭāʾ*) . . . he must bear his iniquity (*wěnāśāʾ ʿăwōnô*)," which could entail capital punishment unless averted by confession and an offering.[26] In Ps 32:5 the speaker proclaims that the weight of his sin has been "lifted off" by God (*nāśāʾtā ʿăwōn ḥaṭṭāʾtî*). With comparable terminology, the psalmist elsewhere laments that his sins (*ʿăwōnōt*) "weigh like a burden too heavy for me" (*kābēd yikbědû mimmennî*; 38:4). The weight of sin is dramatically ritualized in the Day of Atonement event: "Then Aaron shall lay both his hands on the head of the live goat and confess over it all the iniquities (*ʿăwōnōt*) of the people of Israel and all

---

22. Anderson, *Sin*, 24.

23. Ibid., 25.

24. Ibid., 16–26. The examples Anderson gives include Gen 50:17; Exod 10:17; Lev 5:1; 24:15. In Num 11:11–14, the verb *nāśāʾ* means "carry," while it means "remove" in Num 16:15. Though the verb seems to have opposite meanings, a single activity is denoted in both cases: "someone is assuming a burden" (ibid., 19).

25. Unfortunately, Anderson confines himself only to linguistic formulas that have *ʿāwôn* as their object. His study lacks, for example, any substantial discussion of sin as a pollutant of the sanctuary or defilement of the land, a paramount concern in Leviticus (see below).

26. See Jacob Milgrom, *Leviticus 1–16* (AB 3; New York: Doubleday, 1991) 1041.

their transgressions (*pišʿêhem*), all their sins (*ḥaṭṭōʾtām*), putting (*wĕnātān*) them on the head of the goat, and send it away into the wilderness (*midbār*) by means of someone assigned to the task" (Lev 16:21). The accumulation of Israel's sins is borne by the goat and carried into the wilderness, to "Azazel" (v. 10),[27] that is, into oblivion.

According to Anderson, there is no natural antonym for sin as weight: "Nowhere in the Bible do we find virtuous individuals of superhuman moral strength who could carry the sins of others on their backs."[28] That, of course, depends on *which* Bible. In 1 Pet 2:24a we read, "He himself bore (*anēnegken*[29]) our sins in his body on the cross, so that, free from sins, we might live for righteousness." According to this minor epistle, Christ bears the full weight of sin so that we might be released to live in "righteousness," that is, to bear God's image more fully.[30] Atonement, thus, is a matter of removing the *burden* of sin, that is, expiation. Such is the canonical journey of sin's weightiness.

Engulfed by Sin

Sin's weight, however, is not the only aspect of sin's "thingness." Not only does sin bear down, it also rises and fills like an engulfing liquid. The biblical narrative charts, along with the growth of civilization, the proliferation of sin from generation to generation, from Cain to Lamech. In a display of violence against violence, Lamech commits manslaughter and calls for a seventy-sevenfold vengeance, in contrast to Cain's divinely sanctioned sevenfold vengeance (Gen 4:24). Sin ultimately has its fill in the flood narrative, in which all creation becomes "filled with violence" ($\sqrt{ml^{\ni}}$ *hāʾāreṣ ḥāmās*, 6:11b, 13; cf. 1:22, 28). Alternative (Yahwistic) language states that "all flesh had corrupted its ways upon the earth" (v. 12; see also v. 11a). Sin has reached a tipping point; it holds universal sway over creation. It also strikes God with unmitigated grief, prompting divine regret for having created humankind (6:6). A totalizing solution is required. God painfully resolves to "blot out" all humanity and "put an end to all flesh" (6:7, 14). The flood does precisely that. Like the rising tide of sin itself, the waters gush forth to fill the world, all to eradicate sin and effect

---

27. Originally a desert demon but later identified as a place. For detailed discussion, see ibid., 1020–21.

28. Anderson, *Sin*, 9.

29. The verb *anapherō* was often used to translate the Hebrew *nāśāʾ* (e.g., Num 14:33; Deut 14:24; Job 7:13; Isa 53:12; Ezek 36:15). Cf. Heb 7:27; 9:28; 1 Pet 2:5.

30. Such language may have its roots in the final Suffering Servant poem in Isaiah (see esp. 53:5, 10).

what one could call a cosmically extreme makeover. But it does not work, at least not as intended. Sin is not fully washed away; humanity remains sinful. After the waters subside and the aroma of Noah's sacrifice reaches heaven, God makes another resolution, this time to "never again destroy every living creature as I have done" (8:22), a resolution formalized as covenant in Priestly tradition (9:8–17). God's covenant with Noah marks God's unilateral disarmament: the divine warrior's bow is hung in the clouds to serve as a public witness ("sign") to God's covenant of restraint. "Never again" is its refrain (8:21; 9:11, 15). Terence Fretheim puts it well: "For God to promise not to do something again entails an eternal self-limitation regarding the exercise of divine freedom and power. God thereby limits the divine options in dealing with evil in the life of the world. . . . [D]ivine limitation yields real limitation. The route of world annihilation has been set aside as a divine possibility."[31] Such restraint is remarkable given God's acknowledgement that "the inclination of the human heart is evil from youth" (8:21). God's cosmic solution has done nothing to change the human heart. It is God who has changed. Divine forbearance has taken root.

The "fall" forward to the flood and its aftermath reveals a new side of God's character: forbearance, perhaps a more appropriate term than "self-limitation." And with forbearance comes suffering as God decides to "endure a wicked world, while continuing to open the divine heart to that world . . . God's grief is ongoing."[32] But also ongoing is God's compassion. Throughout the Genesis narrative the open, caring heart of God is glimpsed in various acts, both small and large. God makes "garments of skins" for the primal couple after the curse (Gen 3:21), helps Eve give birth to Cain (4:1), protects Cain from murder (vv. 14–15), chooses Noah and his family as the means to save creation (6:8–10, 13–21; 8:1). There is also the brief but touching scene of God shutting Noah in the ark after all had entered (7:16). God reaches out, painfully so, to a sinful world. God's open heart is also God's wounded heart. Grief and sorrow are the result of God's efforts to redirect the course of humanity and creation. The flood failed in this respect. As the human heart remains recalcitrant, God's heart remains wounded. Divine forbearance and loving outreach find their nexus now in suffering. Such is the *theo*-logical legacy of the "fall."

---

31. Fretheim, *God and World*, 83.
32. Ibid.

"Subjected to Futility"

The apocalyptic legacy of the "fall" is found in Paul, particularly in Rom 8, where the present age is contrasted with creation's future glory: "For the creation awaits the revealing of God's children with eager longing; for the creation was subjected to futility (*mataiotēti hē ktisis hypetagē*),[33] not of its own will but by the one who subjected it (*ton hypotaxanta*), in hope that the creation itself will be set free from its enslavement to decay and will obtain the freedom of the glory of the children of God" (Rom 8:19–21).

The word translated "futility" (*mataiotēs*) happens to be the Septuagintal translation of the Hebrew *hebel* (NRSV "vanity"), a widespread motif in Ecclesiastes, attested thirty-eight times. Paul acknowledges that Qoheleth's world of "vanity" remains operative for the time being. He likens the current state of creation to "enslavement" (*douleia*) and "decay" or "ruin" (*phthora*), appropriate extrapolations of Qoheleth's own view of the world, a world running headlong toward its dissolution (Eccl 12:2–8). One wonders whether Paul also has Gen 1–3 in mind with his double reference to creation's "subjection" in Rom 8:20 (*hypotassō*). In Gen 1:28, humankind is "blessed" with the mandate to "subdue" and "have dominion" over creation.[34] Granted Paul's intimate familiarity with the creation accounts, it would seem that the language of dominion in Gen 1 is, as a result of the "fall," twisted from blessing to curse, from salutary command to destructive consequence.[35] "Subduing" creation has become "subjecting" it to "futility," played out also by Cain's violent subjection of his brother. Whether instigated in Paul's exegetical view by Adam or by God (i.e., the proper subject of the aorist participle), God's curse in Gen 3, occasioned by human disobedience, marks the dramatic shift from creation's integrity to its "futility." At the same time, however, subjection provides the foil—put positively, the "hope"—for creation's ultimate redemption. As for the basis of such hope, we now turn to the notion of sacrifice as the defining event of Christ's atoning work.

---

33. KJV: "made subject to vanity."

34. √*kbš*=LXX *katakurieuō* and √*rdh* = LXX *archō*, respectively.

35. See Brendan Byrne, "Creation Groaning: An Earth Bible Reading of Romans 8.18–22," in *Readings from the Perspective of Earth* (ed. Norman C. Habel; Sheffield: Sheffield Academic/Cleveland: Pilgrim, 2000) 193–203.

Sacrifice

The cultic notion of sacrifice discloses another prevalent image for sin, that of stain or more broadly pollution or contamination. From Israel's cultic standpoint, sin was considered an impurity, a "physical substance, an aerial miasma that possessed magnetic attraction for the realm of the sacred."[36] Such was its "thingness" within the Priestly realm, a material force that could even "attack from a distance."[37] Its invasive capacity for contagion gave sin its communal, if not cosmic, scope. The victim of sin was invariably the community, including the land, as well as the sanctuary. The stain of sin, in a word, spreads. Atonement in this connection is a matter of cleansing or purging and, more generally, a matter of restoration of relationship, both horizontally and vertically.[38] In the temple rituals prescribed in Leviticus and elsewhere, those sacrificial acts tied to atonement were the *ḥaṭṭāʾt* ("sin" or better "purification") and the *ʾāšām* ("guilt" or better "reparation") offerings.[39] In contrast to the "well-being" sacrifice (*zebaḥ šĕlāmîm*), these offerings were for those who committed sin.[40] The *ḥaṭṭāʾt* offering, for example, was given by anyone who unintentionally violated any of the prohibitive commandments (Lev 4:2).

Distinctive of the Priestly or Holiness perspective, sin could render both the land and the sanctuary impure.[41] Regarding the latter, the following prescription is given: "You shall set apart the Israelites from their impurity (*ṭumʾâ*), so that they do not die in their impurity (*ṭumʾâ*) by their making impure ($\sqrt{ṭmʾ}$) my tabernacle that is in their midst" (Lev 15:31).[42]

Call it tabernacular degeneration. The solution is cleansing by sacrifice. The blood of the *ḥaṭṭāʾt* and *ʾāšām* offerings served to purge the sanctuary of impurity. Purification of the sanctuary involved prescribed ways of manipulating the blood

---

36. Milgrom, *Leviticus 1–16*, 257. It must be noted, however, that not every impurity was considered the result of sin (e.g., unclean foods and animals [Lev 11:9–45], women in childbirth [12:1–8], skin disease [13:2–59], house mold [14:34–43], bodily discharges [15:2b–32]).

37. Ibid.

38. For the communal dimensions of sin, see the essay by Viktor Ber in this volume.

39. For a condensed discussion of the sacrificial system in Leviticus concerning these two types of offerings, see John H. Hayes, "Atonement in the Book of Leviticus," *Interp* 52.1 (1998) 5–15.

40. Milgrom, *Leviticus*, 149.

41. As for the land, see Lev 18:25–28. The land's response to its defilement is to "vomit out" its inhabitants (18:25, 28; 20:22). In addition, the land, according to Priestly tradition, is to enjoy its own Sabbath every seven years (Lev 25:1–7).

42. See also 20:3; Num 19:13, 20.

of the sacrificed animal: blood was sprinkled or smeared by the officiating priest on certain sancta, most notably the altar but also the curtain that separated the holy of holies from the nave (e.g., Lev 4:6–7, 17–18, 25, 30, 34). In the ordination rites of Aaron and his sons, Moses offered the bull of the *ḥaṭṭāʾt* offering, whose blood was used to "purify the altar" by applying it on its horns (8:14). On the annual Day of Atonement, when the people as a whole were to make atonement for accumulated sins, the *ḥaṭṭāʾt* offerings involved sprinkling blood within the adytum itself and applying it on the altar, thereby "purging (*mikkappēr*) the holy place and the tent of meeting and the altar" (16:20). The technical term *kippēr*, "to purge," consistently has things, rather than persons, as its direct object.[43] Never applied to humans, the blood of sacrifice functioned as a "ritual detergent" that purified the sancta.[44] The cleansing of the sanctuary was, of course, also tied to the offender's forgiveness.[45] The damaging impact of sins upon the sanctuary has led Jacob Milgrom to state the following cultic principle: "[T]he severity of the sin or impurity varies in direct relation to the depth of its penetration into the sanctuary."[46] Put simply, the greater the sin, the greater its incursion into the heart of the sacred.

Priestly theology, thus, treats the sanctuary as a significant player in the atonement process. Not simply the sacred setting of slaughter, the sanctuary itself was the victim of sin and thus the object of atonement. As Milgrom summarizes, "It is only natural that [the Priestly writers] would regard the sanctuary of which they were the stewards as the spiritual barometer to measure and explain God's behavior to his people. The sinner may be unscarred by his evil, but the sanctuary bears the scars and, with its destruction, he too will meet his doom."[47]

From the ancient Priestly perspective, the temple's relationship to God's people was, to borrow from the language of quantum physics, one of "entanglement." Without direct contact, indeed regardless of physical distance, the temple's sacral condition and the people's moral condition were directly correlated, marked by a tight correspondence between human agency and the sanctuary's state of purity (or lack thereof). Foundational to this relationship on the horizontal plane was, of course, God's relationship to the temple. God too had a stake in the temple's sacred

---

43. Milgrom, *Leviticus*, 1040. The basic meaning of the verb, usually translated "atone" or "expiate," is to "wipe" or "rub" (ibid., 1079–81).

44. Ibid., 254.

45. See Hayes, "Atonement," 9–10.

46. Milgrom, *Leviticus*, 257.

47. Ibid., 260.

integrity, for "the God of Israel will not abide in a polluted sanctuary."[48] When the sanctuary became polluted beyond repair, a tipping point was reached, and God would take flight, abandoning the earthly temple, as the prophet Ezekiel vividly recounted (Ezek 11:22; see also Lam 2:7).

The annual Day of Atonement ritual treats sin as both a pollutant of the sacred that required purging and a burden borne by the people to be transferred and, thus, eliminated.[49] In either case, the sins, whether as moral failings or cultic impurities, "disrupt normalcy, creating a reverberation in the divine ecology."[50] For the temple priests God's "ecology" was largely confined to the temple. Nevertheless, in Priestly tradition the temple represented creation and, as noted earlier in Gen 1:1—2:3, the structure of creation reflected that of the temple. The "divine ecology" was not limited to the formal boundaries of sacred space or even to the community. It spanned, no less, heaven and earth. What, then, does the atonement look like in light of the cosmic purview of Priestly tradition? More pointedly, what does atonement do ecologically?

An Ecology of Atonement

Let's begin with a Priestly thought experiment. With all due apologies to Jacob Milgrom, the quotation given above can within the Priestly purview easily be revised to render a chillingly relevant message (see italics): "It is only natural that [the Priestly writers] would regard the *creation* of which they were the stewards as the spiritual barometer to measure and explain God's behavior to his people. The sinner may be unscarred by his evil, but the *creation* bears the scars and, with its destruction, he too will meet his doom."

Substituting *creation* for *sanctuary* is "only natural" in light of Gen 1. How true that creation "bears" the scars of human greed and exploitation, of human violence against creation! How true that our own destruction is bound up with creation's! How true, then, that creation is a "barometer" of our relationship with God!

Foundational for the temple priests was the status of God's residence on Zion. Today, as the world becomes increasingly polluted and depleted, the status of God's relationship with creation is a legitimate, if not urgent, theological concern: Will

---

48. Ibid., 258.

49. The latter act focused on "Israel's moral failings rather than on the sins and impurities that polluted the sanctuary" (ibid., 1069).

50. Hayes, "Atonement," 14, n. 4.

God abandon the earth, God's "footstool' (Isa 66:1), as God did in relation to the temple, according to Ezekiel? Has God already done so, given the look of things? In Christian tradition the answer is a resounding "No!"—an answer founded on Christ's incarnation and, yes, atonement. The tipping point of sin will not and cannot force God's withdrawal from creation (even if it may necessitate our own). In Christ God's solidarity with creation is established once and for all. If "in [Christ] all things in heaven and on earth were created," as well as "through" and "for" Christ (Col 1:16), then God will not abandon creation any more than God will again release the floodwaters. "In [Christ] all things hold together," a declaration grounded in creation but instantiated decisively in the atonement. In Christ God's reconciliation with creation is firmly grounded.

A Reaching Out

The blood of the cross, though freely given, was shed in violence, just as Abel's. As the first "sin" was committed in violence, so Christ's atonement was occasioned by violence. On the cross Christ bore the violence of the world, thereby breaking the death-wielding power of sin and liberating the world from "futility." Christ's death was the sign of God's willingness to suffer and die by human hands. The cross is the sign of God's incarnation in the victim of violence. On the cross God in Christ takes on the violence of sin and does not retaliate. God does not strike back. That itself is an astonishment! The divine warrior keeps the bow hung in the clouds even at the point of death. The cross is the ultimate act of God's forbearance, of God's unilateral disarmament, first enacted with Noah and all creation. God's abiding, grief-stricken concession to human wickedness in Genesis becomes in the Gospels a death sentence. The Lion is the Lamb.

Yet the cross also unveils the passion behind the concession: a love whose ferocity is unleashed in the resurrection, God's power "made perfect in weakness" (2 Cor 12:9). On the cross God does not push back but reaches out, meeting coercion not with coercion but with a suffering, empowering love that embraces the world to transform the world. On the cross God does not take *on* the world but takes it *in*, death and all. With the temple's curtain rent in two,[51] all creation is claimed anew as God's holy sanctuary, and the "gospel" gets "proclaimed to every creature (*pasē ktisei*) under heaven"![52] The atonement does not commend sacrifice for the sake

---

51. Matt 27:51 and Synoptic parallels. The Matthean account in particular invests the rending of the temple curtain with cosmic significance (27:51–52).

52. Col 1:23. My thanks to Stanley Saunders for pointing this out to me.

of sacrifice. It is not the mechanism of satisfaction. The atonement, rather, is the purgative and liberative way of God's passionate love most fully expressed, most fully embodied, a love that advances inexorably from cross to tomb, to hell and back, given to all the world for its reconciliation and renewal. The Lamb is also the Lion.

The Necessity of Newness

If the theological question has been answered decisively in Christ, the Word "made flesh," then what remains is the ecological question, the question about the world made flesh. What does the atonement do ecologically? If the natural sciences have taught us anything, it is that creation, in all its interrelated complexity, is no throwaway world. The natural world consists of myriad interconnected systems, of cycles and feedback loops, both positive and negative. Nothing can actually be thrown away or destroyed, for in fact there is no "away" in this world of ours![53] The wilderness by whatever name, demonic or natural, on land or in the sea, remains an integral part of the "divine ecology." Just ask Job.[54] The natural diversity of life, moreover, plays an indispensable role in human flourishing. Just ask any biologist.[55] The wilderness is no wasteland. Sin sent out into the wilderness will only come back. There is no true elimination, for the scapegoat never really leaves. Nothing is destroyed. Just ask any physicist.[56]

We are now entering what some call the "long emergency" of global warming and its catastrophic effects on life.[57] If anthropogenic degradation of the environment has anything to illustrate theologically, it is the tragedy of sin. The consequence of sin includes "those who have somehow, without intending to commit wrong, set into motion events that will exact the price of responsibility."[58] That would be the *costly* price of responsibility. The scale of suffering on account of sin is often in-

---

53. A vivid sign of this ecological truth is the "Great Garbage Patch" forming in the Pacific Ocean midway between Hawaii and California, a growing accumulation of plastic particles that poses significant risk to marine life. Another is forming in the North Atlantic Ocean (Jocelyn Kaiser, "The Dirt on Ocean Garbage Patches," *Science* 328/5985 [18 June 2010]: 1506).

54. See Job 38–41 and Ps 104.

55. See the collection of scientific essays in *Sustaining Life: How Human Health Depends on Biodiversity* (ed. Eric Chivian and Aaron Bernstein; Oxford: Oxford University Press, 2008).

56. I.e., the first law of thermodynamics.

57. James Howard Kunstler, *The Long Emergency: Surviving the End of Oil, Climate Change, and Other Converging Catastrophes of the Twenty-First Century* (New York: Atlantic Monthly, 2005).

58. Mark E. Biddle, *Missing the Mark: Sin and Its Consequences in Biblical Theology* (Nashville: Abingdon, 2005) 109.

commensurate with the perceived severity of the crime. No truer now! The sin of creation abuse, or as Marjorie Suchocki calls "rebellion against creation,"[59] bears an afterlife that extends far beyond the perpetrator, far beyond a particular industry or company, far beyond a country, far beyond a generation or two.[60] Sin's damaging effects not only linger; they also perpetuate, threatening once again, as it were, to engulf the world.[61] Human abuse of creation has become a sin of biblical proportions.

A totalizing solution is once again needed, but one that does not attempt to wipe all life off the face of the earth. In Christ all the world is "at one" with God. The cross is where divine forbearance and outreaching love intersect most fully. Cosmic in scope like the "fall" and its aftermath, the cross shares in the countless "sacrifices" life has suffered since its beginning over three billion years ago. The "war of nature," as coined by Darwin, entailed countless sacrifices that helped chart the development of life as we know it, of life's beauty and complexity as well as pain and ugliness. Evolution is built on suffering; life has been cruciform since its inception.[62] "Long before humans arrived, the way of nature was already a *via dolorosa*."[63] Christ's sacrifice, to be sure, is categorically different from those suffered by way of evolution and natural disasters, including five massive extinctions. Christ's sacrifice was freely offered in outreaching love for the other. Such love, if it is truly love for the world (John 3:16), must reach back to the beginnings of life and its torturous routes as much as it points forward to the beginnings of a new creation. As there is no sin apart from the whole, so "there is no salvation apart from the whole,"[64] the whole of history and creation.

Looking forward, the cross shares in the suffering wrought by creation's degradation that is only beginning to unfold from our "anthropogenic evil."[65] We are

---

59. Marjorie Hewitt Suchocki, *The Fall to Violence: Original Sin in Relational Theology* (New York: Continuum, 1994) 162.

60. Cf. Exod 20:5; 34:7; Num 14:18.

61. Through positive feedback loops the damages accruing from even the current level of greenhouse gas emissions may last for centuries (David W. Orr, *Down to the Wire: Confronting Climate Collapse* [Oxford: Oxford University Press, 2009] xiii–xiv).

62. See, e.g., Holmes Rolston III, *Science and Religion: A Critical Survey* (Philadelphia/London: Templeton Foundation, 2006 [1987]) 144–45.

63. Holmes Rolston III, "Kenosis and Nature," in *The Work of Love: Creation as Kenosis* (ed. John Polkinghorne; Grand Rapids: Eerdmans, 2001) 60.

64. Attributed to Dorothee Sölle by Catherine Keller, *On the Mystery: Discerning Divinity in Process* (Minneapolis: Fortress, 2008) 144.

65. That is, evil suffered in the nonhuman world as a result of human activity (Deane-Drummond,

all victims in varying degrees as much as we are complicit in various ways. For the second time, as it were, sin's catastrophic reach is most fully realized. The recent Gulf oil spill is but one example of what Robert G. Bea has formulated as a "unified-field theory of catastrophe: A + B = C." A is any natural hazard; B represents the human factors: "the sins of greed, arrogance, laziness and indifference." "Take a hazardous natural environment and flawed human beings and they'll add up to C: catastrophe." The formula smacks of inevitability. Such is sin. "We're the ones who turn a hazard into a disaster," observes Bea.[66] Such may be the hallmark of our species.

The hallmark of Christ's atoning work is its testimony to God's unconditional love and forgiveness in the face of human catastrophe. Christ has borne even the accumulating sin of creation abuse, the weightiest sin of all. But forgiveness alone, even from God, will not prevent the tipping point of our ʿāwōn from crushing creation, of our ḥaṭṭāʾt from engulfing the world. "While it is true . . . that God is eager to forgive and to heal, it is also true that God does not regularly alter the physical and moral principles that give the world its structure,"[67] the world that is as fragile as it is fecund.

Nevertheless, the God who entered the cosmic sanctuary is also the God who purifies it in sacrificial love.[68] When Jesus utters his last words on the cross (John 19:30), "It is finished (*tetelestai*)," reverberations of God's "completion" of creation can be heard (Gen 2:1–3).[69] The cross marks the beginning of the *new* completion, a new Sabbath.[70] For Christ's sacrifice to have its *objective* efficacy, new creation is nothing short of a necessity, for sin can no longer be dispatched into oblivion, for there is no oblivion into which our sins can be sent. But Christ's atonement is for the sake of the world, the world that God so loved. It is the portal to the resurrected Christ, whose body prefigures the new heaven and new earth even as it remains wounded, bearing the "scars" of our abuse. Therein lies the atonement's "logical" necessity, an eco-logical as much as theo-logical necessity. Whether to wash contamination from the cosmic sanctuary or to remove sin's burden from community and creation, either way leads to the renewal of creation itself, and so it must. In

---

Christ and Evolution, 174).

66. Quoted in Bryan Walsh, "The Spreading Stain," *Time* (June 21, 2010) 53.

67. Biddle, *Missing the Mark*, 127.

68. As the "great high priest" who offered his own blood, according to Hebrews (e.g., 4:14; 9:12; 10:19).

69. The Septuagint employs the related verb *synteleō* in Gen 2:1–2.

70. See the theme of Sabbath "rest" in Heb 4:1–11.

the end, through the eco-logic of the atonement, sin is transformed in its defeat, as the world must be utterly transformed, not utterly destroyed. From the Alpha to the Omega, the earth remains as indispensable as Christ's body, transformed but intact. As with creation "in the beginning," the new creation to which the atonement points is a *creatio ex vetere*, not a *creatio ex nihilo* and certainly not a creation from destruction. Rather, it is a creation restored, yet restored to a harmony far greater than before, to a "peace through the blood of his cross" for which creation longingly groans: the lion lying with the lamb and a child to lead them.[71] Such is the astonishing power of the atonement.[72]

---

71. See Isa 11:6–7.

72. My thanks to Brent A. Strawn, Christine Roy Yoder, and Kathleen O'Connor for their helpful comments on an earlier draft of this paper.

RESPONSE TO BROWN

Michael LeFebvre

Professor Brown's paper is a pleasure to read. In it we are led to explore how Christ's atonement relates to the environmental crisis facing the world today. Brown's passion for the subject is evident in the care with which he has written. I am grateful for the opportunity to interact on such a worthy subject treated in such an engaging manner.

As I understand it, one of the goals of this symposium is theological cross-fertilization between the academy and the church. It is from my position in the church that I would like to offer a two-part response to this paper from an able partner in the academy.

In the first part of my response I would like to revisit the Genesis creation account. It is a commonplace that the academic's task is to identify sources behind biblical texts and the theology of those distinct sources. The person in the church benefits from source criticism, but if the Yahwist account represents one theological perspective and the Priestly account another, the church person's primary concern is with the theological school which drew the two together.

In its canonical form we can read the creation/fall account as three episodes of a single story: (1) the Creator's role in the creation week in Gen 1:1—2:3; (2) humanity's role coming out of the creation week in Gen 2:4–24; and (3) the fall in Gen 2:25—3:24.[1] Read together, we find a coherent theology of stewardship binding these episodes into one story. The result is a doctrine of ecology in which the whole is much more than the sum of its sources.

As Brown pointed out, Gen 1 does not begin with nothingness. It begins with natural elements in chaos (*tōhû wābōhû*, 1:2).[2] This is not just a curious detail. Raw nature's chaotic state is the problem which this episode must resolve, and the solution is not a matter of power but of love. There is no doubt God has the power to

---

1. Genesis 2:25 probably belongs with 3:1 because of the play on words between the innocence of the couple (*ʿārôm*) in 2:25 and the craftiness of the serpent (*ʿārûm*) in 3:1.

2. The particular question raised and answered by the doctrine of creation ex nihilo is more clearly addressed by John 1:3 and Heb 11:3 than Gen 1.

manhandle the cosmos. What we marvel at is that the Creator shows his great love for the world by ordering, separating, naming, and blessing it. He delightfully nurtures the primeval chaos into goodness.[3]

At the climax of this good work God adds humanity and then calls the creation "very good" (*ṭôb mĕʾōd,* 1:31). Why does this last addition make everything "very good"? It is because mankind is endowed with the imago dei and in that likeness will "fill the earth and subdue (*kābaš*) it" (1:27–30). This authorization to "subdue" the earth has often been abused, and the earth along with it. Notice, however, it is in God's likeness (and only in God's likeness) that humanity is appointed to natural government. This authority is not license; it is a delightful appointment with strict limits, the limits outlined by the goodness of God himself.

Episode one begins with chaos and concludes with victorious rest. The world is only deemed "very good" (and ready for rest) when the steward is there to love the world week-by-week, as the Creator loved the world in the original week.

As Brown notes, the second episode is not a simple, chronological sequel to episode one, but it is a coherent theological sequel, picking up topically where the first left off. Focus shifts from the goodness of the Creator to examine more closely the steward's role. The first thing that grabs our attention in episode two is that it begins with another scene of nature in chaos: "Now before any plant of the field was in the land and before any crop of the field was sprouting . . ." (2:5).

It is not an absence of vegetation which is the problem. There are no "plants of the field" and no "crops of the field" (*śiaḥ haśśādeh . . . ʿēseb haśśādeh*) in this freshly formed world. The problem is the lack of cultivated plant life—pasturage, orchards, farm fields, and gardens.[4] The reason for this problem is stated: "Yahweh God had not caused rain upon the earth and there was no man to work the soil" (2:5b). This is the problem which must be corrected for the creation to continue enjoying God's goodness.

With that need in view, God provides a regular mist to water the ground (v. 6), and he forms man (v. 7). God himself plants a prototype garden with an earthly sanctuary in its midst (vv. 8–9). Rivers carrying the garden's regular water supply outward into all the surrounding lands with their raw resources (vv. 10–14) tantalize our imagination. What will it be like when the whole world is loved and cared for

---

3. The pronouncement *ṭôb* ("it is good") occurs seven times in Gen 1.

4. *Śiaḥ haśśādeh* may refer to pasturage for animals, while *ʿēseb haśśādeh* refers to field crops for humans. (Theodore Hiebert, *The Yahwist's Landscape: Nature and Religion in Early Israel* [Oxford: Oxford University Press, 1996] 37–38.)

like this edenic prototype? Animals will help in this assignment (vv. 18–20a), but it is the woman who will be an equal partner (vv. 20b–25). The provision of the woman introduces the possibility of offspring—families and communities. Only as societies can humanity fulfill this vocation and express God's love for the whole creation throughout the whole earth and for all time to come.

Finally, episode three recounts the fall. With the introduction of sin, Gen 3 spoils all this wonder so carefully developed. Or does it? The account of the fall is chock full of ironies—like the couple's nakedness turning from a sign of innocence into a display of guilt (ʿārôm in 2:25; ʿêrōm in 3:7, 10–11), the serpent's tempting one created "like God" to become "like God," and so forth. The most amazing irony is the continuation of humanity's vocation. The blessing to form communities is not removed; it is reassigned, though now raising children will be with pain (v. 16). Tending the ground continues to be mankind's godlike privilege, albeit with thorns and thistles (vv. 17–19).[5] Sin corrupts, but does not stop, our vocation "to serve and guard (leʿābdâ ûlešāmrâ)" (2:15) the world.

Let me summarize some points from this canonical reading of Gen 1–3 as it relates to Brown's paper. First, a wholistic reading of the Genesis creation account shows that Christian ecology is not strictly a topic of the atonement. The atonement—Christ's love for the world as Savior—is neither the origin nor the prime pattern for our calling to love the world; his love for the world as Creator is. The atonement disarms the moral obstacles to the ecological success of that love. Atonement disarms the bondage of sin on nature's stewards. Furthermore, Christ's resurrection assures us that all obstacles to ecological success will be fully removed one day. This gives us hope that the renewed heavens and renewed earth are a realistic vision. Christian ecology has its pattern in love long before the atonement; yet the atonement gives hope that loving stewardship is possible and not in vain.

I believe this conclusion is for the most part consistent with Brown's analysis. However, by adding a canonical perspective to this discussion, there is an increased chance for its being embraced in the pews where we desperately need this message to take root. While source criticism is commonplace in academic circles, in the churches many are either confused by or skeptical about source critical treatments of Scripture. By including a canonical interpretation along these lines, as a churchman partnering with an academic, I believe Brown's core message can be reinforced.

---

5. The grace which is already present in the Gen 3 curse is the origin of what is sometimes called "common grace."

This brings me to the second part of my response. Two aspects of atonement are discussed in Brown's paper. The heart of his paper deals with the results of the atonement, but he has much insight to offer on the nature of atonement too. These are two separate topics, and each of them is controversial on its own. It would seem best to focus here on the results of the atonement, leaving controversies about its nature for other projects.

Brown poses arguments (at times, assertions) for a moral theory of the atonement that, in his view, excludes penal substitutionary interpretations. These arguments cannot be adequately fleshed out in a paper of this length, and they add a layer of controversy which seems to me unnecessary for this project. Is it necessary to suggest that penal substitution derives from the "feudal notions" of medieval Europe and stirs "repulsion"? Is it really necessary that we abandon the "economic understanding of the atonement" before we can embrace this fresh emphasis on its ecological implications? Does Ernst Käsemann's conviction that "theological responsibility compels us to abandon the ... tradition which interprets Jesus' death as sacrificial" really belong here?

Instead, I take heart in another statement on the first page of Brown's paper: "any theory of the atonement, whether objective or subjective, penal or moral, simply pales before the gloriously harrowing scene depicted in Revelation in which the slaughtered Lamb is worshipped by angels, elders, *and animals*."[6] I agree. This paper does not need to show how the Lamb's death accomplished atonement (as important a question as that is). What this paper needs to show is that the atonement results in blessings for all creation and that humanity must lead the rest of creation into that praise. That is a message too important for our day to get bogged down in controversies surrounding the nature of atonement.[7]

I view my proposals in this paper as refinements, not rebuttals, to Brown's project. Certainly, there are many points we could (and probably would) differ on—some quite strongly. But there are also things of great importance to collaborate upon in

---

6. Emphasis mine.

7. While preparing for this response, I stumbled across a paper called, "The Ecology of John Calvin." Its author sorts through sermons and writings of the magisterial reformer to piece together what he had to say about sin's impact on creation and the atonement's implications for its renewal. Of course, Calvin never faced the environmental questions now pressing upon the world, and one can hardly be certain what his answers would be from a mere collection of scattered statements on ecological subjects. Nonetheless, this collection of Calvin's comments illustrates that disparate positions on the nature of the atonement (Calvin and Brown would disagree on that subject) do not preclude common ground on the natural world's share in the results of Christ's atonement. (Jason Foster, "The Ecology of John Calvin," *Reformed Perspectives Magazine* 7.51 [Dec 18–24, 2005].)

this paper. I hope these perspectives will help promote this message both within the halls of academia and into the pews of the church.

I close with the prayer of Psalm 72 concerning the Son of David: "Give the king your justice, O God. . . . May he judge your people with righteousness. . . . And let the mountains bear prosperity . . . in righteousness."

EFFECTING THE NEW COVENANT: A (NOT SO) NEW, NEW TESTAMENT MODEL FOR THE ATONEMENT

Michael J. Gorman

That there is no theory or model of the atonement called "covenant," "new covenant," or something very similar is one of the great wonders of the theological world. In this essay, therefore, I aim in a modest way to help in correcting this problem by proposing a new model of the atonement that is really not new at all—the new covenant model. In fact, this model may legitimately lay claim to being the oldest model of the atonement in the Christian tradition, going back to Jesus, the earliest churches, and Paul. I will argue that this is not merely an ancient model in need of rediscovery, but also a more comprehensive, integrated, participatory, communal, and missional model than any of the major models in the tradition.[1]

The Absence of the Obvious

How many images of the atonement are there in the NT? In most recent interpretations, from precise exegetical studies like those of John Carroll and Joel Green in *The Death of Jesus in Early Christianity* to more synthetic, theological treatments like Scot McKnight's *A Community Called Atonement*, the answer is "many."[2] Based on these various images, how many major models or theories of the atonement have developed in the course of the Christian tradition?[3] A standard answer is three—*Christus Victor*, satisfaction (often associated with sacrifice and/or punishment),

---

1. This project is a work in process. It is both too short and too long, and I apologize for both faults. I am deeply grateful to Professors Klyne Snodgrass and Stephen Chester, who presented the paper to the symposium in my absence, due to a family emergency.

2. See John T. Carroll and Joel B. Green. *The Death of Jesus in Early Christianity* (Peabody, MA: Hendrickson, 1995); Scot McKnight, *A Community Called Atonement* (Nashville: Abingdon, 2007).

3. Like many others, I use the term "model of the atonement" as a generic reference to major interpretations of the salvific death of Christ, without committing to a particular understanding of that death (e.g., a substitutionary or expiatory sacrifice for the forgiveness of sins). Two major traditional models, *Christus Victor* and moral influence, for instance, do not really understand Christ's death as an atonement (atoning sacrifice), but they are still called models of the atonement.

and moral influence—though some prefer to separate sacrifice from satisfaction and call it a separate model, yielding four basic models or, by omitting moral influence from the list of true models, retaining three.[4]

These major models have been supplemented in recent years by a variety of new models and by recognition of older models that are not as prominent as the "big three." A volume called *The Nature of the Atonement: Four Views* contains essays treating the *Christus Victor*, penal substitution, healing, and "kaleidoscopic" views, the last being the name given by Joel Green to his proposal that no one model or metaphor suffices to articulate the meaning of the atonement. (He refers vividly to "the church's glossolalia with regard to the soteriological effect of the cross."[5]) In his book *Triune Atonement: Christ's Healing for Sinners, Victims, and the Whole Creation*, Andrew Sung Park prefaces his own contribution (summarized in the subtitle) with a review of eight theories, five traditional and three recent: ransom, *Christus Victor*, satisfaction, moral influence, and penal substitution (all traditional), plus last scapegoat (René Girard), nonviolent narrative *Christus Victor* (J. Denny Weaver), and symbolic (i.e., "the symbolic power of Jesus' blood"—Tillich).[6]

David Brondos, in his *Fortress Introduction to Salvation and the Cross*, considers the role of the cross in ten more general soteriological models, both from the ancient church (e.g., redemption/recapitulation and the union of divine and human natures) and from more recent discussions about such themes as the kingdom of God (Ritschl), reconciliation (Barth), proclamation (Bultmann), and liberation (Sobrino, Ruether). "Covenant" is absent.[7] Peter Schmiechen, in *Saving Power:*

---

4. Paul S. Fiddes (*Past Event and Present Salvation: The Christian Idea of Atonement* [Louisville: Westminster/John Knox, 1989]) acknowledges many images but focuses on four main models: sacrifice, justice, decisive victory (*Christus Victor*), and act of love (moral influence). Colin E. Gunton (*The Actuality of Atonement: A Study of Metaphor, Rationality, and the Christian Tradition* [Grand Rapids: Eerdmans, 1989]) similarly separates sacrifice and justice but omits moral influence, treating three main models, or metaphors: battlefield, justice, sacrifice. McKnight (*Community*, 48) names the "five big metaphors" as incorporation into Christ, ransom or liberation, satisfaction, moral influence, and penal substitution.

5. Joel B. Green, "Kaleidoscopic View" in *The Nature of the Atonement: Four Views* (ed. James Beilby and Paul R. Eddy; Downers Grove: InterVarsity, 2006) 157–85 (165). See also Mark D. Baker and Joel B. Green, *Recovering the Scandal of the Cross: Atonement in New Testament and Contemporary Contexts* (2d ed.; Downers Grove, IL: InterVarsity, 2011), who speak of a "mélange of voices" about the atonement in the NT. McKnight would be sympathetic to this approach.

6. Andrew Sung Park, *Triune Atonement: Christ's Healing for Sinners, Victims, and the Whole Creation* (Louisville: Westminster John Knox, 2009).

7. David Brondos, *Fortress Introduction to Salvation and the Cross* (Minneapolis: Fortress, 2007). As we will see below, Brondos identifies the creation of a new covenant community as the main NT

Theories of Atonement and Forms of the Church, also surveys ten "theories of atonement" under four rubrics, but, again, none of the rubrics or theories contains the word "covenant."[8] In none of these surveys or others with which I am familiar is there a chapter called something like "the new covenant model of the atonement."

The work of the reformed theologian T. F. Torrance comes closest, to my knowledge, to developing such a new covenant model.[9] That a reformed theologian would stress covenant comes as no surprise. However, although covenant is highly significant for Torrance's understanding of atonement, it is apparently not sufficiently developed or stressed to be recognized by others as constituting the core of a model. Thus, apart from an occasional voice like that of Torrance and an additional, fairly narrow, strand of reformed theology, covenant is largely a missing ingredient in the recipe for atonement.[10]

There is one clear exception to this lacuna, which I discovered after completing the original version of this essay: a 2006 book by Wesleyan theologian R. Larry Shelton entitled *Cross and Covenant: Interpreting the Atonement for 21st Century Mission*.[11] Shelton has two main goals in proposing covenant as the key to atonement: greater faithfulness to the biblical witness and greater effectiveness in communicating the faith in the postmodern context. Shelton's proposal is quite similar in substance to the one in this essay, though his work does not appear to have received

---

understanding of the atonement, but he does not develop this thesis or attempt to integrate it with the claims of the traditional or recent models he considers.

8. Peter Schmiechen, *Saving Power: Theories of Atonement and Forms of the Church* (Grand Rapids: Eerdmans, 2005). The four rubrics are Christ died for us (sacrifice, justification, penal substitution); liberation from sin, death, and demonic powers; the purposes of God (renewal/restoration of creation); and reconciliation.

9. Thomas F. Torrance, *Atonement: The Person and Work of Christ* (ed. Robert T. Walker; Milton Keynes, UK: Paternoster, 2009). Torrance's work is quite compatible with many of the directions pursued in this essay.

10. This conservative reformed approach may focus on the extent of the atonement ("limited" or "definite") and/or an entire approach to theology with covenant(s) as the overarching rubric.

11. R. Larry Shelton, *Cross and Covenant: Interpreting the Atonement for 21st Century Mission* (Milton Keynes, UK: Paternoster, 2006); for a summary of his proposal, see 19–35. Shelton had earlier written an article outlining his proposal: "A Covenant Concept of the Atonement," *Wesleyan Theological Journal* 19 (1984) 91–108. He has also summarized the book in a paper delivered at the American Academy of Religion called "Relational Atonement: Covenant Renewal as a Wesleyan Integrating Motif" (http://www.ctr4process.org/affiliations/ort/2008/SheltonL-Relational%20Atonement.pdf), delivered ca. 2008.

much attention to date.[12] One can only hope that his and additional voices for covenant and atonement, including this essay, will begin to alter the situation.[13]

Shelton's volume and other hints at the emergence of covenant notwithstanding, the lack of a theory or model of the atonement called "new covenant" is truly remarkable. After all, according to all three Synoptic Gospels, this appears to have been Jesus' own interpretation of his death on the night before he died, with Luke probably making explicit ("new") what is implicit in Mark and Matthew:

> This is my blood of the *covenant*, which is poured out for many." (Mark 14:24)
>
> "[T]his is my blood of the *covenant*, which is poured out for many for the forgiveness of sins." (Matt 26:28)
>
> "This cup that is poured out for you is the *new covenant* in my blood."(Luke 22:20b)[14]

The scriptural overtones in these accounts are rich and plentiful. The references to blood are obviously echoes of the Passover sacrifice and the Exodus, an event of liberation. Linked with "covenant," they are probably also an echo of the covenant-renewal blood in Exod 24:6–8. Furthermore, the implicit or explicit (in Matthew) connection to forgiveness of sins suggests that Jesus' death fulfills both the Day of Atonement in Lev 16 (plus perhaps the atoning sacrifices more generally [e.g., Lev 4:1—6:7]) and inaugurates the new covenant promised in Jer 31:31–34, which (as we will see below) includes liberation and forgiveness. That is, Jesus' death is the means by which the people of God are liberated, forgiven, and brought into a new

---

12. Shelton argues for an "interpersonal, relational covenant concept of atonement" that is "transcultural" and "community-oriented" (*Cross and Covenant*, 5). Covenant becomes for him the hermeneutical lens for interpreting and incorporating other models and metaphors of the atonement. The project, like this one, understands atonement in deeply participatory, Trinitarian, and missional categories. The lack of attention to Shelton's book may be due in part to its mode of argumentation, which is at times somewhat popular and/or dated. (This is less true of the summary article "Relational Atonement.") The thesis itself is significant and worthy of further development by others.

13. In "Relational Atonement," Shelton draws attention to a paper for the 2009 meeting of the American Academy of Religion by feminist theologian Marit Trelstad, "Atonement through Covenant: A Feminist, Process Approach."

14. Some manuscripts of Luke lack v. 20 and thus the phrase "new covenant," but the RSV, NRSV, NIV, TNIV, NAB, and ESV all retain the verse. In addition, a few manuscripts of Mark and Matthew include the word "new." Space does not permit a discussion of the evidence for the genuineness of this saying attributed to Jesus, which some have questioned because Jesus does not appear to develop the covenant idea. What matters for this discussion is that the evangelists claim that Jesus pronounced these words.

covenant with God. My main point now, however, is that despite its apparent significance to Jesus and the evangelists, (new) covenant is not significant to the Christian theological tradition on the atonement.

This need not be the case. Joel Green, in his "kaleidoscopic" approach to the atonement, briefly emphasizes the Last Supper as "a point of entry into our understanding of Jesus' death"[15] and rightly states that Jesus "developed the meaning of his death in language and images grounded in the constitution of Israel as the covenant people of God (Exod 24:8), the conclusion of the exile (see Zech 9:9–11), and the hope of a new covenant (Jer 31:31–34) so as to mark his death as the inaugural event of covenant renewal."[16] In unfortunate continuity with the theological tradition, however, Green does not develop these observations in his subsequent discussion of the atonement.

In the only canonical account of the Last Supper outside the Gospels, Paul passes on the same kind of tradition we find in the Synoptic Gospels, especially Luke, indicating that both the Last Supper and the present act of its remembrance, the Lord's Supper, narrate an interpretation of Jesus' death centered on the establishment of a new covenant:

> For I received from the Lord what I also handed on to you, that the Lord Jesus on the night when he was betrayed... took the cup also, after supper, saying, "This cup is the *new covenant* in my blood...." (1 Cor 11:23, 25)

Not merely the lack of covenantal language in the "names" of the standard theories of the atonement, but also more broadly the near absence of such language from standard expositions of their content, might suggest that the tradition is blatantly ignoring the interpretation of Jesus himself as well as a very early, pre-Pauline Christian tradition rooted in Jesus' own interpretation.[17]

New covenant language appears in Paul not only in the context of the Last Supper, but also in 2 Cor 3:6. There it seems to serve as a summary of the reality to which Paul's mission is dedicated: he and his team are "ministers of a new covenant." Paul describes this new covenant as one characterized by the Spirit and glory, but references to Christ's death are not far away. Second Corinthians 4 and 5 make it

---

15. Green, "Kaleidoscopic," 165 n.16.

16. Ibid., 165.

17. It is likely that more time has been spent in recent decades discussing the tradition history of the two forms of this tradition—the Markan/Matthean ("covenant"), on the one hand, and the Pauline/Lukan ("new covenant"), on the other—than their common theological content and its theological significance.

clear that the ministry of the new covenant is in a profound sense a re-presentation of the death of Jesus, both in lifestyle and in words. It can only be such if the new covenant itself is inaugurated by the death of Jesus.

Then, of course, there is one book in which covenant is the central theological concept, namely Hebrews. There the word "covenant" appears sixteen times (nearly half of the thirty-three occurrences of "covenant," Greek *diathēkē*, in the NT), with Jesus described as the "mediator" of a "better" (8:6), "new" (9:15; 12:24), and "eternal" (13:20) covenant, which is effected by his blood/death (10:19; 12:24; 13:20; and many other texts). This new covenant is what Jeremiah promised, a promise that Hebrews quotes twice (8:8–13; 10:16–18), the first of which is the longest scriptural quotation in the NT.

These facts alone, it would seem, justify a theory—or a model, which is the language I prefer—of the atonement that we could call "effecting the new covenant," or simply "new covenant." But that model is missing, both from the traditional accounts of the atonement and from more recent revisions of, and additions to, them. As we will see, I do not think that this is because covenant "is not a common category through which the NT writers, apart from the writer of Hebrews, processed their thinking."[18]

The Need for a New, More Comprehensive Model

There are at least four major problems with the traditional models of the atonement as a group. The first is their isolationist, or sectarian, character. Each one is constructed as a kind of stand-alone theory that supposedly tells the whole story and requires the exclusion of other versions of the story. Only rarely, as in the case of Colin Gunton (*The Actuality of the Atonement*), does a theologian try to appropriate and integrate various traditional models.

The second problem derives from the first: the atomistic, or non-integrative, character of the traditional models. They do not naturally pull other aspects of theology into their orbit. "Atonement," however interpreted, often stands apart, separated from ethics, spirituality, ecclesiology, pneumatology, and missiology. In some cases atonement becomes a narrow branch of theology that is almost irrelevant to the actual life of Christian individuals and communities.

---

18. McKnight, *Community*, 74. McKnight rightly suggests, however, that the new covenant theme is significant as an outgrowth of the early-Christian experience of the Spirit.

The third problem is individualism. The traditional models have a nearly exclusive focus on the individual, rather than on both the individual and the community, as the beneficiary of the atonement. Scot McKnight (in *A Community Called Atonement*) and others have, of course, also recognized and begun addressing this problem.

The fourth problem we might call "under-achievement." That is, the models do not *do* enough. We may summarize a model of the atonement in terms of its understanding of the fundamental effect of the cross on a person (or on humanity). In the satisfaction-substitution-penal model(s) the effect is propitiation, expiation, and/or forgiveness; in the *Christus Victor* model the effect is victory and liberation; and in the "moral influence" model the effect is inspiration. In the new covenant model I will propose, the effect is all of the above and more, but that effect is best expressed, not in the rather narrow terms of the traditional models, but in more comprehensive and integrative terms like transformation, participation, and re-creation.[19]

I am not so naive as to think that this proposal is completely comprehensive or new. Regarding the issue of comprehensiveness, a truly comprehensive covenantal model will need to incorporate aspects of other models that are not addressed in any detail here due to space limitations. As for newness, in addition to Shelton's work from a Wesleyan perspective, I am happy to report (as an Anabaptist Wesleyan) that Anabaptist Caleb F. Heppner has seen the lacuna and made an initial attempt to address the problem in a brief online article entitled "A Covenantal View of Atonement."[20] Interestingly, David Brondos, in *Salvation and the Cross*, argues that we need the variety of atonement models in the tradition but also that the basic NT model, which he derives from an analysis of Luke and Paul, is new covenantal.[21] Unfortunately, he does not connect these two basic claims. Furthermore, I will later suggest that there is a close relationship between the new covenant model of atonement and the soteriological model of theosis (or deification: the primarily Eastern-

---

19. So also Shelton, *Cross and Covenant*.

20. See http://www.thepaulpage.com/a-covenantal-view-of-atonement/. He writes in the first paragraph: "In this view Jesus' primary role was not as a substitute or example, but as mediator of a new covenant. If there is a unique theology of atonement that supports an Anabaptist perspective of peace and justice, then this is it." And in the last: "Jesus is the mediator of a new covenant where justice (or righteousness) apart from the law has been revealed. It means that we also become mediators of this justice for all the downtrodden and outcasts of society, for they too have full standing under the New Covenant as God's people." Scott W. Hahn's *Kinship by Covenant: A Canonical Approach to the Fulfillment of God's Saving Promises* (New Haven: Yale University Press, 2009) came to my attention too late to consider.

21. See his summary of the book on 182–84. I disagree with some of the particulars of his interpretations but agree with the overall point.

Christian term for becoming like God by participating in the life of God), which has been much neglected but which is now rightly enjoying renewed attention.[22]

More recent interpretations of the atonement have been proposed by those who have seen similar, or other, problems with the traditional models. Although space does not permit a review of these proposals, to the degree that they offer a more comprehensive, integrative, transformative, participatory, and/or missional interpretation of the atonement, they will likely be compatible with the new covenant model being offered here.

The Prophetic Promise and the Outline of a New Covenant Model

The phrase "new covenant" only appears in the OT in Jer 31:31. This is clearly a classic case of the importance of weighing items rather than counting them when it comes to determining significance. If Paul is a reliable guide, it appears that at least one other prophet, Ezekiel, wrote about the same future reality, for in 2 Cor 3 Paul blends the language of Jer 31 with the language of Ezek 11 and 36.[23] The book of Ezekiel, full of covenant language and the hope of a renewed people, implicitly sanctions this merger. We will therefore consider the relevant portions of these three chapters as guides to the prophetic promise of a new covenant, first articulated during the Exile.[24] The relevant passages are the following:

> Jer 31:31-34: [31]The days are surely coming, says the Lord, when I will make a new covenant with the house of Israel and the house of Judah. [32]It will not be like the covenant that I made with their ancestors when I took them by the hand to bring them out of the land of Egypt—a covenant that they broke [LXX = 38:32: "in which they did not remain"], though I was their husband, says the Lord. [33]But this is the covenant that I will make with the house of Israel after those days, says the Lord: I will put my law within them, and I will write it on their hearts; and I will be their God, and they shall be my people. [34]No longer shall they teach one another, or say to each

---

22. So also Shelton, *Cross and Covenant*, though he does not use the language of theosis.

23. See especially Carol Kern Stockhausen, *Moses' Veil and the Glory of the New Covenant* (An Bib 116; Rome: Pontifical Biblical Institute, 1989) 42-71. Other Second Temple Jewish writers apparently made the same connections.

24. Jack R. Lundbom (*Jeremiah 21-36* [AB 21B; New York: Doubleday, 2004] 466) lists additional new covenant texts (without that precise term, but often with "everlasting covenant") in Jeremiah (24:7; 32:38-40; 50:5) and Ezekiel (16:60; 34:25; 36:27-28; 37:26), as well as (Second and Third) Isaiah (42:6; 49:8; 54:10; 55:1-5; 59:21; 61:8) and Malachi (3:1).

> other, "Know the Lord," for they shall all know me, from the least of them to the greatest, says the Lord; for I will forgive their iniquity, and remember their sin no more.

> Ezek 11:17–20: [17]Therefore say: Thus says the Lord God: I will gather you from the peoples, and assemble you out of the countries where you have been scattered, and I will give you the land of Israel. [18]When they come there, they will remove from it all its detestable things and all its abominations. [19]I will give them one heart, and put a new spirit within them; I will remove the heart of stone from their flesh and give them a heart of flesh, [20]so that they may follow my statutes and keep my ordinances and obey them. Then they shall be my people, and I will be their God.

> Ezek 36:23–28: [23]I will sanctify my great name, which has been profaned among the nations, and which you have profaned among them; and the nations shall know that I am the Lord, says the Lord God, when through you I display my holiness before their eyes. [24]I will take you from the nations, and gather you from all the countries, and bring you into your own land. 25I will sprinkle clean water upon you, and you shall be clean from all your uncleannesses, and from all your idols I will cleanse you. [26]A new heart I will give you, and a new spirit I will put within you; and I will remove from your body the heart of stone and give you a heart of flesh. [27]I will put my spirit within you, and make you follow my statutes and be careful to observe my ordinances. [28]Then you shall live in the land that I gave to your ancestors; and you shall be my people, and I will be your God.

When we read these texts we find that the new covenant is a transformative, even a creative, act that generates a renewed covenant people of God. More specifically, we can say that this new covenant people will have several characteristics. The community of the new covenant is:

1. liberated (having experienced a new Exodus)
2. restored and unified (Israel and Judah together; gathered from the peoples; returned to the land of Israel; one heart)
3. forgiven, cleansed from unholiness and idolatry/infidelity to YHWH
4. sanctified

5. existing in a mutual covenantal relationship with YHWH ("I will be their/your God, and they/you shall be my people"[25]) characterized by community-wide faithfulness, intimacy, and knowledge

6. internally empowered and enlivened (law/new spirit/God's Spirit within; heart of flesh, not stone) to keep the law/covenant

7. bearing witness to YHWH's holiness

8. permanent, i.e., partners in an everlasting covenant[26]

We can summarize these in eight adjectives: liberated, restored, forgiven, sanctified, covenantally faithful, empowered, missional, and permanent.[27] According to the exilic prophets Jeremiah and Ezekiel, this will be the nature of the new covenant community. It is a comprehensive vision, to be sure.

There has been some debate about what precisely is new about the new covenant. Suggestions include its apparent unconditional character, interiority, gracious pronouncement of forgiveness, intimacy, universality, permanence, and requirements.[28] There can be little doubt that the images of interiority—new heart and indwelling Spirit/Law—and permanence are critical to both the prophets and the NT writers. Without minimizing either of those emphases, I would suggest that what is critical and new is not one particular aspect but the *total character* of the new covenant just outlined.

Of course the understanding of this new covenant, and the community it calls into existence, will be dramatically affected by the story of Christ, especially by his death that brings about the new covenant. That is to say, the cross of Christ does not only effect the new covenant; it also effects a "fracture" of traditional understandings of the new covenant.[29] For example, covenant faithfulness and holiness will take on a cruciform shape, meaning sacrificial self-giving, sometimes even to

---

25. This is the fundamental "covenantal formula"; it appears in all three of our texts. See also Exod 6:7; Lev 26:12; Deut 29:13; Jer 7:23; 11:4; 24:7; 30:22; 32:38; 38:33; 39:38; Ezek 11:20; 14:11; 37:23, 27; Zech 8:8; 2 Cor 6:16; Heb 8:10; Rev 21:7.

26. For a similar analysis, see Stockhausen, *Moses' Veil*, 63. Permanence is implicit in these texts, more explicit in corollary texts.

27. See my *Apostle of the Crucified Lord: A Theological Introduction to Paul and His Letters* (Grand Rapids: Eerdmans, 2004) 115–30, for somewhat similar language to characterize Paul's spirituality.

28. See discussion in, e.g., Lundbom, *Jeremiah 21–36*, 466–71.

29. For the great discontinuities caused by the cross, see Roy A. Harrisville, *Fracture: The Cross as Irreconcilable in the Language and Thought of the Biblical Writers* (Grand Rapids: Eerdmans, 2006).

the point of death. Moreover, the reconstituted community will unite, not merely Israel and Judah, but Jews and Gentiles. Nonetheless, the key elements of the vision of Jeremiah and Ezekiel will remain, even if reshaped.

Before exploring the way in which the death of Christ both effects and affects the new covenant promised by the prophets, we need to pause to consider the content of the covenant obligations that a new covenant community will be empowered to fulfill.

The Vertical and Horizontal Demands of the Covenant[30]

In his *Theology of the Old Testament* Walter Brueggemann says that for Israel the demands of covenant relations may be summarized in one requirement: love for people as the expression of love for God.[31] Perhaps Brueggemann goes too far in conflating love for God and love for others, but he is clearly right that both are fundamental to covenantal life and that they are inseparable. We may refer to these two inseparable categories of the covenant as the vertical (God-oriented) and horizontal (human-oriented) dimensions, the two tables of the Law given to Moses (Exod 31:18). The covenant expectation, as summarized in Mic 6:8, is a practical symbiosis of vertical and horizontal love.[32]

According to the Synoptic Gospels (Mark 12:28–34; cf. Matt 22:36–40 and Luke 10:25–28), Jesus understood the covenant obligations in this twofold way. Other Second Temple Jews had a similar understanding, including the author(s) of *Jubilees* and of the *Testaments of the Twelve Patriarchs*, as well as both Philo and Josephus.[33] Thus the covenant-keeping that the new covenant will effect can be summarized in two phrases: love of God and love of neighbor. Since the love of God in the Bible means both loyalty/obedience and intimacy/communion, we may use the

---

30. The following two paragraphs draw from my discussion of this topic in *Inhabiting the Cruciform God: Kenosis, Justification, and Theosis in Paul's Narrative Soteriology* (Grand Rapids: Eerdmans, 2009) 48–49.

31. Walter Brueggemann, *Theology of The Old Testament: Testimony, Dispute, Advocacy* (Minneapolis: Fortress, 1997) 424; cf. 429 and the entire discussion of "Israel's Covenant Obligation" (417–34).

32. Ibid., 460–61.

33. See, e.g., *Jubilees* 20:2; *Testament of Issachar* 5:2; *Testament of Dan* 5:3; *Testament of Benjamin* 3:3–5. Early Christian tradition continued this understanding: *Didache* 1.1; Justin, *Dialogue*, 93.2; Theophilus, *Ad Autolycum* 2.34. See David E. Aune, "Following the Lamb: Discipleship in the Apocalypse," in *Patterns of Discipleship in the New Testament* (ed. Richard N. Longenecker; Grand Rapids: Eerdmans, 1996) 269–84 (281).

word "faithfulness" to connote these senses in one word. God aims to create a liberated and forgiven community, a faithful and loving people empowered by the Spirit to bear witness to the holy character of God. That is, God wants to form a people in his own image. The new covenant will mean a new creation; the image of God will be restored, not just in individuals but in a people.

We will now examine several NT writings that bear witness to, and can help us articulate, a new covenant model of the atonement: the Synoptic Gospels (with attention primarily to Mark), John, the writings of Paul, Hebrews, and Revelation. The danger of attempting to articulate a more comprehensive understanding of the atonement is that in trying to say much one ends up saying too little. In this essay, therefore, I will note the various aspects of the new covenant effected by Jesus' death but will focus especially on the nature of participation in it as an integrated life of cruciform vertical and horizontal love.

Effecting the New Covenant in the Synoptic Gospels

Cross and New Covenant in Mark

What is the significance of the cross in the Gospel of Mark? This is the Synoptic Gospel that most fully fits Martin Kähler's description of a gospel as "a passion narrative with an extended introduction," so there is much that could be said. The shadow of the cross reaches back from ch. 15 to at least ch. 2. Although Jesus' healing and teaching dominate the first half of the gospel, his suffering and dying take center stage beginning in ch. 8.

Those looking for evidence of the New Testament's sacrificial or substitutionary view of the atonement have found a showcase text in Mark 10:45, which paradoxically combines the image of Son of Man (Dan 7) and Suffering Servant (Isa 53).[34] But this text is not merely, or even primarily, about the mechanics of atonement. Its christological claim is linked to a summons to discipleship. This is in fact the case in all three of the passion predictions in Mark (of which 10:45 is part of the third) and therefore in all of the Synoptic Gospels, since Matthew and Luke take them up. Jesus calls his disciples to a life of "taking up their cross" (Mark 8:34 par.) that is analogous to his own death and can therefore be termed "cruciform existence" or "cruciformity." According to the corollaries of the three passion predictions, it consists of self-denial—losing oneself as the path to finding oneself—in witness to the gospel (8:31–34 par.); hospitality to the weak and marginalized, represented by children

---

34. See Joel Marcus, *Mark 8–16* (AB; New Haven: Yale University Press, 2009) 754–57.

(9:31–37 par.); and service to others rather than domination (10:32–45 par.), all with the possibility of suffering (13:9–13 par.). Discipleship will be a life of "danger and dishonor . . . shame and suffering."[35]

The call to cruciform discipleship is, in fact, a call to covenant faithfulness, a summons to embody the two tables of the Law. We see this clearly in the story of the encounter of Jesus with the man who wanted to know what he had to do to "inherit eternal life" (10:17–22, shortly before the third passion prediction). After Jesus replies with a recitation of the requirements of the second table of the Law and the man claims his compliance with them from his youth (10:19–20), Jesus informs him that he lacks one thing, and that to fulfill that one thing the man must sell his possessions, give the proceeds to the poor, and follow Jesus (10:21). The promise that the man would thereafter "have treasure in heaven" suggests that the thing he lacks, and will now gain, has something to do with his relationship with heaven, with God, and therefore with the first table of the Law. The fulfillment of that table takes place by following Jesus, as if Jesus somehow functions in the role of God, the proper focus of life's commitments and direction. At the same time, this radical love for God is not separated from love for others; in fact, the two are inextricably interconnected, as giving to the poor and having treasure in heaven are here two sides of the same coin of discipleship. In fact, we could say that following Jesus is the way to simultaneously fulfill—really fulfill—both tables of the Law: love of neighbor, especially the poor, and love of God. Moreover, in caring for the poor, Jesus' disciples become not only Christlike, but also, as the Scriptures of Israel make clear, Godlike, for God is the God who attends to the needs of the poor and oppressed.

Having heard the three summonses to cruciform discipleship, along with the story of the man seeking eternal life, the audience of Mark's gospel, whether ancient or contemporary, is more than likely overwhelmed by the cost of being part of the people of the covenant reconstituted around Jesus. Thus, upon finally hearing the words of Jesus at the Last Supper—"This is my blood of the covenant, which is poured out for many" (14:24)—the audience can breathe a sigh of relief. Why? Because Jesus' imminent death will create the covenant community that the entire gospel narrative has described: a community of missional, self-giving, loyal-to-God disciples who are able and willing to suffer and die for their commitment. To be sure, the death will not create such a community apart from the resurrection (which Jesus has also predicted three times), but it is Jesus' death that is the covenant-creating

---

35. Morna D. Hooker, *Not Ashamed of the Gospel: New Testament Interpretations of the Death of Christ* (Grand Rapids: Eerdmans, 1994) 54.

and community-creating act. As Morna Hooker has written, "[Jesus'] reference to the covenant takes us back to the covenant made between God and his people on Sinai, which established them as his people . . . Jesus' blood seals a new covenant, and in doing so establishes a new community . . . [T]hrough Christ's death a new people of God is created.[36] Hooker continues: "The death of Jesus is the beginning of something new: it is the ransom which creates a new people, the means of establishing a new covenant . . ."[37]

The cross as revelation of Christ's identity as Son of God (15:39) is, at least implicitly, a profound theological statement of the inseparability of act and being. The Son of God did what he did in life and in death because that is what it means to be the Son of God. Thus, discipleship is not merely following the Son of God who arbitrarily died, but following the one who has died because that is the fullest manifestation of the self-giving nature of the Son of God, and thus of God himself. Therefore, to follow Christ in the way of the cross is more akin to participating in the being or life or story of God—God's narrative identity, we might say—than to following someone at a distance or even imitating a master. To be the new covenant people is truly a new experience of knowing, loving, and being like God.

Cross and New Covenant in Matthew

Matthew is the only gospel that specifically says that Jesus' blood is spilled for the forgiveness of sins (26:28). As noted earlier, in this dominical claim we should probably hear echoes of at least three scriptural texts and themes—the Passover/Exodus, the blood of the covenant (Exod 24:6–8), and the new covenant and its forgiveness (Jer 31:31–34)—plus, in light of Matthew's ransom text (20:28 = Mark 10:45), the suffering servant's death (Isa 53:12).

We would be wrong, however, to conclude that the covenant about which Jesus speaks in Matthew is reducible to the forgiveness of sins in some narrow (i.e., "vertical" only) sense. Rather, receiving God's forgiveness is part of existence as a community of salt and light (5:13–16) that can also practice forgiveness (5:21–24; 18:15–20) and its associated virtues, such as deeds of mercy and compassion (9:13 and 12:7, citing Hos 6:6; cf. 5:7; 23:23; 25:31–46) like those of their Master (9:36; 14:14; 15:32; 18:33; 20:34). Although the Last Supper text is an explicit statement of

---

36. Ibid., 59.

37. Ibid., 67. According to Hooker (55), the ransom text echoes the redemption from Egypt and from Exile more than Isa 53.

the purpose of Christ's death (like the "ransom" text), to limit that purpose to the vertical relationship would be to negate the message of the rest of the Gospel.

This forgiven and forgiving new covenant community embodies, indeed fulfills, the two tables of the Law. As Richard Hays persuasively argues, the Matthean audience is being called to follow the one whose "hermeneutic of mercy" and claim to fulfill the law (5:17–18) yield for his disciples a mandate to love God and neighbor (22:34–40, based on Mark 12:28–34). Matthew's specific point is that ". . . everything else in the Torah 'hangs' upon them [the two love commands]; everything else must be derivable from them. In consequence, the double love command becomes a hermeneutical filter—virtually synonymous with Hosea 6:6—that governs the community's entire construal of the Law."[38]

Matthew famously concludes with the Great Commission text (28:16–20). This too needs to be understood in connection with the covenant inaugurated by Jesus' death. Disciples, members of the new covenant community, are sent out to make more disciples who similarly fulfill the Law by obeying Jesus. This missional activity, and implicitly the life of double-commandment discipleship as a whole, is not done alone but by means of the power of the always-present Jesus (28:20), the one who is the covenant-God with us (1:23).

Cross and New Covenant in Luke

Not only does Luke lack the phrase "poured out for many for the forgiveness of sins" in his account of the Last Supper, but he also famously omits (intentionally or not) the Markan/Matthean ransom text when he places the call to discipleship from the third passion prediction in the context of the Last Supper (22:24–30). These and other features of Luke have caused significant confusion and, in some quarters, consternation around the question of Luke's theology of the cross. Is it an atoning, sacrificial, redemptive event? Is his death a death for sins or only the death of a martyr and prophet?

The new covenant model both alleviates some of our distress and refocuses our interest. Luke is the only Synoptic writer who uses the precise phrase "*new* covenant." According to the prophetic tradition, the new covenant includes the forgiveness of sins; it is highly likely, then, that Luke's account implies forgiveness and thus

---

38. Richard B. Hays, *The Moral Vision of the New Testament: Community, Cross, New Creation; A Contemporary Introduction to New Testament Ethics* (San Francisco: HarperCollins, 1996) 101, in a section called "The Hermeneutic of Mercy" (99–101).

an atoning death (especially in light of the word of forgiveness in 23:34).[39] But Luke's associating Jesus' death with the new covenant is more comprehensive than a word or act of forgiveness. As John Carroll and Joel Green have said, "The cup after the meal is a metaphor for a new covenant enacted through the blood Jesus spills 'on your behalf.' Jesus here interprets his death as an event enabling a new covenantal loyalty, a gift creating a new covenantal community (cf. also Acts 20:28). His self-sacrifice is a means of benefaction for the community of his followers."[40]

Here Carroll and Green point out at least two significant elements of a "benefaction" that is, in fact, a transformation: the creation of a "new covenantal community" and the enabling of a "new covenantal loyalty," two of the main features of the new covenant and of the proposal being advocated in this essay.

Furthermore, we see in Luke's handling of the three Markan passion predictions and their corollary calls to discipleship the especially close connection Luke envisions between the death of Jesus and the countercultural cruciform and missional existence of disciples. Disciples need to (1) take up their cross *daily* (9:23; "daily" only in Luke); (2) follow Jesus and share his mission, even to Jerusalem, without hesitation or distraction (9:43b–62); and (3) remember *on the very eve of Jesus' death* that they are called to forsake the cultural norms of hubris and domination to embrace cross-shaped service (22:24–30).[41] It is as such a community, empowered by the Spirit, that they will bear witness (24:48), as Acts will relate in detail.

Effecting the New Covenant in John

John has a rather full theology of Christ's death. Craig Koester finds four Johannine themes about Jesus' death: an expression of love, a sacrifice for sins, victory over sin, and revelation of divine glory.[42] Several texts in the so-called "farewell discourse" (or "discourses") of chs. 13–17 express these themes about Christ's death. However, although speaking of John 13–17 as the farewell discourse tells us something about

---

39. On the assumption that this verse is original to the gospel.

40. John Carroll and Joel B Green, *The Death of Jesus in Early Christianity*, 69.

41. In Luke the second Markan passion prediction and its immediate aftermath (Luke 9:43b–50) become the segue to the narrative of Jesus' journey to Jerusalem (9:51—18:14), which itself begins with another call to discipleship and a sending out (9:51—10:20). Luke actually splits the third Markan passion prediction and discipleship call into two parts, leaving the prediction in the Markan narrative context (Luke 18:31-34) but moving the call to the Last Supper (Luke 22:24-30).

42. Craig R. Koester, *The Word of Life: A Theology of John's Gospel* (Grand Rapids: Eerdmans, 2008) 110–23. The first three of these, interestingly, correspond quite closely to the three traditional models of the atonement.

the form and basic rhetorical function of these chapters, the phrase says very little about their theological content and function.

John 13–17 constitutes more than just a farewell discourse. Rekha Chennattu calls them "discipleship discourses." She argues (independently from the present writer) that John 13–17 draws heavily on OT covenant motifs. The discourses constitute Jesus' teaching about his forming a new covenant community of disciples marked especially by a relationship of intimacy and covenant-keeping vis-à-vis God and of love for one another. They will share in the divine mission enacted in him, with similar obligations and risks. John 20–21, Chennattu contends, actualizes the promissory teaching given in chs. 13–17.[43]

Chennattu's observations are insightful and her argument compelling. Although the word "covenant" does not appear in John 13–17, it is clear that Jesus is assembling a community of committed and loyal friends (15:13–15) who will be the core group of a new covenant community that embodies his divine mission after his death. He is saying to them, in effect, "We (Father, Son, and Spirit) will be your God, and you will be our people." In these chapters we find community and covenant as well as cruciformity, charismatic empowerment, and mission.

Chennattu's work needs to be supplemented by emphasizing more forcefully and consistently the close connection in John 13–17 between covenant discipleship and Jesus' death. These chapters are, in effect, an extended commentary on the synoptic claim that Jesus' death creates the new covenant community. They contain a description of the community formed precisely by that death.[44] It is a community of forgiven people restored to covenant relationship with God, empowered by the Spirit to live in Christlike, cruciform loyalty to God and love for one another in spite of persecution, and sent out on a Christlike mission. John 13–17 tells us why Christ died or, narratively speaking within the Gospel itself, why Christ will die. In both the promissory discourse (chs. 13–17) and the narrative of fulfillment (chs. 20–21), we encounter a missional community of atonement.

The discourse is given as Jesus' hour to depart, to die and return to his Father, has arrived (13:1). The event narrated in these chapters that gives rise to the entire

---

43. Rekha M. Chennattu, *Johannine Discipleship as a Covenant Relationship* (Peabody, MA: Hendrickson, 2006). Chennattu also discusses the handful of other scholars who have dealt similarly with this subject.

44. In the Synoptics, teaching about the shape of the covenant community is presented primarily before the narrative of Jesus' last meal, whereas in John such teaching comes during and after the meal. The overall narrative effect is the same: the death of Jesus creates the kind of covenant community he calls for in his teaching.

discourse is Jesus' parabolic action of foot washing. Put the other way around, the farewell discourse is an extended commentary on the foot washing.

The enacted parable of foot washing is given two distinct but inseparable interpretations by Jesus. First, it is a unique act of cleansing that only Jesus can perform and that is mandatory for a relationship with him (13:8b–10). Second, it is a paradigmatic act of servant-love that is mandatory for his disciples to replicate (13:12–17). Both Jesus, who speaks in the narrative, and John, who has constructed the narrative, move seamlessly from one interpretation to the other. Indeed, while it is not altogether clear to what "doing these things" refers (13:17), the most likely referent of the plural is both being washed and washing. Disciples benefit from the servant-Jesus' death as cleansing from sin and imitate it as loving care for others. Both Jesus and John see these two aspects of his death as inherently inseparable. The gift is also demand. *There is no cleansing without discipleship, no vertical relationship without horizontal relationships, no atonement without ethics.*

Moreover, the horizontal dimension of this covenant life is not independently defined and described; it grows organically out of the one act of Jesus' self-giving death. Thus, Jesus explains the second interpretation of his death as a "new commandment" (13:34), not because the commandment to love is new, but because its shape is new. It is now Christlike, cruciform love: "As I have loved you" (13:34; 15:12–13). The self-giving of Jesus in death embodies the love of God (see John 3:16) that both liberates and binds. It liberates people from sin and binds them to God in a covenant relationship that similarly seeks the good of the other. The liberated and bound community, that is, the cleansed and covenanted community, is in the process of becoming like the loving God revealed in the loving death of Jesus (see 13:1b). As Chennattu emphasizes, the *imitatio Dei* was an integral part of the covenantal relationship between the people and God: "You shall be holy for I am holy."[45]

Two major issues must still be addressed at least briefly. First, is this love truly Godlike and Christlike if it is only directed toward fellow disciples, toward "one another"? Second, is an ethic of imitation, especially imitation of self-giving love, simply a "new commandment" that will remain unrealized due to human sin?

To deal first with the second question, Jesus in John does not present us merely with an ethic of commandment and imitation. It is better described as a spirituality of mutual indwelling that makes possible the fulfilling of the obligation of imitation, not dissimilar from what we will find in Paul. Already in John 14, when Jesus refers to the requirement of keeping his commandments as the demonstration of love for

---

45. Chennattu, *Johannine Discipleship*, 59–61.

him and the Father, he makes it clear that the disciples can do nothing on their own power but will have the indwelling presence of Jesus in the person of the Spirit/Advocate (14:17–20, 26, 28). The nature of this relationship is further disclosed in ch. 15, in which Jesus speaks of a reciprocal residency between himself and his disciples: "Abide in me as I abide in you. Just as the branch cannot bear fruit by itself unless it abides in the vine, neither can you unless you abide in me" (15:4). This does not decrease the force of the expectation. It is still a matter of commandments, or covenantal obligations, but it does alter the manner in which the obligations are fulfilled. The prophetic language of the new covenant, made effective by the indwelling of the Spirit or the law within, is behind this formulation of covenantal requirements here even as it will be in Paul.[46] *But the prophetic promises of mutual covenant relationship and (one-way) interiority have merged to become mutual indwelling.* We are moving beyond imitation toward theosis: becoming like God by participating in the life of God.

Now to address the first question: Is love for one another sufficient? What about love for outsiders generally and for enemies in particular? I think here we must consider two things: the Johannine context of (current or coming) persecution and the missional impetus of ch. 17. When a community is being persecuted, it is critical that it sustain itself in love. The community of disciples in John is going to be pursued, persecuted (15:18–21; 16:33; 17:11–16). It will die without an ethos of mutual love, support, and unity, as Jesus himself knows (17:11–16). But equally important is the corollary ethos of mission. The disciples will share in Jesus' fate because they share in his mission, which is in fact God's mission. Following the promises of persecution in chs. 15–17, Jesus does not order his disciples to flee or hide but to join him in his mission of bringing eternal life to the world. He prays to his Father, "As you have sent me into the world, so I have sent them into the world" (17:18) and asks only for their protection (17:15). Their internal love and unity, therefore, is not merely an end in itself but a means to the success of the mission, of the *missio Dei* (17:21–23). The upshot of all this is that the disciples are in fact called to love the world, even the world that hates and persecutes them, because they participate in the world-centered love and mission of God manifested in the Son, especially in his death (3:14–17).

To summarize the theological importance of the farewell discourse in relation to the atonement, the death of Jesus will create a community of committed friends of Jesus who indwell him and are indwelt by him/his Spirit. Within this relationship

---

46. The Holy Spirit is "John's answer" to Jeremiah's promise (Lundbom, *Jeremiah 21–36*, 478).

they will participate in his death in four ways: receiving his forgiveness, fulfilling the obligations of a covenant relationship by continuing his self-giving love for others, experiencing hatred and persecution similar to that which caused his death, and extending God's mission to the world. That is, as a community of atonement they are a covenantal, cruciform, charismatic, missional community.

Effecting the New Covenant in Paul

Much could be said regarding Paul's interpretation of the cross, though explicit references to the new covenant are fewer than one might expect.[47] We will need to limit ourselves to a small selection of texts from three different letters, all of which bear, explicitly or implicitly, on the connection between the cross and the new covenant and on the significance of that connection. Before considering those texts, however, we need to mention one important book that has, unfortunately, received less attention than it deserves: T .J. Deidun's *New Covenant Morality in Paul*, published in 1981.[48]

Deidun argues that the new covenant, promised by Jeremiah and Ezekiel and fulfilled by God through Christ in the giving of the Spirit, is the center of Paul's theology. Paul's morality, he argues, "was coloured from the very beginning by his interpretation of Ex. 36,27 and Jr. 31,31ss."[49] Deidun finds strong evidence that Paul uses the language of Jeremiah and Ezekiel, not only in 2 Cor 3, but also in his earliest letter (1 Thess 4:8-9). Moreover, he argues compellingly that Paul refers throughout his letters to the content of the new covenant: being God's holy people empowered by the Spirit to forsake idolatry and immorality and to love God and others (especially fellow believers). Although there are a few areas of Deidun's work with which I would quibble, it is overall a persuasive argument. What is absent from the book is a clear and consistent connection between new covenant and Christ's death.[50] That will be our focus now.

---

47. Lundbom (*Jeremiah 21-36*, 475) suggests that Paul would have referred to Jer 31 more often except that he wanted to establish a "more ancient base [the Abrahamic promises] for the new faith in Christ." Nevertheless, he argues, especially regarding Romans, that Paul's lack of new covenant language should not be confused with lack of new covenant theology (476).

48. T. J. Deidun, *New Covenant Morality in Paul* (AnBib 89; Rome: Biblical Institute Press, 1981). Another often overlooked but important work, which interprets Romans in terms of the new covenant, is R. David Kaylor, *Paul's Covenant Community: Jew and Gentile in Romans* (Atlanta: John Knox, 1988).

49. Deidun, *New Covenant Morality*, 228.

50. For Deidun, the cross in Paul functions primarily as Christ's exemplary self-offering, which is also the demonstration of the love of God, and which becomes the ongoing work of the Spirit in believ-

Second Corinthians 3–5

We begin our consideration of Paul by making some connections between 2 Cor 3–4 and 2 Cor 5. As already noted, the term "new covenant" appears in 2 Cor 3:6 (the only occurrence in Paul besides the account of the Last Supper in 1 Cor 11:25): "[God] who has made us competent to be ministers of a new covenant, not of letter but of spirit; for the letter kills, but the Spirit gives life."[51] This verse is part of an extended description of Christian ministry (specifically, Paul's) and, within that, also of Christian existence more generally. Paul describes the Corinthians who benefit from the ministry of the new covenant as a community formed by the Spirit of God (3:3). This covenant is one that brings about life, righteousness/justification, and glory rather than death and condemnation (3:6–11). We know implicitly in 2 Cor 3–4, and explicitly elsewhere in Paul, that he is referring to the effects of preaching the gospel, which is the word of the cross (Rom 1:16–17 in light of 3:21–26; Rom 5:12–21; 1 Cor 1:18–25; 2 Cor 5:14–21). Those who participate in this new covenant are in the process of being transformed into the image of Christ (3:18; 4:4). It was the death of Christ that brought this new covenant of life and glory into existence, and, paradoxically, it is the death of Christ that continues to define Christian existence, especially Christian ministry. It entails "always carrying in the body the death of Jesus, so that the life of Jesus may also be made visible in our bodies" (2 Cor 4:10). Those who minister on behalf of the God of this covenant will embody in daily life the very act that effected the new covenant, and the communities they form will also take on a cruciform shape.[52] The work of the Spirit is to form cruciform communities. (See also, e.g., Phil 2:1–4 in light of Phil 2:6–8).

Despite the rather narrow context that generates 2 Cor 3–4, it would be difficult to find a fuller description of the transformative nature of the atonement. Christ's death is covenant-effecting, community-creating, empowering, paradigmatic, and mission-generating. When we turn to 2 Cor 5:14–21, we see a parallel and equally full description.

The death of Christ is his act of love, and that love expressed in death continues to motivate those who minister to others (5:14). That act of love had human transformation as its purpose, as is evident in Greek *hina* clauses. Paul explains this

---

ers. While this is all true for Paul, there is more that needs to be said.

51.. The NRSV here curiously fails to recognize that "spirit" is a reference to the "Spirit," i.e., the Spirit of God.

52. See Michael J. Gorman, *Cruciformity: Paul's Narrative Spirituality of the Cross* (Grand Rapids: Eerdmans, 2001).

purpose in two different ways: "And he died for all, so that (*hina*) those who live might live no longer for themselves, but for him who died and was raised for them (5:15); and "For our sake he made him to be sin who knew no sin, so that (*hina*) in him we might become the righteousness of God" (5:21).

All of this drives Paul once again to use the word "new," but this time it is "new creation" (5:17) rather than "new covenant." Yet the two are closely related.[53] The prophetic promises that God will bring about a new covenant (and thus a new people) and also bring about a new creation are both being fulfilled in and through Christ, inaugurated by his death and resurrection. Paul summarizes that covenant-effecting, community-creating act in the word "reconciliation" (5:18–20). It is clear that this reconciliation involves forgiveness ("not counting their trespasses against them" 5:19), but also more. As in Matthew's account of the Last Supper, forgiveness is the prerequisite for participation in the new creation/covenant, the start of the transformation into the righteousness of God. Christ did not die merely to forgive sins, or to create a people who know themselves to be forgiven. Rather, he died to create a covenant-keeping people, a people that embodies the kind of divine righteousness displayed in Christ's incarnation and death. The ministry of the new covenant is a ministry of righteousness/justice (3:9; Greek *dikaiosynēs*; NRSV "justification.").

Richard Hays has recently offered the following important comment on 2 Cor 5:21:

> Notice carefully what Paul actually says here: Not "so that we might know about the righteousness of God." Not "so that we might believe in the righteousness of God." Not "so that we might proclaim the righteousness of God." Not even "so that we might be justified by the righteousness of God." Rather, he says, "so that we might *become* the righteousness of God." Our commission from God is that we as a community are called to embody the righteousness of God in the world—to incarnate it, if you will—in such a way that the message of reconciliation is made visible in our midst. And of course reconciliation made visible is something that can appear only in practices that show unity, love, mercy, forgiveness and a self-giving grace that the world could not even dream of apart from Christ.[54]

---

53. See, e.g., Ralph P. Martin, *2 Corinthians* (WBC 40; Dallas: Word, 1986) 152–53.

54. From a sermon preached June 1, 2010 and based on his *Moral Vision*, 24; see http://www.faithandleadership.com/sermons/the-word-reconciliation, 2. There has been some debate about the identity of the "we" that becomes the righteousness of God, but Katherine Grieb makes a compelling case (against N. T. Wright) that the "we" refers to all those in Christ. See A. Katherine Grieb, "'So That in Him We Might Become the Righteousness of God' (2 Cor 5:21): Some Theological Reflections on the Church Becoming Justice," *Ex Auditu* 22 (2006) 58–80. Unless we want to posit a new version of

Not only do I agree with Hays, but also, with Morna Hooker and others, I have argued that 5:21 is about justification understood as transformation; there is nothing about "imputation" here. In fact, what Hooker calls the Pauline patterns of interchange—Christ became what we were so that we might become what he is—constitute the Pauline basis for the early Christian doctrine of theosis.[55] This takes place, not by imitation, but by indwelling, being "in him." For Paul this indwelling is not a one-way relationship but mutual: we in Christ, Christ in us; we in the Spirit, the Spirit in us (see, e.g., Rom 8:1–17). The new covenant promise of interiority has been fulfilled but also altered, as in John, to become mutual indwelling.[56]

Some may think that the idea of God reconciling us to himself (5:18) restricts the notion of reconciliation to the vertical realm. But that interpretation flies in the face of the evidence of Second Corinthians as a whole. In this letter Paul is at pains to effect reconciliation between himself and the Corinthians, an effort not only grounded in his gospel of reconciliation but also presented as an essential part of that gospel. How can Paul, or the Corinthians, claim to themselves or others that they are reconciled to God if they are not reconciled to one another? That is the narrative logic and theo-logic of Second Corinthians, especially chs. 1–7.

Moreover, for Paul the *message* of reconciliation and righteousness is also a *mission* of reconciliation and righteousness (5:20—6:2). Though the text may put the primary emphasis on Paul's apostolic mission team as "ambassadors for Christ" (5:20), it is difficult to think that Paul wants the righteous, reconciled community in Christ to be anything less than a community of righteousness/justice and reconciliation in and for the world.[57]

Once again, we see in Paul the transformative nature of the atonement: Christ's death is God's re-creative, transformative, righteousness-effecting, covenant-producing, community-creating, empowering, paradigmatic, mission-generating act.

---

limited atonement—Christ died only for Paul and other ministers—then we must conclude that some of the "we" texts in Second Corinthians clearly and deliberately refer to all believers, and preeminent among them is 5:21.

55. Morna D. Hooker, *From Adam to Christ: Essays on Paul* (Cambridge: Cambridge University Press, 1990; repr. Eugene, OR: Wipf and Stock, n.d.) 13–69; Michael J. Gorman, *Inhabiting the Cruciform God: Kenosis, Justification, and Theosis in Paul's Narrative Soteriology* (Grand Rapids: Eerdmans, 2009). Interest in this aspect of Paul is on the rise. In *Inhabiting*, I define theosis, especially in Paul, as "transformative participation in the kenotic, cruciform character of God through Spirit-enabled conformity to the incarnate, crucified, and resurrected/glorified Christ" (7).

56. Chronologically, this probably happened first in Paul's spirituality/theology.

57. See Grieb, "'So That in Him.'"

Galatians

Before turning to the other occurrence of "new covenant" in Paul (1 Cor 11:25), we briefly consider new covenant theology in Galatians. Three brief but highly significant points will have to suffice. Elsewhere I have developed these points at greater length.[58]

First, in his discussion of justification, Paul is in part defining the nature of the (new) covenant community: who is in, why, and how. The "Israel of God" (6:16) is defined, not as the community of the circumcised, but as those Gentiles and Jews, men and women, slaves and free (3:28) who have received the eschatological gift of the Spirit, which is now in and among them, as Jeremiah and Ezekiel promised (and, for that matter, Abraham; see 3:6–18). This Spirit is, of course, the Spirit of God, but also—and this is crucial for Paul—the Spirit of the Son (4:6; cf. Rom 8:9).

Second, the members of this new covenant community have received the Spirit of the Son, the Messiah, by responding in faith to the proclamation of the gospel of the crucified Messiah (3:1–5), which means participation in the death of Jesus the Son of God/Messiah (2:15–21).[59] Paul does not spell out the mechanics of this event, but he makes it clear that there is a close association between expressing faith that leads to justification, being crucified with Christ, and receiving the Spirit; the three are essentially one. *In fact, this may well be Paul's most innovative and important contribution to the theology of the new covenant: the "new spirit" that comes to dwell in the people is the Spirit of the crucified Messiah; it is, therefore, the cruciform Spirit, the spirit of cruciformity.*[60]

Third, if we understand the occurrences of the noun *pistis* ("faith," "faithfulness") in Gal 2:15–21 as references to Christ's own faith (i.e., faithfulness), then Paul characterizes Jesus' death as an act of both faithfulness toward God (2:16 [twice], 20) and love for us (2:20).[61] It is thus the quintessential act of covenantal fulfillment, the paradigmatic symbiosis of the vertical and the horizontal requirements of the covenant. To live in the Son/Messiah, and to have the Spirit of the faithful and loving

---

58. See Gorman, *Cruciformity*, especially 122–54, 214–67; and *Inhabiting the Cruciform God*, 40–104.

59. For a philosophically oriented treatment of the atonement that relies heavily on the motif of participation found in Paul, see Tim Bayne and Greg Restall: "A Participatory Theory of the Atonement," in *New Waves in Philosophy of Religion* (ed. Yujin Nagasawa and Erik Wielenberg; Hampshire, UK: Palgrave, 2008) 150–66 (available also at http://consequently.org/papers/pa.pdf).

60. See Gorman, *Cruciformity*, 50–62.

61. See Gorman, *Cruciformity*, 95–121, and *Inhabiting the Cruciform God*, 40–104.

Son/Messiah within, means that the covenant community will be people of "faith working through love" (5:6). It will be impossible to separate the vertical from the horizontal, or the spiritual from the ethical and missional.

Galatians, to summarize, demonstrates that for Paul participation in the faithful and loving, covenant-fulfilling Christ—and that alone—is the basis for reception of the Spirit and membership in the new covenant community. Furthermore, this participation is the reason why the community and all those within in it are both required and able to fulfill the covenantal requirements of faithfulness and love (see 5:14; cf. Rom 13:8–10[62]).

First Corinthians 10–11

One of several concrete manifestations of the significance of this cruciform communal covenant-keeping in Paul may be found in his discussion of the Lord's Supper in 1 Cor 10–11. Elsewhere I have suggested that Paul makes four key theological claims about Lord's Supper: it is (1) "not a sequence of private meals but an experience of solidarity or fellowship (*koinōnia*)" with both Christ and one another; (2) an "event of memory," meaning not recollection but present appropriation and participation; (3) "an act of proclamation—a parabolic sermon"; and (4) a "foretaste of the future messianic banquet."[63] To these four we may now add the following: the Lord's Supper for Paul is also a microcosm of the new covenant life effected by the cross.

In 1 Cor 10 Paul concludes his discussion of believers and meat offered to idols by pronouncing the Lord's Supper as an exclusive meal: "You cannot drink the cup of the Lord and the cup of demons. You cannot partake of the table of the Lord and the table of demons" (10:21). One cannot be in relationship/partnership/fellowship with the Lord Christ and Lord Serapis or whomever. Attempting to do so violates the "vertical" dimension of the new covenant, loving the Lord; it is idolatry (10:7, 14).

In 11:17–34 Paul, from a very different angle, asserts that the Corinthians are no longer celebrating the Lord's Supper (11:20). That is, he says to them, "Your practice (intentional or not) of separate meals and times, plus the consequent disdain for the lowly, subverts the realities to which the meal points—Christ's past atoning death, Christ's present role as host and communion partner, Christ's future return,

---

62. Rom 8:13–14 shows that Paul refers to the second table when speaking of love as fulfilling the Law.

63. Gorman, *Apostle of the Crucified Lord*, 268–69 (original emphasis omitted).

Christ as Lord, the inherent connection between the cross and the weak, and the unity of the church."

Focusing simply on the first of these, we can say that the Corinthians have failed to be a "community called atonement." Why? Because they have their doctrine of the atonement wrong? No, or at least, that is not the reason Paul gives. They have misunderstood the atonement by their inappropriate exclusion of some in the community (10:21–22), that is, by their failure to fulfill the horizontal demands of the new covenant. This horizontal failure is likely grounded in the vertical failure. The Lord's Supper at Corinth looks like a symposium offered by, to, and with any other first-century deity, performed in a context where inclusivity of deities (Tuesday, Serapis; Wednesday, Asclepius; and so on) and exclusivity of humans (honored peers, yes; their slaves, no) are the norms. That is not the way of the Lord and banquet host who was crucified on a cross.

Ironically, the Corinthians have rendered the Lord's Supper null and void by making its exclusive (i.e. vertical) dimension inclusive, and its inclusive (i.e. horizontal) dimension exclusive. In two distinct but inseparable ways, the Corinthians have failed to understand and practice the ritual that connects them to the atonement and that embodies the atonement in concrete practices.

The only way these Pauline pronouncements make any sense is if the new covenant in Jesus' blood creates—or is meant to create—a community in which the vertical and horizontal are seamlessly merged and concretely practiced. Paul assumes the inseparability of orthodoxy and orthopraxy, and he assumes the inseparability of the vertical and the horizontal in the atonement. Some may be tempted to say, "Paul is talking about ethics, not atonement." Therein lies the kind of problem that Paul addresses; ethics is not a separate category! Ethics is atonement in action, not as a supplement, but as constitutive of atonement itself. The horizontal is not the *result* of atonement, it is one of the *components* of atonement.

Effecting the New Covenant in Hebrews

Significant attention has been paid to the theology of covenant and sacrifice in Hebrews, and some serious concerns about that theology have been raised. One concern is that Hebrews endorses supersessionism, which seems to some to be inherent in the notion of a new and better covenant. Another concern is that Hebrews endorses violence by grounding this new and better covenant in blood and sacrifice.[64]

---

64. See, e.g., Stephen Finlan, *Options on Atonement in Christian Thought* (Collegeville, MN:

Rather than reexamine the theology of covenant and sacrifice per se in Hebrews, I wish to answer these two charges and simultaneously also to discuss the contribution of Hebrews to the new covenant model of atonement. I wish to consider not the *mechanics* of the new covenant in Hebrews but the *effect*.

Hebrews, like Revelation (see below), is a summons to covenant faithfulness.[65] It is also a warning that even participation in the blessings of the (new) covenant does not guarantee final salvation. Thus according to Hebrews it is possible to "lose" one's salvation, one's part in the new covenant (6:1–8; 10:19–39). This possibility would seem to call into question the efficacy of Christ's supposedly once-for-all (7:27; 9:12), new-covenant-effecting sacrificial death, rendering it nothing better than the repeated animal sacrifices it allegedly replaced (see 9:12–22; 10:1–4, 11). But Hebrews does not allow us to draw that conclusion.

Rather, the author of Hebrews makes it clear that the purpose of Christ's death, and the evidence of genuine participation in the new and permanent covenant it inaugurated, is—not surprisingly—permanence. The prophecy of Jeremiah, quoted at length in Heb 8, is a promise that the fate of Israel and Judah will not be repeated in the new and different covenant, "for they did not continue in my covenant" (Heb 8:9, referring to Jer 31:32 in the LXX [38:32]). The new covenant offers a permanent place, "an eternal inheritance" (9:15). The death of Christ is not just a *one*-time offering but an *all*-time offering (10:14). Moreover, because Christ's death was the ultimate demonstration of his faithfulness despite shame and suffering (12:1–3; cf. 2:17; 3:1–6), associating with his death in faith means sharing in his faithfulness, even in the face of persecution.

Those who benefit from and participate in Christ's one-time, for-all-time, faithful self-offering must therefore remain permanently faithful to the new covenant it effects. This requirement does not, however, entail a form of Pelagianism, for it is the promissory character of the new covenant and of the God who has established this new covenant that makes permanent covenant faithfulness possible: "Let us hold fast to the confession of our hope without wavering, for he who has promised [i.e., promised permanence in Jer 31] is faithful" (10:23). The human responsibility is to assemble together to promote this covenant faithfulness as well as "love and good deeds" within the covenant community (10:24–25).

The new covenant community is called to be permanently loyal and loving, yet when it falters it must be warned. Its allegedly "supersessionist" status is better

---

Liturgical, 2007) 44–53.

65. So also Harold W. Attridge, *Hebrews* (Hermeneia; Philadelphia: Fortress, 1989) 13, 21–23.

understood as participation in the promised new covenant activity of God, and it is not a status to be taken for granted or viewed with either pride in self or disdain toward others.

Effecting the New Covenant in Revelation

In contrast to Hebrews the word "covenant" appears in the book of Revelation only once, and it is in reference to the ark of the covenant (11:19). Nonetheless, there is a strong emphasis in the book on covenant faithfulness in connection to Jesus' death.

The central figure of the book of Revelation is Jesus as the Lamb; he is referred to as the Lamb twenty-eight times, meaning the slaughtered Lamb (5:6, 9, 12; 13:8). In addition to the possible sacrificial connotations of that image, Jesus' death in Revelation should above all be viewed as an act of faithful witness, the culmination of his loyalty to God. Indeed, Jesus is called "the faithful witness" in the same breath as he is called the one who "loves us and freed us from our sins by his blood" (1:5); he is also called "the faithful and true witness" (3:14), and simply "Faithful and True" (19:11). Thus, John can speak of the faith(fulness) of Jesus (14:12) and possibly also of the witness of Jesus (1:9; NRSV "testimony").

Throughout Revelation disciples are depicted as those who share—or who should share—in the faithfulness, witness, suffering, and possibly even slaughter of Jesus. "Be faithful until death," Jesus tells the church at Smyrna (2:10), while the church at Pergamum is commended for its faithfulness, as is their deceased brother Antipas, the sole named martyr in Revelation: "my witness, my faithful one" (2:13). All the martyrs now in heaven were slaughtered for their witness (NRSV "testimony"; 6:9; cf. 18:24). Faith (*pistis*) as a virtue in Revelation means not assent or even trust but faithfulness, and it is coupled with endurance (*hypomonē*; 2:19; 13:10; cf. 14:12), suggesting in combination also "resistance." The opposite of faith/*pistis*, therefore, is faithlessness (21:8).

Therefore, the sacrificial, liberating death of Jesus is also the faithful, witness-bearing death of Jesus, and it has created a people who are forgiven and liberated by his death in order to share in that death—whether figuratively or literally—as his faithful witnesses. In other words, Jesus' death has created a new covenant, faithful, cruciform, and missional multinational (5:9) people. The role of Christ's death—his "blood"—in this is absolutely critical. It is by his blood that Christ "ransomed saints for God" (5:9), and it is by "washing" in his blood that the saints survive the great ordeal, or tribulation (7:14), and are victorious, or "conquer" (12:11). John seems to ascribe a kind of power to Christ's death. It may well be that John wants us to understand that part of the role of the Spirit who continually speaks (2:7, etc.) to the churches is to make the faithful death of Jesus palpably present to the communities so that they replicate the faithfulness of Jesus exhibited in his death.[66] This is certainly a central aspect of "being in the Spirit" in Revelation (e.g., 1:10; 4:2): participating in the ongoing heavenly worship of the slaughtered Lamb (ch. 5) and thereby preparing for ongoing public witness to that Lamb.

With good reason, then, Charles Talbert has characterized Revelation as a summons to first-commandment faithfulness.[67] Yet while the vertical dimension of the covenant—loyalty to God and the faithful, slaughtered Lamb—is clearly the emphasis in Revelation, the book does not lack a summons to the horizontal dimension of the covenant. In fact, both dimensions appear to be combined in several places. One place is the message to Ephesus that criticizes the church for having abandoned "the love [they] had at first" (2:4). Some interpreters think the lost love is love for God, or for both God and others, but in the message the Ephesians' loyalty to and love for God/Christ is evident; they "are enduring patiently and bearing up for the sake of [Christ's] name" (2:3). The love they need to regain, therefore, is for one another.

Similarly, John combines the vertical and horizontal in describing the faithful as those who "keep the commandments of God and hold the testimony of Jesus" (12:17), which is better translated "maintain the witness to Jesus" or "maintain the witness of Jesus."[68] Further, the saints' "endurance" or "resistance" is defined as "keep[ing] the commandments of God and hold[ing] fast to the faith of Jesus" (14:12). David Aune argues that in Revelation "the commandments of God" serves as a summary of the Law's ethical requirements (i.e., the second table). If he is right, as I think he is, then in these two texts as well as in ch. 2, John describes covenant faithfulness as the inseparable vertical and horizontal practices of bearing faithful witness to and like Jesus and fulfilling obligations of the Law to others.[69]

One last point needs to be made about Revelation. Despite its images of a slaughtered Lamb whose blood effects ransom, liberation, and victory (not to mention its graphic images of divine judgment), the book does not—or at least does not

---

66. The close association of the Spirit with the slaughtered Lamb is evident in Rev 5:6.

67. See Charles Talbert, *The Apocalypse: A Reading of the Revelation of John* (Louisville: Westminster John Knox, 1994) 11.

68. See Aune, "Following the Lamb," 282.

69. For further treatment of these themes in Revelation, see Michael J. Gorman, *Reading Revelation Responsibly: Uncivil Worship and Witness: Following the Lamb into the New Creation* (Eugene, OR: Cascade, 2011).

intend to—produce a violent people. In fact, just the opposite is the case; the faithful are called to accept suffering and death if necessary, but not to inflict it (13:9–10). The new covenant people is a community of non-violence.[70]

The New Covenant Model in Relation to Traditional and Recent Models of the Atonement

Having concluded our (necessarily incomplete) consideration of the new covenant model of the atonement in the NT witnesses, we may now briefly consider the relationship of this model to other models of the atonement, both traditional and more recent. Space does not permit an extensive discussion, though such a discussion will obviously be needed as the conversation continues.

Christus Victor/Apocalyptic Interpretations

We have seen from the discussion of Jeremiah that the new covenant will be the result, like the Mosaic covenant, of a liberation, a (new) Exodus. No doubt this is implied in the Last Supper, and it is of course present in NT texts that speak of liberation of human beings from the powers, from sin and death, and from the devil. This theme is therefore inherently part of the new covenant model. Its presence implies that covenantal and apocalyptic understandings of atonement can—indeed, must—co-exist.

The promise of the new covenant is ultimately to deliver people into a form of covenantal life that the Mosaic covenant prescribed but did not fully provide. New Testament writers, especially Paul, attribute this, not to some inherent flaw in the first covenant, but to the power of the forces arrayed against humanity. Christ's victory in his death and resurrection provides the liberation from these powers that humans need to start afresh and to live in the new age of the new covenant.

---

70. Richard Hays insightfully comments on this issue: "A work that places the Lamb that was slaughtered at the center of its praise and worship can hardly be used to validate violence and coercion. . . . As a paradigm for the action of the faithful community, Jesus stands as the faithful witness who conquers through suffering. . . . Those who read the battle [or, we might add, sacrificial] imagery of Revelation with a literalist bent fail to grasp the way in which the symbolic logic of the work as a whole dismantles the symbolism of violence" (*The Moral Vision of the New Testament*, 185). See further discussion in Gorman, *Reading Revelation Responsibly*, especially ch. 8.

Satisfaction/Sacrificial/Penal Interpretations

The new covenant model can incorporate a sacrificial model of the atonement, carefully articulated, as a partial explanation of what Christ's death effects and how it effects it. This is true for at least three reasons.

First, the same NT writers who use new covenant language also use the language of sacrifice. Forgiveness of sins via the sacrifice of Christ is an essential, but not a sufficient, dimension of an atonement model rooted in the NT texts. To suggest that the new covenant model and the sacrificial model are mutually exclusive would be to ignore the evidence of the NT itself. The prophetic promise of a forgiven covenantal people is realized in the sacrificial death of Christ.

Second, as T. F. Torrance (among others) points out, the sacrificial system in the OT is itself an emblem of God's covenantal faithfulness and mercy, an expression of God's hospitality, in the apt phraseology of Hans Boersma.[71] The sacrifice of Christ, therefore, must be viewed by us as it is viewed by the NT writers: as the ultimate expression of God's covenantal love. Now, however, the reach of that love extends beyond Israel to all peoples; this is part of the newness of the new covenant as it is articulated in the writings of the NT. The death of Christ should not be seen as the expression of divine anger or even wrath, but as the expression of divine love. It is the gift of God's Son and, at least in some sense, the gift of God's own self: "God was in Christ . . ." (2 Cor 5:19). If that is the major emphasis from the satisfaction/sacrificial/penal kind of atonement models, then there may also be room for the satisfaction and penal components as minor sub-plots in the atonement narrative, but only if they can be clearly found in the NT texts, and only if they retain their minor role in relation to divine, covenantal love.

Third, the death of Christ is also the manifestation of Christ's own love, an act of self-giving and self-sacrifice. Christ is both the gift, i.e. from God, and the giver, i.e. the one who gives himself in covenant love.[72] Beneficiaries of the new covenant who receive this gift are also participants in it. The recipients of the gift become like the gift and the giver. This leads us to the question of participation and theosis, for theosis is the consequence of a divine act of giving and self-giving that manifests the very character of God.

---

71. See, e.g., Torrance, *Atonement*, 38–39. On this divine hospitality, see Hans Boersma, *Violence, Hospitality, and the Cross* (Grand Rapids: Baker Academic, 2004).

72. In fact, Christ should be seen as the gift in two ways: as gift from God the Father as giver and as gift from himself as giver.

Incarnational/Participatory/Theosis

When I first told my friend Richard Hays about my plans to do this paper, he—knowing very well my interest in participation and theosis—immediately asked, "What does that have to do with theosis?" My response was and remains essentially this: in becoming part of the new covenant community that takes on the Christlike holiness of God by the work of the Spirit, and specifically the divine character traits of faithfulness and love, we are drawn into the very life of the Triune God. We are drawn into God's being-expressed-in-acts, God's narrative identity, and that is participation. That is theosis.

A number of recent proposals for new models of the atonement have stressed its incarnational, participatory, and theotic nature. Similar approaches to justification and atonement in Paul, including especially the work of Morna Hooker, Richard Hays, and myself (all noted above), as well as Douglas Campbell and Udo Schnelle, reinforce this more participationist understanding of salvation and atonement.[73] The new covenant model, it should be clear, resonates deeply with these new directions.

Moral Influence Interpretations

The moral influence model of the atonement is the weakest of the traditional models. Nonetheless, the new covenant model clearly includes the best of the moral influence model. The cross is the quintessential act of covenant fulfillment, and particularly of love of neighbor, even of enemy. By the work of the Spirit within—though not merely by inspiration or imitation—the community of the new covenant is able to reincarnate, even if imperfectly, the divine love and hospitality that are the motivation behind and the substance of the cross.

Nonviolent Atonement Interpretations

As noted above, the new covenant model emphasizes Jesus' death as an act of divine, self-giving love. We may now be more specific. It is not an act of violence but of love that generates a covenant community of love and nonviolence. This is one of the new developments in the New Testament's appropriation of the new covenant tradition: the emphasis on nonviolence and reconciliation.

---

73. See Douglas A. Campbell, *The Deliverance of God: An Apocalyptic Rereading of Justification* (Grand Rapids: Eerdmans, 2009) and Udo Schnelle, *Apostle Paul: His Life and Theology* (trans. M. Eugene Boring; Grand Rapids: Baker, 2005 [2003]).

There is not a scrap of evidence that the images of sacrifice and ransom in the NT created a violent people among the first recipients. If it is true that "by their fruits you shall know them," then perhaps calling atonement by sacrifice inherently violent is a grave error. On the other hand, if we include the reception history and impact history of such biblical images among their "fruits," as indeed we must, then we will rightly come to the conclusion that those images, when wrongly interpreted and appropriated, have the potential to inspire or underwrite violence.

Conclusion

The new covenant model is indeed more comprehensive, integrated, participatory, communal, and missional than any of the major models in the tradition. The NT writers apparently were far less concerned about the mechanics of the atonement than about the results, but the new covenant model incorporates other models of the atonement that do depict the mechanics, some of which are hinted at in the prophetic promises themselves.

Our primary goal in the preceding pages has been to rediscover the features of a new covenant model of the atonement in various parts of the NT. The basic claim has been that the NT writers we have considered view the several aspects of the promised new covenant as having been effected by the death of Jesus. This is not to assert that any or all of these writers had, or could articulate if asked, a systematic doctrine of the atonement that they would label "the new covenant model of the atonement." Rather, we have found that these writers, in various ways—sometimes deliberately, sometimes perhaps not—interpreted the death of Jesus in ways that correspond to those aspects of the new covenant found especially in Jeremiah and Ezekiel. The prophets expected a new covenant people who would be liberated, restored, forgiven, sanctified, covenantally faithful, empowered, missional, and permanent. The NT writers are convinced that Jesus' death created that people.

At the risk of neglecting the differences and distinctives among these writers, we may now summarize our findings, and thus the new covenant model of the atonement in the NT. *Christ's death effected the new covenant, meaning specifically the creation of a covenant community of forgiven and reconciled disciples, inhabited and empowered by the Spirit to embody a new covenant spirituality of cruciform loyalty to God and love for others, thereby participating in the life of God and in God's forgiving, reconciling, and covenanting mission to the world.*

I believe that this kind of holistic, communal, participatory, missional model of the atonement—incorporating various metaphors for its "mechanics"—is precisely what the church needs to appropriate, articulate, and actualize today.[74]

---

74. I wish to thank my student and research assistant Kurt Pfund for his help with this essay.

RESPONSE TO GORMAN

Troy W. Martin

First, let me thank Prof. Gorman for his stimulating and engaging paper that proposes a "new covenant model" of the atonement to replace or, perhaps better, to complement other theories of the atonement. Gorman says his paper is both too short and too long. His paper is indeed too long for the time allotted to it at this symposium. We could spend the remainder of our time discussing his paper and still not be able to address all the significant issues it raises. His paper is too long for me to offer an adequate response in the even shorter time that I have been allotted. I want to concentrate on a few ways in which his paper is too short before describing what I consider to be the real significance and enduring contribution of what he has written.

The paper is too short in its criticism of prior theories of the atonement for their lack of focus on covenant language. Gorman begins his criticism by stating, "That there is no theory or model of the atonement called 'covenant,' 'new covenant,' or something very similar is one of the great wonders of the theological world." His statement is obviously correct, but the lack of the term *covenant* in the names of these theories does not necessarily demonstrate that they are devoid of new covenant content. For instance, Gorman notes that John 13–17 does not contain the word *covenant* but nevertheless develops many covenant motifs. His criticism may indeed be right that "(new) covenant is not significant to the Christian theological tradition on the atonement." However, his argument that the term *covenant* does not occur at all in the titles of theories of the atonement and only seldom in the substance of these theories is insufficient to prove his point. It would be helpful if his "too short" paper would demonstrate which new covenant themes, or if indeed all of them, are missing from the substance and not just the titles of these theories.[1]

---

1. Gorman himself recognizes this when he writes, "Not merely the lack of covenantal language in the 'names' of the standard theories of the atonement but also, more broadly, the near absence of such language from standard expositions of their content, might suggest that the tradition is blatantly ignoring the interpretation of Jesus himself as well as a very early, pre-Pauline Christian tradition rooted in Jesus' own interpretation." His paper needs to demonstrate that not just language but themes and motifs are lacking as well.

The paper is also too short in its explanation for the lack of a covenant emphasis in these theories. Gorman's demonstration that "(new) covenant" language figures prominently in atonement contexts in the NT but not in the subsequent theological discussion invites an explanation as to why subsequent theological theories on the atonement ignored this emphasis. He offers a negative explanation when he writes, "But the [new covenant] model is missing, both from the traditional accounts of the atonement and from more recent revisions of, and additions to, them. As we will see, I do not think that this is because covenant 'is not a common category through which the NT writers . . . processed their thinking.'" If this lack of emphasis is not caused by the NT writers, then what is the reason for this lack? Immediately following his negative explanation, he discusses four major problems with the traditional theories of the atonement. I am not certain if he intends this discussion of the problems to be an explanation for the lack of covenant language in these theories. These problems seem more to be the result of their failure to integrate covenantal language than the cause itself. We need further help to understand why covenant language is missing from the traditional theories of the atonement.

Nevertheless, I think the paper implicitly offers an explanation in his preference for the term *model* rather than for the term *theory* in reference to the atonement. I would like to make Gorman's implicit explanation explicit by using Aristotle's four causes as an analytical tool. Everyone is familiar with Aristotle's material, efficient, formal, and final causes. The material cause of a statue is the stone from which it is made. The efficient causes are the tools or instruments as well as the agent or agents necessary to sculpt the statue. The formal cause is the pattern according to which it is made, and the final cause is the purpose for which it is made, perhaps to grace someone's garden.

Gorman's decision to use the term *model* rather than *theory* indicates that his proposal offers a formal rather than an efficient cause for the atonement. The new covenant is the form or model that atonement takes, and this form is distinct from the form of the old covenant on which it is based and out of which it arises. Thus, he describes the "outline" of the new covenant model as well as the "characteristics" and "nature" of the new covenant people. Furthermore, he mentions the "vision" and "images" of this new community and the "cruciform shape" of the new covenant, as well as its "vertical (God-oriented) and horizontal (human-oriented) dimensions." He summarizes his model of the atonement by writing, "That is, God wants to form a people in his own image. The new covenant will be a new creation; the image of God will be restored, and not just in individuals, but in a people." This language is formal language as it describes the form of the new covenant or the new covenant community. What is proposed is a formal cause for the atonement.

In contrast to the formal cause of his model, however, traditional theories of the atonement address the efficient causes. The theories of *Christus Victor*, of satisfaction, and of moral influence all attempt to explain the "how" rather than the "form" of the atonement. They attempt to answer the question of how the broken relationship between sinful humans and a holy God is restored. In the *Christus Victor* theory the power of sin and evil is obliterated, and sinful humans are liberated to rejoin a holy God. In the satisfaction theory Jesus' sacrificial death allays a holy God's wrath so that sinful humans can be forgiven, ransomed, and restored. In the moral influence theory the imitation of Jesus enables sinful humans to improve and eventually to be worthy of relating to a holy God. Each of these theories and their variations explain how atonement occurs, and they thus address the efficient cause of the atonement in contrast to the formal cause of the new covenant model proposed by Gorman.

His paper works with this distinction but only implicitly. After describing the need for and the form of the new covenant model, the majority of his paper addresses the topic entitled "Effecting the New Covenant." The term *effecting* refers to the efficient cause, and he identifies this cause as the death of Jesus. At the end of this long section he makes an insightful comment, "The NT writers were far less concerned about the mechanics of the atonement than about the results. If that is true, then the new covenant model ought to be able to incorporate various other models of the atonement that highlight one or another of the metaphors that depict the mechanics." By "mechanics" Gorman refers, I think, to the efficient causes of the atonement, and he recognizes that his formal new covenant model does not necessarily exclude the efficient causes addressed by the traditional theories of the atonement.

Even though his paper is too short to enable us to understand why covenant language is missing from the traditional theories of the atonement, it nevertheless offers an implicit explanation that can now be stated explicitly in terms of Aristotelian causes. The traditional theories of the atonement fail to include the new covenant model because they address a different cause of the atonement. Whereas Gorman's model provides the formal cause, these theories present the efficient causes of the atonement, and it is not surprising that they lack extended discussions of the new covenant model proposed by Gorman.

Finally, the paper is too short in its consideration of the human person that is the object or beneficiary of the atonement. In particular, his new covenant model simply assumes an ancient and medieval understanding of the human condition and does not consider the modern psychological shift that has occurred in the conception of the human person.[2] At least since the time of Jerome, theories of the atonement have been based on the assumption that humans have a viable conscience capable of more or less determining right and wrong. In his theological reflections Thomas Aquinas among others accepts this assumption and describes the human problem as a willful decision to pursue the wrong and reject the right.

For theologians, therefore, the human problem is thus primarily an intellectual problem or a problem of the conscious will, and humans require convincing to reverse their thinking. In the *Christus Victor* theory the power of Christ convinces humans to abandon the folly of the transient wrong and embrace the enduring value of the right. In the satisfaction theory the sacrifice of Christ convinces humans to repent of the wrong and turn to the right. In the moral influence theory the example of Christ convinces humans to adopt the right and avoid the wrong. Gorman's new covenant model assumes that humans are capable of choosing to leave the wrong, noncovenantal group of humans and join the right group known as the new covenant community. At the risk of oversimplifying, all of these theories and models of the atonement assess the human problem primarily as faulty thinking or rebellious willfulness, with guilt or conviction playing an essential motivational role to effect change. Each of these theories envisions and depends for the appropriation of the atonement upon a human with a viable conscience.

Sigmund Freud and subsequent psychologists, however, have undermined this assumption that all humans possess a viable conscience. Psychologists estimate that at least four percent of the population has no conscience at all and is incapable of determining right from wrong. A significantly larger proportion of the population has such a deformed conscience that it is also unable to distinguish right from wrong in any way approximating what the rest of us think. In particular, those with a Narcissistic Personality Disorder are incapable of feeling empathy toward others and of accepting responsibility for their actions. They are thus capable of treating others in the most inhuman ways since their basis for determining right and wrong is whatever enhances or detracts from their projected self image. At no time, however, do those with no conscience or those with such a deformed conscience feel any

---

2. For a concise discussion of the relationship between theology and psychology on this issue, see Martha Stout, *The Sociopath Next Door: The Ruthless Versus the Rest of Us* (New York: Broadway, 2005) 26–32.

guilt or think that they have done anything wrong. If anything is wrong, it is always someone else's fault.

Gorman's paper is too short in that he does not explain how his new covenant model of the atonement relates to this significant proportion of the human population. In the first part of his paper he describes the form of the new community as "liberated, restored, forgiven, sanctified, covenantally faithful, empowered, missional, and permanent." It would be helpful if his paper explained how those without conscience or those with a severely deformed conscience could ever appropriate or fit into this form. It seems they are excluded by the very nature of their deficient or defective conscience. In the second and larger part of his paper he discusses the death of Jesus as the efficient cause of this new community. He states, "Jesus' imminent death will create the covenant community that the entire gospel narrative has described: a community of missional, self-giving, loyal-to-God disciples who are able and willing to suffer and die for their commitment." Later, he describes Jesus' death as a creative transformation "of a 'new covenantal community' and the enabling of a 'new covenantal loyalty.'" In this part of his paper, however, he never explains how Jesus' death transforms or enables those with little or no conscience to become this community. More is needed.

All the other theories of the atonement, however, also fail to address the modern psychological view of a human without a conscience at all or with a severely deficient one. Theologians in general and biblical theologians in particular need to relate the appropriation of the atonement to this psychological assessment of the human condition and stop assuming a prior antiquated conception based on the assumption of a viable conscience in all humans. The simple response that God's grace has the power to heal or restore the deficient or defective conscience will appear naïve to psychologists who know the almost hopeless prognosis for these people. Psychologists also have the right to request from theologians case studies of those diagnosed with such conditions that were subsequently "cured" by God's grace. The following are my questions to Gorman and to all of us participating in this symposium on the atonement. Do we have any data to corroborate the simple response that God's grace is capable of healing such people? Do we have any proof that the atonement reaches these hopeless people or, in terms of the subjective appropriation, are we left with a modern version of a limited atonement?

Lest we think that this problem raised by the modern psychological assessment of the human population is simply an annoyance for our theological theories or models of the atonement, let me place this problem in a pastoral context. In a church of 500 members, as many as twenty may have no conscience at all, and many dozens more may have a severely deficient conscience. How does a pastor relate the atonement to such a significant number of these members? What hope can a pastor give to the father forced to make the agonizing decision to institutionalize his son, who has been diagnosed as having no conscience. After speaking to a Christian gathering about the Narcissistic Personality Disorder, I was caught off-guard by a man who approached me and stated that he was one and wanted to know what to do now. I must confess that my decades of theological training and study left me without an adequate response.

I have often thought of the pastor of the church in Wichita, Kansas, and how he ministered after the arrest and conviction of a prominent member of his congregation as the BTK serial killer. On which theory or model of the atonement did he base his pastoral response to this man so devoid of conscience? I realize this example may border on sensationalism, but it was nonetheless a reality for this pastor in Wichita. If the psychologists are correct in their assessment of the human condition, many other pastors in less extreme, less notorious, and less publicized cases face no less perplexing predicaments that demand a pastoral response.[3] What help do our theories or models of the atonement offer to pastors dealing with those in their congregations who possess deficient or defective consciences?

My daughter and I have written a manuscript entitled "I Promise to Hate, Despise, and Abuse You Till Death Do Us Part: Marriage in a Narcissistic Age." We have sent it to several readers for comments, and their primary concern is that we fail to explain how God's grace deals with the narcissist whose lack of empathy creates tortuous, toxic marriages. Our manuscript does not contain an explanation because we do not know. I explained to one of my readers that I would be attending a symposium on the atonement at North Park Theological Seminary and that I would ask those there how to respond to him. He seemed pleased, and I am making good on that promise now. I am hoping that all of you will help me formulate a response to him.

I hope that I have not been unfair in pointing out that Gorman's paper does not relate his model of the atonement to such people since other theories and models

---

3. Lest the BTK example seem an aberration, consider the recent case of Robert Courtney, a pharmacist in Kansas City, who for years diluted drugs for cancer patients so he could donate a million dollars to his church. Of course, examples of this problem can be multiplied if instances of sexual abuse in the church are perpetrated by those with defective or deficient consciences. The problem of how to relate the appropriation of the atonement to those not possessing a viable conscience is not an aberration but a very real crisis that invites a theological response.

also do not address this problem and I myself have not been able to do so either. I would really like to know how the atonement relates to people whom psychologists diagnose as having no conscience or a deficient conscience, and I wish Gorman would expand his "too short" paper to address this issue. I also invite the rest of us as well to reflect on this issue in the remainder of this symposium.

Permit me to conclude with what I consider to be the real significance and enduring contribution of what Gorman has written. He has accurately assessed that prior theories of the atonement have concentrated too much on what he calls the "mechanics" and what I call the efficient causes of the atonement. He has correctly perceived that the formal cause of the atonement deserves more attention, and he has reasonably proposed the new covenant as this formal cause. In all this I heartily concur with him and think he has done us all an invaluable service by helping us to begin thinking about the formal aspect of the atonement and how the efficient causes relate to this formal cause. In conclusion, I would simply like to say to him, "Thank you for your stimulating and engaging paper."

RESPONSE TO MARTIN

Michael J. Gorman

I want to express my gratitude to Troy Martin for his response to my paper. I especially appreciate his eagerness to run with my self-critique about the length of the paper and to milk that admission for all its worth. On a more serious note, I am grateful to him for the seriousness with which he has taken, not only my paper, but also and more importantly the pastoral implications of the atonement. Nevertheless, I fear that Martin has misunderstood, or perhaps underestimated, three important aspects of my proposal.

First, I fear he misinterprets my use of the word "model." My use, and even preference, for this term is hardly original or unique, as the title and text of Linda Peacore's essay for this symposium indicates, not to mention a host of other recent treatments of the atonement. I cannot speak for others, but I prefer the term for two reasons: it conveys something less speculative than "theory" and more concrete than "metaphor," and it suggests a holistic, more comprehensive approach to atonement—we might say an architecture of atonement—that moves beyond the narrowly focused traditional theories. In other words, the dictionary definition I have in mind for "model" is closer to "description of a complex reality" than "pattern." I do not prefer the term because it implies a "form of the new covenant or the new covenant community" and thus a formal, rather than an efficient, cause.

Second, I fear that Martin underestimates the comprehensive character of my proposal with respect to causes. Although most discussions of the atonement are not framed in the language of Aristotle's four causes, for the sake of argument I will grant the helpfulness of such language for the moment. While I do not know what the *material* cause of the atonement might be, my proposal clearly addresses the other three causes. Martin has already stressed the element of the *formal* cause. As for the *final* cause, I would suggest that it is the existence of a faithful and loyal covenant people to be God's own and to participate in God's mission. Furthermore, the very title of my essay—"Effecting the New Covenant"—also strongly suggests an *efficient* cause. That efficient cause is, as in the theories Martin discusses, the death of Jesus, understood in my proposal to effect forgiveness of sins, to liberate from sin's power, to establish a new covenant, and to create a new people. Indeed, I contend in the essay that "in the new covenant model I will propose, the effect is all of the above [propitiation, expiation, and/or forgiveness; victory and liberation; inspiration] and more, but that effect is best expressed, not in the rather narrow terms of the traditional models, but in more comprehensive and integrative terms like transformation, participation, and re-creation." In this regard, my proposal has certain resonances with the work of Gregory of Nyssa, as presented in this volume by Hans Boersma, who refers to the de-emphasis on "mechanics" in Gregory. In other words, like some other interpreters of atonement, both ancient and contemporary, I do not find preoccupation with the details of the "how"—the "mechanics"—to be particularly helpful or biblical, but that is not the same as recognizing no efficient cause.

Third, and very briefly, I fear that Martin renders my proposal Pelagian and individualistic when it is neither. His concern about people without a viable conscience is an important one for atonement theology, and I appreciate his raising it. Still, it is not clear to me that a model of the atonement that stresses divine initiative and the work of the Spirit corresponds to an anthropology focused on the intellectual character of the primary human problem, with the alleged solution being a change in thinking and a conscious choice to "join the right group." It seems to me that, unlike many atonement theories with no connection to pneumatology or ecclesiology, the new covenant proposal may prove to be fertile ground for exploring the question of atonement for those who are disabled, whether with respect to conscience or otherwise.

To conclude, I appreciate Martin's pushing me to try to clarify my position in a few respects, and I value his appreciation of the new covenant proposal, even if he perhaps mistakenly limits that proposal to the formal cause of the atonement. For my part, I would like to repeat the last line from my essay to indicate where I see the proposal's significance: I believe that this kind of holistic, communal, participatory, missional model of the atonement—incorporating various metaphors for its "mechanics"—is precisely what the church needs to appropriate, articulate, and actualize today.

"ANYONE HUNG ON A TREE IS UNDER GOD'S CURSE" (DEUTERONOMY 21:23): JESUS' CRUCIFIXION AND INTERRELIGIOUS EXEGETICAL DEBATE IN LATE ANTIQUITY

Peter W. Martens

It is difficult to convey to a contemporary audience the scandal associated with crucifixion in Greco-Roman antiquity. Crucifixion was a form of execution customarily reserved for the lower classes, slaves included, and for crimes particularly violent and treacherous. It was, moreover, a profoundly humiliating form of death. The criminal was usually crucified naked in a prominent public setting, and often not granted the dignity of burial.[1] Jesus and his followers were certainly not immune to the shame attached to his crucifixion. In one of the earliest Christian writings, the apostle Paul admitted that "the message about the cross is foolishness," but that he nevertheless proclaimed "Christ crucified, a stumbling block to Jews and foolishness to Gentiles" (1 Cor 1:18, 23, NRSV). As late as the turn of the ninth century, we still find Christians admonished by their leaders "not to be shamed of the pains Christ suffered for us."[2] While most Christians today do not have such a visceral response to Jesus' death, throughout most of their history the stigmatization associated with the crucified Jesus was deeply felt by his followers.

Yet these followers faced a more daunting task than rehabilitating their crucified Lord from the societal shame of crucifixion. This form of death also raised an acute theological problem. In the Torah nothing less than a curse from God was pronounced on anyone who hung from a tree:

> When someone is convicted of a crime punishable by death and is executed, and you hang him on a tree, his corpse must not remain all night upon the tree; you shall bury him that same day, for anyone hung on a tree is under God's curse (Deut 21:22–23).

---

1. For more on crucifixion in antiquity, see M. Hengel, *Crucifixion in the Ancient World and the Folly of the Message of the Cross* (trans. J. Bowden; Philadelphia: Fortress, 1977).

2. Theodore Abu Qurrah, *On Our Salvation*, B90. Translation: *Theodore Abu Qurrah* (trans. J. C. Lamoreaux; Library of the Christian East, vol. 1; Provo: Brigham Young University Press, 2005).

This verse complicated the picture considerably for Jesus' followers. If its reference to hanging was understood as inclusive of crucifixion (as it usually was), Deut 21:23 exacerbated the contemptible shame already associated with Jesus' death. He experienced more than a humiliating demise; he experienced God's condemnation.

In his Letter to the Galatians the Apostle Paul offered the earliest Christian retrieval of this verse. In a move that many in his audience would surely have seen as counterintuitive, he *applied* Deut 21:23 to Jesus' death, yet in such a way that did not undermine but rather paradoxically *endorsed* his messianic credentials. In the space of a few short lines the apostle contested that it was not a contradiction to insist that Jesus suffered God's condemnation when he was ingloriously executed on a tree. The crucified Jesus was indeed cursed in accordance with Deut 21:23, but he was still the "Christ," i.e., Messiah. Moreover, his death became a blessing, since "by becoming a curse for us," he "redeemed us from the curse of the law" (Gal 3:13).

My central concern in this paper is to trace the reception of Paul's condensed, and perhaps even cryptic, use of Deut 21:23 through several late antique authors. I will offer a selective history of the interpretation of this verse, focusing on the exegetical work of Justin Martyr (writing in the middle of the second century in Greek), Augustine (late fourth century in Latin), and Theodore Abu Qurrah (turn of the ninth century in Arabic). Despite the chronological and linguistic distances that separate these authors from one other, they bear a striking familial resemblance. Each refracted this verse christologically, thus following (and developing) Paul's exegetical precedent in his Letter to the Galatians. Each in turn accepted the concomitant challenge of grappling with the paradoxical possibility that God could curse his Messiah. As we will also see, each developed a similar strategy to the apostle for making sense of this ostensible contradiction. If Jesus experienced—so their arguments ran—a vicarious death (i.e., a death undergone on behalf of sinful people), he could in fact be God's Messiah who also experienced divine condemnation. These authors provide us a glimpse into the emergence of the early Christian doctrine of Jesus' vicarious atonement and how it was shaped by a Pauline retrieval of Deut 21:23.

Yet it is important to stress that each of these authors also shared a polemical context. When we canvass the panoramic religious landscape of late antiquity, it is conspicuous how often Deut 21:23 surfaced in the interreligious conflicts about the identity of Jesus. Vicarious atonement was only one of many possible interpretations of this verse; expressed otherwise, Paul's reading of the Torah's curse did not win universal approval. The aforementioned Christian exegetes offer a convenient reference point for surveying some of the diversity surrounding the reception of this verse. The accounts of Jesus' death that emerge in the writings of Justin, Augustine, and Theodore were all shaped by these theologians' debates with the rival interpretations of Deut 21:23 in Judaism, Manicheanism, and Islam, respectively. As will become increasingly clear in the course of this paper, the Torah's curse was seized in a number of different ways in late antiquity. In addition to those who followed Paul in applying this verse to Jesus to generate a sympathetic portrait of him, we will discover two other important approaches to this verse: those who applied it to Jesus to generate a critical portrait of him, and those who distanced the verse from him in order to promote a sympathetic view. The heterogeneous reception of Deut 21:23 turns out to be a convenient marker for late antique religious diversity.

Before turning to my argument, I should note that I intend for this paper to enter into an implicit dialogue with Gustaf Aulén's modern classic, *Christus Victor*.[3] Alongside this work I too wish to challenge the traditional narrative that the early church did little to forward a doctrine of atonement. We find, in fact, serious, sustained reflection on the theological significance of Jesus' death in early Christianity. Moreover, the traditional claim that we must wait for Anselm of Canterbury to find a developed account of atonement is also deeply misleading, and indeed, in ways even Aulén did not imagine. As we will see below, it is intriguing to consider the possibility that Anselm's account of atonement was actually derivative of Theodore abu Qurrah's earlier version. At the same time, I also wish to complicate in two ways the picture of the atonement that we have inherited from Aulén. First, he pressed his readers to acknowledge not simply the presence of a "Christus Victor" model of atonement in early Christianity, but that "that there can be no dispute that it is the dominant idea of the Atonement throughout the early church period . . . It was, in fact, the ruling idea of the Atonement for the first thousand years of Christian history."[4] This paper will suggest that this claim is inflated. Indeed, we will see that what is often considered a typically Protestant idea—penal substitution—actually played a significant role in early Christian reflection on Jesus' death. Second, this paper will also contend that Jesus' death was more integral to late antique interreligious disputes than Aulén himself recognized. By attending to the interreligious

---

3. G. Aulén, *Christus Victor: An Historical Study of the Three Main Types of the Idea of Atonement* (trans. by A. G. Hebert; London: SPCK, 1931; reprint: Eugene, OR: Wipf & Stock, 2003).

4. Ibid., 6. By the "Christus Victor" idea of atonement, Aulén signified "Divine conflict and victory," that Christ "fights against and triumphs over the evil powers of the world, the 'tyrants' under which mankind is in bondage and suffering, and in Him God reconciles the world to Himself" (p. 4).

milieu in which one Christian approach to the atonement emerged, we grasp more clearly the circumstances and challenges its authors faced when developing their accounts of Jesus' death.

Justin's *Dialogue with Trypho*[5]

Justin tells us that he was from Flavia Neapolis in the Roman province of Syria Palestina (*1 Apology* 1.1). As best we can tell, he was probably born in the first decade of the second century and spent some time in Ephesus before heading to Rome where he set up a school.[6] Justin offers us a rare glimpse into his formative years in the opening autobiographical paragraphs of the *Dialogue with Trypho*.[7] There he recalls how, as a young man, he sought initiation into the ranks of the philosophers. After studying with a Stoic, a Peripatetic (i.e., Aristotelian), and a Pythagorean, each of whom left him for different reasons unsatisfied, he turned to the Platonists "whose reputation was great" (2.6). However, one day while Justin was going for a walk by the sea, he tells us that he met "a respectable old man" who pushed him to concede the weaknesses in Platonic philosophy and look, in turn, more closely at the Hebrew prophets. These exalted God and made known his Son, the Christ (7.3). After this man departed, Justin tells of his conversion to the true philosophy of Christ. "But my spirit was immediately set on fire, and an affection for the prophets, and for those who are friends of Christ, took hold of me; while pondering on his words, I discovered that his was the only sure and useful philosophy" (8.1). Moreover, Justin continued, it was his desire "that everyone would be of the same sentiments as I, and never fall away from the Savior's words" (8.2). This wish captures well the tenor of Justin's surviving writings. His undisputed works include the two *Apologies* (composed roughly in 153) and the later *Dialogue with Trypho*. In each of these works we see Justin joining the already well-established tradition of Christian apologetic discourse, as he sought to offer a learned defense of the Christian faith against the prevailing criticisms of it in his day.

---

5. Translation: *St. Justin Martyr, Dialogue with Trypho* (trans. T. B. Falls; rev. T. P. Halton; ed. M. Slusser; Selections from the Fathers of the Church 3; Washington: Catholic University of America Press, 2003). Unless otherwise noted the numbers in parentheses refer to Justin's *Dialogue with Trypho*.

6. For introductions to Justin's life, see L. W. Barnard, *Justin Martyr: His Life and Thought* (Cambridge: Cambridge University Press, 1967); E. F. Osborn, *Justin Martyr* (Tübingen: Mohr Siebeck, 1973); S. Parvis and P. Foster, eds., *Justin Martyr and His Worlds* (Minneapolis: Fortress, 2007).

7. Some have read these opening paragraphs as reliable autobiography whereas others see them as rhetorical fiction. For commentary, see J. C. M. van Winden, *An Early Christian Philosopher: Justin Martyr's Dialogue with Trypho, chapters One to Nine* (Philosophia Patrum 1; Leiden: Brill, 1971).

Trypho's Interpretation of Deuteronomy 21:23

The *Dialogue with Trypho* recalls a conversation that transpired over the course of two days, shortly after the Bar Kochba revolt in Palestine in 132–135 (1.3; 9.3). In the opening chapter of this work we are introduced to Justin's interlocutor, Trypho, who identifies himself as a "Hebrew of the circumcision" (1.3). One morning when Justin was out for a walk, he met Trypho who consented to his request that he be given a chance to defend his Christian way of life (9.1–3). What ensues in the *Dialogue* is a lengthy, digressive, and at times repetitious debate. At the same time, the conversation continually returns to three broad areas of concern: the role of the Jewish ceremonial law (particularly its injunctions to observe circumcision and the Sabbath), the identity of Jesus (especially whether he was the anticipated Messiah), and the status of Christians as the New Israel. Trypho and Justin pursue this debate exegetically, each contending that the correct interpretation of their shared Scriptures— i.e., the law and prophets, or what would later be termed in Christian circles the "Old Testament"—supports the conflicting practices and beliefs of their respective communities.

In the opening paragraphs of the *Dialogue* we are introduced to one of Trypho's leading objections, i.e., that Christians place their "hope in a crucified man" (10.3). Indeed, throughout this work there is one epithet that both Trypho and Justin consistently attribute to Jesus: he is the "crucified Christ" (11.4–5).[8] This telling designation hints at one of the central questions in the *Dialogue*: whether the law and prophets indicated that the Jewish Messiah would experience the suffering of crucifixion. Trypho rejects this as a possibility based upon the words in Deut 21:23:

> But we doubt whether the Christ should be so shamefully crucified, for the Law declares that "he who is crucified is to be accursed [Deut 21:23]." Consequently, you will find it very difficult to convince me on this point. It is indeed evident that the Scriptures state that Christ was to suffer, but you will have to show us, if you can, whether it was to be the form of suffering cursed by the Law (89.2).[9]

Trypho's argument is straightforward. While he admits that there are passages in the law and prophets that announce that the Christ was to suffer, he disputes that the Christ would undergo the form of suffering that the law specifically pronounced

---

8. Justin speaks of the "crucified" Jesus, Christ, Savior, etc. at 49.8; 73.2; 110.3; 112.2; 116.1; 117.5, *passim*. Trypho speaks similarly at 38.1; 46.1.

9. See also 39.7; 90.1 for the same objection.

cursed: crucifixion. Since Jesus suffered this fate, the conclusion for Trypho follows: he died as an accursed enemy of God and was clearly not the Messiah (93.4).

Justin's Reply

Justin intermittently works out several responses to Trypho's objection (chs. 90–112). The response that is of most interest to us is his engagement with Paul's argument in Galatians. Justin was aware that already prior to Trypho Paul had applied Deut 21:23 to Jesus. Whereas Trypho saw in this verse a disqualification of Jesus as God's Messiah, the apostle applied it to Jesus with the intent of commending some facet of his death. Justin cautiously explores Paul's reading of this verse in chapter 95 of the *Dialogue*.

While he never refers to Paul's letters by name in this work, the circumstantial evidence in this section strongly points to Justin's engagement with Gal 3. First, when he cites Deut 21:23, he tellingly offers a non-Septuagintal reading that coincides with Paul's rendering of this verse in Gal 3:13 (96.1).[10] Second, Justin retraces the steps in Paul's argument in Gal 3 by citing, with the apostle, Deut 27:26. For both authors this verse immediately precedes and sets the stage for the difficult claim that Jesus died under a curse: "Cursed be everyone that abides not in the words of the book of the Law so as to do them" (Deut 27:26/Gal 3:10). Justin expounds upon this verse by clarifying the scope of this curse:

> Not even you [Trypho] will dare to assert that anyone ever fulfilled all the precepts of the Law exactly; some have kept them more than others, some less. But, if those who are subject to the Law are certainly under a curse, because they have not kept the whole Law, how much more so will all the Gentiles evidently be cursed, since they commit idolatry, seduce youths, and perform other wicked deeds (95.1)?

Having explained the extent of this particular curse of the law, Justin finally moves, as Paul did, to the curse of Jesus' crucifixion. For his part, the apostle writes—succinctly—that "Christ redeemed us from the curse of the law by becoming a curse for us—for it is written, 'Cursed is he who hangs on a tree' [Deut 21:23]" (Gal 3:13). Justin offers the following gloss on Paul's succinct use of Deut 21:23: "the Father of the Universe willed that His Christ should shoulder the curses of the whole human race" (95.2). This gloss is interesting because we see Justin both softening *and*

---

10. See K. S. O'Brien, "The Curse of the Law (Galatians 3.13): Crucifixion, Persecution, and Deuteronomy 21.22–23," *Journal for the Study of the New Testament* 29 (2006) 55–76.

sharpening Paul's language. By claiming that Christ "shoulders" (*anadechomai*: "to accept, receive; to take upon oneself") the curses of the human race, he mollifies the forcefulness of Paul's diction. Justin is not comfortable claiming with the apostle that Christ was or became a curse (or became sin—cf. 2 Cor 10:21). In fact, he repeatedly insists that Jesus was *not* cursed by God (93.4; 94.5; 96.1; 111.2). This insistence almost certainly stems from Justin's conviction that the divine curse was a response to someone's guilt, a guilt Justin emphatically insists Jesus had not incurred ("the most just and immaculate and sinless Christ" [110.6]). At the same time, the claim that Christ "shoulders" the curses of the human race clarifies for Justin the sense in which he fell under a curse at his crucifixion. He was not himself guilty, as if he had violated a divine command, but rather took upon himself the curses of those who were guilty. Justin provides his readers very little else in the immediate literary context that might explain what he means by Jesus accepting vicariously human curses.[11]

Under Paul's influence, then, Justin applies Deut 21:23 to Jesus' crucifixion, but in a manner decidedly different from Trypho. Whereas Trypho's interpretation of this verse sanctioned his rejection of Jesus as the Messiah, Justin's interpretation bolstered Jesus' credentials. Jesus (the sinless one) vicariously accepted the curses of others who were legitimately under a divine curse. In this way he was at the same time God's Messiah and the subject of God's condemnation.

Augustine's *Against Faustus a Manichean*[12]

Augustine was born in 354 in Thagaste in the North African Roman province of Numidia.[13] With the support of his parents, friends, and relatives, he enjoyed a lengthy education that eventually took him to Carthage. It was there at the age of eighteen that he became deeply influenced by Cicero's *Hortensius* (a work now lost). This book gave rise to a quest that would eventually lead Augustine to the Christian

---

11. Note, however, that he is alluding to a theme that often surfaces elsewhere in the *Dialogue*: that at his crucifixion Jesus underwent a fate properly intended for the human race. See in particular Justin's affinity for the suffering servant passages in Isaiah: 13.2–9; 32.2; 43.3; 89.3; 1 *Apology* 50.

12. Translation: *Answer to Faustus, A Manichean (Contra Faustum Manichaeum)* (trans. R. Teske; ed. B. Ramsey; The Works of Saint Augustine: A Translation for the 21st Century, I/20; Hyde Park: New City, 2007). Unless otherwise indicated, numbers in parentheses refer to this work.

13. For a brief overview of Augustine's life, see R. A. Markus, "Life, Culture, and Controversies of Augustine," in *Augustine Through the Ages: An Encyclopedia* (ed. A. D. Fitzgerald; Grand Rapids: Eerdmans, 1999) 498–504. For knowledge of Augustine's life there is no replacement for reading his *Confessions*.

faith. Its immediate effect was to spur him to leave behind his desire for worldly success and embark upon a quest for wisdom. Shaped no doubt by his mother's devout Christianity, Augustine turned his attention to the Christian Scriptures, though he judged these writings lacking in the style of authors like Cicero and Quintilian. Thus it was at this time that he joined the Manichees in 372/373, a movement that traced its origins back to its founder Mani, the third century Mesopotamian sage. Even though Manicheanism was frequently legislated against in the Roman empire, it flourished in North Africa where it was widely propagated by its preachers, often in debate with Catholic Christians. Augustine would remain with this community for nearly a decade.[14] However, he became increasingly disenchanted with this movement, which he would later call in the *Confessions* "a vast myth and a long lie."[15] Pivotal in his move away from Manicheanism was his encounter with Faustus.

Faustus was born around 340 in Milevis in Numidia (1.1). He was a convert to Manicheanism from a pagan background, and by 382 had risen in rank to become a Manichean bishop (13.1; 15.1; 18.2; 19.5; 23.2). Augustine was fascinated by his reputation and admired his eloquence, but when the two finally met in Carthage, Augustine ultimately left disappointed by Faustus' inability to answer his pressing questions about Manichean Christianity.[16] Faustus was condemned as a Manichee in 385/386 and exiled to a desolate Mediterranean island for a year. We know little else of his life, except that he probably wrote a book called *The Chapters* sometime between his exile and death in 390. This work provides us a reliable glimpse into many of the contours of North African Manicheanism, though arguably the central thrust of the work is a polemic against the OT which he saw as contradictory to the NT. Faustus' work only survives in the quotations of it in Augustine's *Contra Faustum Manichaeum*.

Against Faustus is Augustine's longest anti-Manichean writing, composed on the occasion of a request from several of "the brothers" who had stumbled upon Faustus' book and desired an intelligent response (1.1). This work belongs to the large corpus of anti-Manichean writings that occupied Augustine for nearly twenty years after his baptism in 387.[17] It was probably written at the very end of the fourth

---

14. For a helpful discussion of the appeal of Manicheaism to Augustine, see S. N. C. Lieu, *Manichaeism in the Later Roman Empire and Medieval China: A Historical Survey* (Manchester: Manchester University Press, 1985) 117–53.

15. *Confessions* 4.8.13 (trans. H. Chadwick; Oxford: Oxford University Press, 1991).

16. *Confessions* 5.3.3; 5.6.10—5.7.13.

17. See J. K. Coyle, "Anti-Manichean Works," in *Augustine Through the Ages*, 39–41.

century, a few years after he was ordained bishop of Hippo. In each of its thirty-three books he first cites an excerpt from Faustus' text and then offers his own response to Faustus' reply. As noted above, Faustus is critical of the OT. He laments the morals of its leading figures that are in contrast to the ethical teachings of the NT (e.g., 22.5). He highlights the selective adherence to its laws by Christians, noting especially their rejection of its ceremonial precepts (e.g. 6.1). He insists that Christians only take an interest in prophecies that they think point to Jesus as the Messiah, ignoring all others (e.g. 22.2; 32.1). Indeed, Faustus insists that he has found no prophecies of Christ in the OT (e.g. 22.1). So profound is the disconnect between the Testaments that there are passages in the OT that actually slander Jesus. It is in this context that Faustus raises the particularly contentious Deut 21:23.

Faustus' Interpretation of Deuteronomy 21:23

For most of the fourteenth book of *Against Faustus* Augustine offers a detailed refutation of his opponent's reading of this verse. As is his pattern throughout this work, he begins with Faustus' own text. Faustus is responding to the Catholic query, "Why do you not accept Moses?" His reply is concise and to the point: "We despise Moses more because by the harsh abuse of his curse he hurt Christ, the Son of God, who hung upon a tree for the sake of our salvation." "After all," Faustus resumes, Moses "says that everyone who hangs on a tree is cursed (Deut 21:23)." Indeed, he continues, Moses "does not even say that they are cursed in the ordinary sense, that is, cursed only in the eyes of human beings, but that they are cursed by God" (14.1). Faustus anticipates the objection that apparently surfaced among many Christians in his day that Moses' curse did not apply to Jesus since there is "a big difference between being hanged and being crucified" (14.1). But Faustus counters that since the Apostle Paul applied Deut 21:23 to Jesus' death in Gal 3, this confirms Moses' curse was indeed relevant to Jesus. As a result, Faustus concludes, there is only one unflattering verdict that can be reached about Moses. Whether he "knowingly and willingly" cursed Christ, or did so "unwillingly and in ignorance," the result will be the same: he "blasphemed God" with the "venom of his lips" (14.1).

It is instructive to compare Trypho's and Faustus' respective interpretations of Deut 21:23. Both share the view that Moses disqualified from the ranks of Messiah those who died on a tree. The principle difference between their readings is that Trypho thinks this critique was *legitimate*, and thus on the authority of Moses, rejects Jesus as the Messiah. Faustus, on the other hand, thinks Moses' critique was *misguided*, and thus inverts Trypho's argument: on the authority of Jesus' saving death on a tree, he rejects Moses as a prophet of God (14.1).[18] As we will see below, Augustine pursues a similar exegetical strategy to Justin by subverting the underlying assumption jointly held by Trypho and Faustus: that Moses was disqualifying Jesus in the first place. To do so Augustine will offer an interpretation of Deut 21:23 that resembles Justin's reading analyzed above, though he develops it more thoroughly and relies far more explicitly on the Pauline corpus.

Augustine's Rebuttal

Augustine initially responds to Faustus' reading of Deut 21:23 with puzzlement. He calls into question his opponent's sincerity when he criticizes Moses, since on a number of occasions in *The Chapters* Faustus clearly denied the reality of Jesus' death. "[W]e confess," Faustus writes, "that he suffered only apparently and did not really die" (29.1). Or again, "[i]n any case, for us, Jesus did not die" (26.2).[19] In light of statements such as these, Augustine wonders why Faustus and other Manicheans "are angry at Moses, since his curse did not affect their Christ" (14.2). They seem only to "pretend to be angry at Moses who cursed the fictitious death of Christ—I am saying this in according with the way they think" (14.2). Augustine's confusion was understandable. There was already a significant Gnostic tradition within the Christian ambit (broadly conceived) that denied Jesus was crucified in the first place.[20] Faustus was apparently part of (or at least sympathetic to) this tradition, and so it was hardly clear why he was chastising Moses for cursing those who died on a tree, when Faustus did not think Jesus had ever died.

---

18. Shortly thereafter he adds that Moses was "lacking in divine inspiration" and "prophetic power." There follows in this section several other arguments Faustus raises against the cogency of Moses cursing those who are crucified, as well as the ramifications of the other curses Moses pronounced.

19. See also 5.5; 14.12; 26.1; 26.6; 28.2; 29.1–3; 32.22. There are, however, significant difficulties in interpreting Faustus' Christology (and indeed the Christology in other Manichean writings). A fundamental problem in Faustus and other Manichean writings are passages that seem to speak of multiple Christs. See most clearly *Contra Faustum* 20.2 where Faustus appears to speak of three Christs (and Augustine's response at 20.11: "Finally, tell us how many Christs you say that there are"). The matter is complicated further by passages where Faustus seems to think Jesus suffered and was crucified. He speaks of Jesus who "suffered of his own will" (16.4); claims he believes Jesus' "mystical crucifixion" (32.7) and speaks of the "suffering Jesus . . . hanging from every tree" (20.2). For an orientation to the figure(s) of Jesus in the Manichean movement, including Faustus, see M. Franzmann, *Jesus in the Manichaean Writings* (London: T. & T. Clark, 2003).

20. See, for example, the denial of Jesus' crucifixion in *The Second Treatise of the Great Seth*, *The Apocalypse of Peter*, *The Gospel of Judas*, and *Acts of John*.

But Augustine quickly leaves this criticism behind to pursue his own interpretation of the great mystery Moses "piously" pronounced when he said, "Cursed is everyone who hangs on a tree." Augustine agrees with Faustus that he cannot quickly exonerate Moses as some Christians want to do by claiming that the curse does not apply to Jesus. He admits that "ignorant people" in the church make this claim, insisting that Moses was actually cursing Judas. Their ignorance, in Augustine's opinion, is twofold: first, they do not know how Judas hung himself—was it from a tree or from a rock? and second, they have forgotten that Paul approvingly applied Deut 21:23 to Jesus' crucifixion in his Letter to the Galatians (14.8). Augustine, thus, squarely faces the challenge of showing how Moses fittingly cursed Jesus, but not in such a way that Jesus was thought to have committed a prior sin that merited the divine curse of crucifixion.

Fundamental to Augustine's labyrinthine interpretation of Deut 21:23 is the distinction between evil actions and death. When the Scriptures speak of Jesus as "sin" or "curse," these words are used more flexibly than Faustus allows. Augustine begins by arguing that the term "sin" is used polysemically in Scripture, i.e., it is a word with the same spelling and pronunciation, but with distinct, yet related meanings. He illustrates how polysemes surface in everyday discourse. For instance, "tongue" refers properly to the muscle in the mouth, but it can also refer to what this tongue produces, a language like Greek or Latin. Or again, the word "hand" refers to a distinct body part, but it also indicates writing, the product of the moving hand. So it is with "sin." It technically and properly refers to an "evil action that deserves punishment." However, it also has a second sense: "death itself, which sin has brought about, is also called sin" (14.3).[21] Readers of Scripture need to be especially alert to these two distinct senses of the term. It is almost certainly the case that the Pauline passage Augustine cites a few paragraphs later drives the foregoing lexical analysis: "Him who did not know sin he *made sin* our behalf so that we might be the righteousness of God in him" (2 Cor 5:21) (14.5). If Faustus is willing to claim that Jesus was crucified "for the sake of our salvation" (14.1), then he will agree with Augustine that Paul surely did not mean that Jesus was "made sin" in the customary sense of this word so that his crucifixion was a divine punishment justly administered for some sort of guilt he had incurred. Rather, Paul means that he was made to experience *death*, the

---

21. Note also the following statement: "Hence, death is itself called sin not because a person sins when he dies but because the fact that he dies came about as a result of sin" (14.3). Augustine's reference to Gen 2:17 ("On whatever day you touch it you shall die the death") is used to support this relationship between sin and death (14.4).

punishment of sin. "Christ, therefore, did not commit that sin for which he would have been worthy of death, but he took on for us *that other sin*, that is, the death that sin inflicted upon human nature" (14.3, italics mine).[22]

The term "curse" is equally fluid in Scripture. Unfortunately, Augustine does not parse this term as carefully, but the basic thrust of his lexicography is the same. To say that someone is cursed could mean that person performed an evil act, since sin elicited the curse God pronounced in the second chapter of Genesis. But to call someone cursed could also mean that the curse has gone into effect and that person has experienced God's punishment of sin, death.[23] Thus when Moses wrote, "Cursed for God is everyone who hangs on a tree," Augustine insists he was not slandering Jesus as a sinner, as Faustus surmised, as if the curse of crucifixion pointed to its underlying cause, Jesus' guilt. Moses was, rather, using curse in a different sense, commenting only on Jesus' death itself. Moses

> intended to convey nothing else than that everyone who hangs upon a tree is mortal and dying. For he could have said, "Cursed is everyone who is mortal," or, "Cursed is everyone who dies." ... By crying out "Cursed," therefore, he cried out nothing else than that he [Jesus] truly died, since he knew that the death of sinful man, which he took on without sin, came from that curse by which it was said, "On whatever day you touch it you shall die the death" (Gen 2:17) (14.7; cf. also 14.4).

Thus Augustine argues that the forceful, indeed scandalous, language in Scripture—that Jesus was "made sin" or "cursed"—needs to be carefully scrutinized.

---

22. Augustine bolsters this distinction by reminding his readers of how the virgin birth ensured that the Son assumed both a sinless *and* a mortal human nature. The Son could not have assumed *immortal* human nature, since he was born of the Virgin Mary, and thus ultimately, born of Adam. It is a postlapsarian humanity already under the curse of death—in short a mortal human nature—that the Son assumed. But precisely because he was born of a virgin and was not the product of a sexual union by which original sin was transmitted, the Son assumed mortal yet not *sinful* flesh (14.4; 14.5).

23. On the term "curse" applying to both sin and its punishment, death, note esp.: "every sin is a curse—either the sin itself, which is committed with the result that punishment follows, or the punishment, which is called sin in another sense, because it was produced by sin" (14.4). On Augustine's preferred association of cursing with death in the case of Jesus, note his juxtaposition of 2 Cor 5:15 with Gal 3:13 "And for this reason the apostle said confidently of Christ, 'He became a curse for us' (Gal 3:13), just as he was not afraid to say, 'He died for all' (2 Cor 5:15). For 'he died' (2 Cor 5:15) means the same thing as 'he was cursed'" (14.4). Augustine's reply to Faustus is, at points, difficult to decipher since alongside seeing Jesus' death *as the curse* Moses spoke of (the dominant interpretation in book 14), Augustine intermingles another interpretation: that Moses *cursed* the death that afflicted human nature when Christ died. "[D]eath was condemned so that it would not reign and was cursed in order that it might perish" (14.3).

Terms like "sin" and "curse" are used ambiguously to refer either to an evil action itself or the punishment of this action, death. This distinction is, of course, crucial for the response to Faustus. In the case of Deut 21:23, to say Jesus was "cursed" when he hung on the tree is to say that he underwent death, the punishment or result of sin, *not* that he was a sinner. Such an interpretation challenges Faustus' contention that Moses was unfairly criticizing Jesus. He was, rather, simply prophesying the manner of his death, and in so doing, neither impugned himself nor slandered Jesus.

Augustine has a good deal more to say in response to Faustus's interpretation of Deut 21:23, but one final aspect of his retrieval of this verse should not be overlooked. He repeatedly insists in book 14 of *Against Faustus* that there is a cause-effect relationship between sin and death. This relationship holds for humans in the sense that *their* death is the punishment for *their* sin. Yet Augustine has been arguing that Jesus, even though he was sinless, experienced the punishment of sin. If the cause-effect relationship between sin and death is not to be destroyed, the question surfaces concerning whose punishment Christ endured if he was without guilt? Augustine answers this question by again leaning heavily on Paul. He cites three passages in succession to highlight that Christ was punished vicariously, i.e., he accepted the punishment of someone else who was legitimately guilty, the sinful human race: "Our old self was crucified along with him" (Rom 6:6); "He died for all" (2 Cor 5:15); and then, tellingly, the lines in Paul's Letter to the Galatians that immediately precede his citation of Deut 21:23, "He became a curse for us" (Gal 3:13). Augustine reads all of these passages the same way: "Christ took on our punishment without guilt so that he might in that way destroy our guilt and also end our punishment" (14.4).[24]

Augustine's retrieval of Deut 21:23 is, like Justin's, informed by Paul's application of the verse in Gal 3:13 to Jesus' crucifixion. However, whereas Justin does not explicitly cite Deut 21:23 when he comments on its applicability to Jesus' death, Augustine clearly acknowledges Pauline precedent and strives to decipher it. In his attempt to exonerate both Moses and Jesus, he makes two points. He argues that Moses' and Paul's language is fluid enough to warrant reading the "curse" as a reference not to Jesus' sin, as Faustus would have it, but to his death. Then he argues that the death he experienced as punishment for sin was, as several Pauline passages additionally suggest, the punishment for the sins of the human race. This interpreta-

---

24. Christ "was ever blessed in his righteousness but cursed on account of our sins in the death he took on from our punishment" (14.6). Or again, "admit that he took on the punishment of our sin without our sin" (14.7).

tion is certainly more developed than Justin's, but it still bears important affinities. For Justin, Jesus "shouldered the curse" of the human race, a statement that implies not only his innocence, Augustine's first point, but also the vicariousness of this act, Augustine's second point. Either way, both Justin and Augustine challenge their interlocutors by denying that Moses was rejecting Jesus as Messiah when he called him cursed by God.

Theodore Abu Qurrah's, *On Our Salvation*[25]

Muhammad was born around 570 in the town of Mecca. We know little of his early years. By the age of six he was orphaned, after which he lived under the guardianship of his grandfather, and after the grandfather's death, his uncle. In his twenties he worked as a trader for Khadija, a wealthy widow fifteen years his senior, to whom he was eventually married. According to Muhammad, when he was forty years old he was meditating in a cave outside Mecca when he received a revelation from an angel: "Read in the name of your Lord."[26] When he replied that he could not read, the angel revealed to him the opening lines of the Qur'an. With each subsequent revelation, Muhammad recited what he received, and so gradually over the course of the rest of his life the entire text of the Qur'an was revealed. These revelations were memorized and subsequently written down by his followers. According to this traditional account, shortly after his death in 632 all these revelations were gathered together and arranged in one written document.[27]

The Denial of Jesus' Death in Islam

There is a famous passage in the Qur'an that denies, or seemingly so, Jesus' crucifixion. In the fourth Sura the following statement is attributed to the "People of the Book," which in this context refers to the Jews: "We have killed the Messiah, Jesus, son of Mary, the Messenger of God." Immediately thereafter the Qur'an disputes this claim:

---

25. Translation: *Theodore Abu Qurrah* (trans. J. C. Lamoreaux; Library of the Christian East, vol. 1; Provo: Brigham Young University Press, 2005) 129–49. The designation in parentheses refers to the marginal notations in this translation.

26. Qur'an 96:1–5; for a translation see *The Qur'an* (trans. M. A. S. Abdel Haleem; Oxford: Oxford University Press, 2004).

27. For orientations of the life of Mohammad, see the introduction to the aforementioned translation.

They did not kill him, nor did they crucify him, though it was made to appear like that to them. Those that disagreed about him are full of doubt, with no knowledge to follow, only supposition: they certainly did not kill him, God raised him up to Himself. God is almighty and wise.[28]

While this passage has elicited tremendous (and often diverging) interpretations throughout the years, a significant trajectory of Muslim commentary on this verse has read it as a denial of Jesus' death.[29] Jesus was a great prophet (Q 2:87; 2:253; 4:171) who was, rather, saved by God from the scandal of crucifixion and raised alive into heaven.[30] Within the first two centuries of Islam, there is not only strong evidence for the Muslim revulsion of the symbol of the Christian cross, but also early commentary on the aforementioned Qur'anic verse that consistently points to a denial of Jesus' crucifixion.[31] Even Christian writers heard the Muslim position this way. John of Damascus, who held important positions in the Islamic court, wrote a chapter on Islam in his *On Heresies* (the second part of his trilogy, *The Fount of Knowledge*, written toward the middle of the eighth century). In this work he rehearses his view of what the Qur'an says about Jesus' death, "that the Jews, having themselves transgressed the Law, wanted to crucify him, and having arrested him they crucified his shadow; but Christ himself was not crucified (they say), nor did he die, for God took him unto Himself in heaven, because He loved him."[32]

What is particularly noteworthy for our purposes is how early Muslim apologists sought both corroboration of their denial of Jesus' death and critique of the opposing Christian view by turning to the OT. Several authors noted Moses' curse on the crucified in Deut 21:23 and thus puzzled over how Christians could claim someone as great as Jesus suffered this fate. Perhaps the most famous example comes

---

28. Qur'an 4:157-58.

29. N. Robinson, *Christ in Islam and Christianity: the Representation of Jesus in the Qur'an and the Classical Muslim Commentaries* (Hampshire: Macmillan, 1991) 127-41.

30. For two recent studies that explore the death of Jesus in Islam, see T. Lawson, *The Crucifixion and the Qur'an: A Study in the History of Muslim Thought* (Oxford: Oneworld, 2009); and A. H. M. Zahniser, *The Mission and Death of Jesus in Islam and Christianity* (Maryknoll: Orbis, 2008).

31. M. N. Swanson, *Folly to the* Hunafa: *The Cross of Christ in Arabic Christian-Muslim Controversy in the Eighth and Ninth Centuries A.D.* (Dissertation at the Pontificio Istituto di Studi Arabi e d'Islamistica; Rome: 1992) 65-95; 102-10.

32. Trans. by M. N. Swanson, "Folly to the *Hunafa*: The Crucifixion in Early Christian-Muslim Controversy," in *The Encounter of Eastern Christianity with Early Islam* (ed. E. Grypeou, M. Swanson, and D. Thomas; History of Christian-Muslim Relations, vol. 5; Leiden: Brill, 2006) 240. For other eighth century Christian responses to the Qur'anic denial of Jesus' crucifixion, see the entire article (237-56).

from pseudo-Umar's *Letter to Leo,* which dates to the late ninth century. The author writes:

> You still pretend that Jesus . . . revealed to him [Moses] the Torah, even though you read in that same Torah that any man who is crucified is cursed (cf. Deut 21:23). Did Jesus therefore curse himself when he already knew that he would be crucified, as you yourselves pretend? May God keep us from such an affirmation! On the contrary, God "raised him up to Himself and God is powerful and wise (Q 4:158)."[33]

This Muslim author claims an internal contradiction in Christian Christology: that Jesus both inspired the Torah which claims the crucified is cursed and underwent this form of death. For this author the resolution to this contradiction is that the Torah's curse on the crucified does not befall Jesus. Rather, with the Qur'an, he was spared this fate and raised up to God.[34] We see here yet another late antique reading of Deut 21:23 with reference to Jesus. For this author the Torah's curse on the crucified does not lead to Trypho's conclusion, that Jesus was, in fact, an accursed enemy of God (the Torah is relevant); nor does it lead to Faustus' conclusion that the Torah's curse slanders Jesus because his death is saving (the Torah is erroneous). Rather, this Muslim author reaches a different conclusion: the Torah's curse is *irrelevant* to Jesus since he was not crucified.

Theodore's Reply

Theodore Abu Qurrah is perhaps most well-known for his defense of the Christian faith against Islam. Muslims ruled the Near East already a century before his birth. Theodore appears to have been born in Edessa in northern Mesopotamia around the middle of the eighth century. Some reports place him in his early years as a monk in the Judaean monastery of Mar Sabas, though this claim is disputed. Less contentious is that he was the Melkite (i.e., Chalcedonian) bishop of Haran, a town not far from his native Edessa. In his surviving writings, Theodore comes across as an enthusiastic polemicist. He defended the Chalcedonian doctrine against both Nestorian and Monophysite Christologies. He was also one of the earliest Christian

---

33. J. M. Gaudeul, *Encounters and Clashes: Islam and Christianity in History. II, Texts* (Rome: P.I.S.A.I., 2000) 153.46 (modification of punctuation and spelling of proper names). For orientation to the correspondence between "Umar" and "Leo," see Gaudeul, *Encounters and Clashes. I, A Survey* (Rome: P.I.S.A.I., 2000) 81–86.

34. For other Islamic uses of Deut 21:23, see M. N. Swanson, *Folly to the* Hunafa, 128.

theologians to write in Arabic, and many of his writings were infused with a critique of Islamic theology.[35]

In his treatise *On Our Salvation* Theodore offers his most sustained account of the salvation that came through Jesus' death.[36] While he does not specify his audience, it is hard to imagine that Theodore was not responding at some level to the Islamic denial of the historicity of the crucifixion.[37] In this work Theodore offers an elaborate account of the centrality of Jesus' death for the Christian faith and in so doing also notes the way in which this death was a "curse." In what follows I will rely primarily on this treatise, though I will also intersperse relevant materials from two other works, *On the Death of Christ* and *That We Have Five Enemies from Whom the Savior Saved us, by Way of Question and Answer*.[38]

"God revealed the law to Moses on Mount Sinai, in it establishing precepts for human beings and laying down penalties for those who transgress those precepts" (B83). This is the way Theodore opens *On Our Salvation*. He specifies that the law commands that humans love God with all their hearts, might, souls, and wills (cf. Deut 6:5). However, if it is the case that God always requires (in keeping with the ability granted us) that *all* our effort be devoted to obedience, it is also clear, Theodore notes, that "there is no way of making amends for those who fall short—even for a moment—of the maximum of their ability in obeying God" (B83–84). What Theodore means is that the law continually requires the maximum love and obedience of humans. Thus, when someone sins, it is impossible to make subsequent restitution, since in addition to offering the maximum that is continuously stipulated in the law, the sinner would have to offer something *more* than this maximum to make up for the past sin. But this is obviously impossible. The most anyone can do after sinning is to try to keep up with the law's ongoing expectations. Theodore concludes that sinners live in a difficult situation and says, "the penalty God imposed for any sort of disobedience is hanging over the heads of those who have fallen into that disobedience: those who have been disobedient are not in any way able to pay for themselves the required penalty and they have absolutely no escape from it" (B83).

---

35. For a brief orientation to Theodore's life, see J. C. Lamoreaux, "Introduction," in *Theodore Abu Qurrah*, xi–xxv.

36. On the three treatises that make up this work, see J. C. Lamoreaux, "Introduction," xxxii–xxxiii. As readers familiar with Anselm's *Cur Deus Homo* will undoubtedly detect, the similarities between Anselm's text and Theodore's are striking.

37. On the Qur'anic language and allusions in *On Our Salvation*, see M. N. Swanson, *Folly to the Hunafa*, 211–17.

38. J. C. Lamoreaux, *Theodore Abu Qurrah*, 109–28; 249–54.

If this is the situation, what course of action might the sinner expect from God? Theodore canvasses two options, one of which is impossible (so he argues) and the other undesirable. The first scenario is that God "will forgive our sins freely and mercifully remit the penalty we owe for them" (B84). Theodore offers a number of arguments against this option, most prominently, that if God mercifully rescinds the law's penalty, this "makes God's law void and God himself one who does things in vain, in that he imposes a law but does not demand full payment of its claims" (B85). Theodore repeatedly reminds his readers of this point. If God were not to demand back from sinners the love and obedience that the law originally stipulates, it makes little sense for God to have drawn up this law in the first place. "God does not do things without purpose, as if he were jesting with us" (*Five Enemies*, PG1468). This sort of mercy comes at the expense of God's justice. If God is going to proclaim a law, then this law must be enforced.

This leads Theodore to the other scenario which, while not impossible, is most unwelcome: that God will in fact "demand—and justly so—that we give him full payment, in which case we go to eternal damnation" (B84). In other words, if God is going to insist justly that sinners make the payment that the law demands, an impossibility for Theodore given the lofty expectations of the law, then an inescapably grim consequence follows: God will punish the sinner with death. As he reminds his readers more explicitly in his treatise *Five Enemies*, the punishment for eating from the forbidden tree is Genesis was death (Gen 2.17) (PG1461). "We, having transgressed the law of God a myriad of times, deserve to die a myriad of times" (PG1468).

The human situation sketched out by Theodore in the opening paragraphs of *On Our Salvation* is that of a gradual deterioration to death. God's law establishes fair precepts that humans do not meet, and thus they justly incur the penalty of repayment. But, since they cannot make retroactive amends for past wrongs, this penalty continually hangs (and grows) over their heads. God does not blithely wipe this penalty out, since it would render the law pointless and ultimately would render God unjust. Thus, the just course of action is for God to insist that the penalty be paid. Since humans are incapable of paying, they will eventually experience the law's final punishment, the condemnation of death. Theodore drives his readers into a cul-de-sac: the inevitable yet just consequence of their sin is the punishment of death. Thus, the only way out is a third course of divine action that allows humans to somehow avoid their punishment yet *also* simultaneously preserves God's justice.

The solution Theodore proposes rests in the ministry of God's Son. Theodore offers his readers an imaginary speech in which God looks down upon the fallen human race, laments the law's just punishment which all deserve, and then turns to his Son, requesting that he become incarnate and experience on their behalf the punishments humans merit for their sins. "[W]hen the Father saw that Adam and his children had fallen into sin and were being jostled about in it as if by waves and that through it destruction had overwhelmed them, he said to his Son,

> I see that Adam, who is in our image and likeness (cf. Gen 1:26–28), as well as his offspring, have come under sin's dominion. The just claim of sin that stands against them has excluded them from the state of blessedness for which they were created. The law cannot be made void, however; it must receive its claims in full, from every single human being. Come, take a body. Through it, manifest yourself in the world and expose yourself to the punishments that human beings merit because of their sins. Let those punishments befall you, for when this happens there will be forgiveness of sins for those who, for their sins, offer to me your pains. For them there will be an escape from every punishment they merit because of my law (B87).

Here Theodore offers a particularly clear statement of the incarnate Son's vicarious death: he exposed himself to the law's just punishment on behalf of the human race that merited it, so that they could escape their eventual punishment.[39] Theodore is particular careful to insist that the Son was not undergoing a punishment he *also* merited. Rather, the Son took flesh from the virgin Mary who had been purified by the Holy Spirit "of all stains of sin" (B88) and throughout his life "rendered what was due" (*Five Enemies*, PG1468). It thus follows that he did not need, on account of his own genealogy and conduct, to undergo the punishment for sin. The death he voluntarily accepted was on behalf of others. "He went forth into the world and allowed himself to experience the punishment that each of us merited because of our sins, namely, being beaten, being humiliated, being crucified, and experiencing death" (B86).

Theodore intersperses several important reflections on why the punishment experienced by someone who had the constitution of the incarnate Son was crucial for salvation (i.e., why something more than an animal, indeed more than a mere man was needed). It was vital that the divine Son who had taken on flesh experi-

---

39. Or, as Theodore says in his treatise, *On the Death of Christ*, the pains Jesus underwent were to "provide the law with a substitute for the punishments God requires from all of us" (B52).

ence this punishment if it was to be effective. Theodore also discusses the ways in which humans can appropriate the Son's punishment on their behalf. The emphasis is on faith and offering the pains of the Son on their behalf. Moreover, he offers several scriptural *testimonia* to buttress his account of vicarious punishment. Not surprisingly, the passages include those about the suffering servant being wounded for the sake of our sins (Isa 53:2–7) and the lamb of God who bears sins (John 1:29). What is important for our purposes, however, is Theodore's assessment of the Deuteronomic curse.

While he does not explicitly cite Deut 21:23, he retrieves both Paul's argument *and* his nomenclature of the "curse" in Gal 3 to convey clearly enough how he understood Jesus to be cursed on the tree. Indeed, I think the case can be made that Theodore's elaborate account of Jesus' saving death in *On Our Salvation* reads as an extended commentary on Gal 3:10–13. First, his lengthy argument for the human predicament under God's law—that all fall under the sanction of punishment—strongly mirrors the apostle's claim in Gal 3:10 that those who fail to obey all that is in the law are under the law's curse. Second, confirmation that Theodore has the third chapter of Galatians in mind can be found in both *On Our Salvation* and *Five Enemies* where he *does* cite the words of the first part of Gal 3:13, Christ "delivered us from the curse of the law by becoming a curse for us."[40] In both treatises it is clear from the larger argumentative context already outlined above that Theodore understands the law's curse to be its pronouncement of the death sentence on the sinner and that Christ delivered us from this curse by accepting this sentence on our behalf. Finally, Theodore does not shy away in both of the aforementioned works from asserting that the curse Jesus became for our sakes transpired not simply at his "death," but more specifically when he was "crucified" (B86; B90; PG1468). This is precisely the claim Paul makes in the second part of Gal 3:13 when he cites Deut 21:23 to confirm Jesus became the curse when he was hung on the tree.

In an Islamic milieu where the Deuteronomic curse could be used to deny the historicity of Jesus' death, Theodore replies with an alternative interpretation that uses this verse to defend his death. For Theodore, the quandary humanity (or is it God?) faces, is how God can forgive sinners, allowing them to sidestep the punishment for their sins that they have legitimately merited, yet still uphold the law's demand for punishment. Theodore proposes a solution that strikingly foreshadows the later work of Anselm in *Cur Deus Homo*. In whatever way God is going to save, his

---

40. Note that the "five enemies" he has in mind in this latter treatise are death, the devil, *the curse and condemnation of the law*, sin, and hell.

justice must be merciful and his mercy just, i.e., God must be just with respect to the law's righteous demands but also simultaneously merciful to humans.[41] As we have seen in the emerging proposal, Theodore approaches the Deuteronomic curse that falls upon the crucified through the Pauline lens of Gal 3. The Son delivers humanity from the curse of the law, the punishment of death for sin, by willingly accepting its punishment when he is crucified. In this way he becomes the curse announced in Deut 21:23. Here there is justice, since "God does not forgive anyone's sin until he receives the whole punishment required by the dictates of the law" (*Death of Christ*, B51). But there is also mercy (B85; B88). Theodore draws *On Our Salvation* to a close with a beautiful meditation on the term "gospel": "It is thus that his [Christ's] summons is called the 'gospel,' that is, the 'good news,' for it proclaims to humanity the good news about how Christ saved them from that from which they were unable to save themselves. We give praise to Christ for his immeasurable grace" (B90).

Conclusion

In this paper I have examined a thin trajectory of the history of interpretation of Deut 21:23 that has hopefully conveyed, despite its selectivity, some of the richness associated with the reception of this verse in late antiquity. The exegetical disputes Justin, Augustine, and Theodore conducted with their theological opponents reveal how the Torah's curse was ultimately seized in three different ways to promote three correspondingly distinctive portraits of Jesus and his death. First, Trypho *applied* Deut 21:23 directly to Jesus to assert that he was justly cursed by God and, thus, that he could not have been the anticipated Messiah. In his hands the verse supported a critical portrait of Jesus. Second, several others offered instead a sympathetic portrait by reversing Trypho's strategy. They *distanced* the verse from Jesus so as to remove him from the divine curse. God was just in *not* cursing Jesus. In early fifth century North Africa, several Christians contended that Moses' curse was wrongly interpreted as referring to Jesus' crucifixion. It referred instead to Judas' hanging. Faustus argued that Moses' curse on the crucified was erroneous and thus that Jesus escaped his misguided condemnation. In Islam and earlier in several Gnostic traditions, this curse was distanced from Jesus more radically: he never died, and so Moses' curse was irrelevant.

---

41. This juxtaposition of justice and mercy is stated concisely as follows: "In this manner, he [the Son] made it possible for God to have mercy on us, without making null and void his justice, but instead satisfying it by allowing it to receive its rights, and without allowing his mercy to be ineffective" (*Five Enemies*, PG1468–69).

Yet as we have seen in this paper, another set of interpretations of this contentious verse emerged in early Christianity, inspired by Paul's use of Deut 21:23 in his Letter to the Galatians. Third, Justin, Augustine, and Theodore were not willing to compromise the apostle's exegetical legacy: they sought to *apply* this verse to Jesus in order to promote a *sympathetic* portrait of him. But there was nothing straightforward about such a reading. These Christians needed to articulate how God could justly curse the crucified Jesus, but not in such a way that impugned the Messiah's credentials. They needed, in other words, to demonstrate that what for most others in the late antique world was a contradiction—God cursed the Messiah—was, in fact, a paradox. Among all the groups surveyed in this paper, only Justin, Augustine, and Theodore were willing to entertain this possibility. Each in turn proposed a similar strategy for meeting this new challenge. If Jesus was envisioned as a blameless representative of the sinful human race, then he experienced his death vicariously by accepting on behalf of guilty people the punishment they, and not he, justly deserved. Such a proposal allowed these authors to retrieve Deut 21:23 in a way that embraced Paul's exegetical precedent while also explicitly vindicating the character of God's Messiah.

"HAPPILY EVER AFTER?" PAUL PETER WALDENSTRÖM: BE YE RECONCILED TO GOD

Michelle A. Clifton-Soderstrom

Imagine Dante's *Inferno*. Existing in various levels of the underworld, human beings are consumed by such sins as lust, gluttony, greed, envy, violence, anger, and betrayal. They tremble at the gates of hell, wallow in the marshes of the Styx, and submit to the whims of the Minotaur. They are reaping what they have sown. Ascent evades them. Even for those who have not read the first volume of the *Divine Comedy*, these images are familiar to any who have dared to imagine punishment without a Savior.

Hell is a terrible ending, and fortunately Dante's epic poem provides reflection on paradise as well. Journeying in the octave of Easter, Beatrice guides Dante from Mount Purgatory through the spheres of heaven to the abode of God. The comedy closes with Dante's epiphany of the two natures of Christ, his soul aligned with God's, happily ever after.

The attention given the two most widely-read books of the trilogy, the *Inferno* and the *Paradiso*, mirrors a temptation in Evangelical thought to gloss over themes in the middle volume—*Purgatorio*—and to interpret the central aspects of God's character and work in categories of sin and punishment, on the one hand, and salvation and deliverance on the other. "Why did Jesus have to die such a horrible death?" the church has asked from its inception. In the words of the great reformer Martin Luther, "Christ died for all of our evils which were supposed to oppress and torment us eternally!"[1] Christ died once and for all, suffering punishment on behalf of humanity. The Christian story is one that dares to imagine punishment *with* a savior.

I would argue, however, that more serious theological reflection is needed on punishment in the church's theology of the atonement. Surely, the gospel is more complex than the idea that unbelievers will be justly punished and believers will be glorified. The Christian life is not built around the dichotomous endings of hell or heaven; we live in the *meantime*. Further, though Christ did indeed die once and for all, are not Christians called to participate in his death in an ongoing way? Is this call

---

1. Martin Luther, *Luther's Works: Lectures on Galatians Chapters 1-4, 1535* (eds. J. Pelikan and W. A. Hanson; St. Louis: Concordia, 1963) 290.

a punishment? Perhaps, but it is not the ending. Christ's work on the cross signifies the power and purpose of a greater end. This end is reconciliation, and it defines the church's ministry now and God's consummation in the not yet. In contrast to punishment as the central focus of the cross, this paper offers analysis and reflection on the relationship between the atonement and the church's ministry of reconciliation as it participates in God's good ending.

The Atonement and Punishment: Potential Problems

The theological questions that Christians ask around Christ's death, resurrection, and second advent have to do with the complex doctrine of the atonement. Any theory of the atonement must deal with humanity's relationship with God and the question of how God draws humans to himself given the existence of sin. While answers range considerably, as the Symposium papers suggest, some theologies of the atonement proceed from the standpoint that humans owe God a debt for their sins. Because they are incapable of paying such a debt and because sin has violated creation, God is wrathful. The only appropriate punishment for sin is death, and God's solution is to send his Son to be punished in our stead. Christ becomes our substitute, paying the debt we accrued from sin by dying on the cross, thereby appeasing God's wrath toward human beings and opening up the possibility for eternal life.

This view, called "penal substitution,"[2] is faced with significant challenges, as much scholarly literature over the last hundred and fifty years suggests. Among the difficulties are theological questions of God's punishment, wrath, sacrifice, and substituting death. Broadly speaking, critics hold that the penal substitutionary view has an inadequate doctrine of the Trinity, that it sunders the cross from ethics, that it misunderstands the nature of Christ's death as substitutionary, and that it wrongly portrays God's wrath over and against God's love.[3] Penal substitution's critics have

---

2. For representatives of the penal substitution view, I work with the writings of John Stott, J. I. Packer, Leon Morris, and Thomas Schreiner. I also use Christina Baxter's work characterizing classic representations of penal substitution. See her article "The Cursed Beloved: A Reconsideration of Penal Substitution" in *Atonement Today* (ed. John Goldingay; London: SPCK, 1995) 54–72.

3. Some of the strongest critiques of penal substitution include Rita Nakashima Brock, "And a Little Child Will Lead Us: Christology and Child Abuse," in *Christianity, Patriarchy, and Abuse: A Feminist Critique* (ed. Joanne Carlson Brown and Carole Bohn; New York: Pilgrim, 1989); C. H. Dodd, *The Epistle of Paul to the Romans* (London: Hodder & Stoughton, 1932); Dorothee Soelle, *Christ the Representative: An Essay in Theology After the 'Death of God'* (London: SCM, 1967); Mark Lewis Taylor, "American Torture and the Body of Christ: Making and Remaking Worlds," in *Cross Examinations:*

important moral questions regarding how we understand the cross. Yet, some of them fall short in bridging the theological and biblical grounds of the atonement, and therefore miss key difficulties in God's work of overcoming the barrier of sin and drawing near to his people.[4]

Penal substitution conceptualizes well some aspects of God's dealings with sin, such as the importance of Christ's death for our salvation, the gravity of God's hatred toward sin, and the immensity of God's love expressed in Christ's willingness to be an atoning sacrifice. However, penal substitution's subscription to an inherent connection between "penalty" and "substitution" leads to a perilous flaw. If one takes to its logical end the belief that penalty is the just system behind Christ's death in combination with a narrow or exclusive view of Christ's death as substitution, Christians are left with a distorted perspective on the relationship between repentance and forgiveness as defining moments of the cross and of the work of reconciliation.

In an effort to locate the above theological problems in penal substitution and examine the implications of these problems in the life and mission of the church, I engage the work of Swedish Lutheran biblical scholar Paul Peter Waldenström (1838–1917).[5] Waldenström ministered and wrote in Sweden in the late nineteenth

---

Readings on the Meaning of the Cross Today (ed. Marit Trelstad; Minneapolis: Fortress, 2006) 259–63; Vincent Taylor, *Jesus and His Sacrifice* (London: Macmillan, 1937) idem, *The Atonement in New Testament Teaching* (London: Epworth, 1940) idem, *Forgiveness and Reconciliation: A Study of New Testament Theology* (London: Macmillan, 1946); J. Denny Weaver, *The Nonviolent Atonement* (Grand Rapids: Eerdmans, 2001); Delores S. Williams, *Sisters in the Wilderness: The Challenge of Womanist God-Talk* (Maryknoll: Orbis, 1993).

4. While their concerns about penal substitution are well placed—namely those regarding punishment and violence, substitution and the relationship between the Father and the Son, and questions of women's relationship to sacrifice, they neglect some of the biblical depth to the concepts of wrath, substitution, and sacrifice, and for this reason their critiques remain unconvincing to many Evangelical audiences. This point is only tangential to this paper, however.

5. Born in northern Sweden, Waldenström was a key leader in the Swedish Free Church movement, and he eventually advocated for a break from the state church of Sweden. His emphasis on strong biblicism over and above creedal confessions, alongside his vital evangelical piety, led him to join other "Mission Friends" in forming the Swedish Mission Covenant in 1878. Many of these same mission-minded Christians immigrated to the United States, eventually forming the Swedish Evangelical Mission Covenant of America in 1885 (today known as the Evangelical Covenant Church). Waldenström was ordained in the Lutheran Church of Sweden in 1864 and served as a pastor and educator throughout his life. He earned his doctorate from Uppsala University and later received an honorary doctorate from Yale University. Waldenström published his sermon on the atonement ("Sermon for the Twentieth Sunday after Trinity") in the *The Pietist* in 1872, provoking widespread theological debate. (An English translation is available in *Our Covenant* 34 (1961). After extended controversy with the authorities, he resigned from the state church. His work with the Mission Friends led to his becoming president of the Swedish Mission Covenant in 1904.

and early twentieth centuries. A forerunner of the Mission Covenant churches in Sweden and the United States, Waldenström remains influential in the biblical and theological work of the Evangelical Covenant Church today. As a biblical scholar, he developed the tensions around the questions of God's wrath, God's sacrifice, and God's work of reconciliation guided by one simple question: "Where is it written?" His attention to these scriptural themes aids my analysis of penalty and substitution and offers a constructive pathway to understanding the church's work of repentance and forgiveness.

Paul Peter Waldenström: His Argument[6]

In Waldenström's period, penal substitution was the principal view of Christ's atoning work on the cross. It was common for both clergy and laity to speak of an angry God being reconciled through Christ's death. Waldenström, however, was not convinced. Specifically, he was not persuaded that the penal substitution view addressed the atonement in a way that represented God, Jesus Christ, and humanity as revealed in Scripture.[7] Waldenström considered as heathen the idea that God needed to be repaid or appeased because it not only painted the picture of God as cruel, it also was articulated in terms of human legal systems. Most importantly, Waldenström thought the view of penal substitution was absent from the biblical account. He launched a two-year study of the atonement in the Old and New Testaments ending with his sermon on the atonement published in *The Pietist*.[8]

Waldenström summarized his study of the atonement in the following five theses:

1) The fall of humanity into sin occasioned no change in the disposition of God.

---

6. Parts of this section are taken from my article "Where is it Written? Understanding the Cross and the Church's Ministry of Love," *Covenant Companion* (April, 2008) 13–15.

7. The Evangelical context of Waldenström's period includes both the prevalence of penal substitution (e.g., from such preachers and thinkers as Charles Simeon, D. L. Moody, Charles Finney, Charles Haddon Spurgeon, and Charles Hodge) and the challenge of liberal theology (e.g., F. Schleiermacher, Horace Bushnell, and John McLeod Campbell). For more on the historical development, see Ian J. Shaw and Brian H. Edwards, *The Divine Substitute: The Atonement in the Bible and History* (St. Louis: Buswell Library, 2006).

8. Paul Peter Waldenström, "Be Ye Reconciled to God, A Look at the Atonement," *The Pietist*, 1872. (See n. 5 above.) He also wrote a text called *The Reconciliation: Who Was to be Reconciled? God or Man? Or God and Man?* (trans. J. G. Princell; Chicago: John Martenson, 1888).

2) It was neither God's wrath nor vindictiveness toward us after the fall that blocked the way of salvation.

3) The change brought about by our fall into sin occurred only in humanity in that we became sinful and therefore separated from God.

4) We therefore needed reconciliation but not for the purpose of appeasing God's wrath in order to render God merciful; rather it was to blot out and take away our sin so as to render us righteous again.

5) Jesus Christ accomplished this reconciliation.[9]

From Waldenström's study of Scripture, two distinctive emphases emerged: 1) the atonement is to blot out sin, i.e., to sanctify sinners from their sins, and 2) the atonement is the reconciliation of sinners to God.

Broadly speaking, Waldenström's work offers notable differences from other liberal[10] and twentieth-century critiques of penal substitution, and this paper calls attention to these as it also addresses the problems of penal substitution. First, penal substitution opponents polarize God's love with God's wrath, arguing that the two cannot exist together. Waldenström, however, frames God's wrath in the categories of penal substitution scholars, noting that wrath is an aspect of God's holiness or righteousness. Second, unlike strong penal substitution opponents, Waldenström puts forth an understanding of sacrifice that includes propitiation and debt—words not easily accepted by penal substitution critics. Third, Waldenström's understanding of grace is strongly anchored in his view of human sin. In concert with St. Augustine, who believed that humans could comprehend the greatness of God through grace powerful enough to forgive human sin, Waldenström believed that the power of the cross lay in the promise of forgiveness in the context of profound sin.

God's Wrath

A chief issue allied with penal substitution is the question of God's wrath, its existence, and how the cross affects it (or not). Can God really be both wrathful and

---

9. Donald C. Frisk, *Covenant Affirmations: This We Believe* (Chicago: Covenant Publications, 2003) 100–1.

10. I use the term "liberal" in a technical sense denoting that tradition following Schleiermacher and, in particular, the view that radically doubts the centrality of the cross. This view is summarized well in Reinhold Niebuhr's comment: "A God without wrath brought men without sin into a kingdom without judgment through the ministration of a Christ without a cross." Quoted in Shaw and Edwards, *The Divine Substitute*, 120.

loving toward human beings? Does not one preclude or inhibit the other? Some theologians reason that wrath cannot co-exist within a loving God. Others, arguing with C. H. Dodd, note the presence of wrath in Scripture, yet do not attribute it to God's character. Dodd's perspective maintains that while God exhibits wrath, it is impersonal and "an inevitable process of cause and effect in a moral universe."[11] Dodd and others in this camp stress that God's wrath, while it exists, is not directed toward sinners individually.

Penal substitution argues that God's wrath is not only biblical,[12] but wrath is also part of God's holiness and response to sin. God's wrath and love are two aspects of the divine nature.[13] In fact, the two *must* remain aspects of God's nature because God cannot tolerate sin. In this view the atoning work on the cross shows the manner in which God's love and wrath relate through the category of penalty. Specifically, Jesus' death appeases God's wrath because death is the most just penalty for sin. The argument is that sin is linked to death (Rom 3:23), sin requires a penalty (not merely natural consequences), and, in agreement with St. Anselm, an innocent person is the only one who can take on the penalty that our sins deserve.[14] In the words of John Stott, "The Bible everywhere views human death not as a *natural* but as a *penal* event. . . . Throughout scripture, then, death (both physical and spiritual) is seen as divine judgment on human disobedience."[15]

Like the penal substitution view, Waldenström recognizes the existence of God's wrath as anger toward sin and the barrier that it creates. Wrath is a just response to human sin, and it exists in the backdrop of God's love. Not only are God's love and wrath compatible, they are God's righteous response to his desire for creation. Further, love and wrath exist equally in the Father and the Son. He writes, "The love of God and the love of the Lamb are one, and the wrath of God and the wrath of the Lamb are one."[16] God's wrath is not an impediment to his love. His wrath toward sin

---

11. Dodd, *The Epistle of Paul to the Romans*, 23. This view is also held by A. T. Hanson in *The Wrath of the Lamb* (London: SPCK, 1959).

12. Texts cited include Num 16:46; Ps 2:5; 6:1; Jer 25:15; Lam 4:11; Zeph 1:15; Matt 3:7; Rom 1:18; 1 Thess 1:10; Rev 6:17.

13. John R. W. Stott, *The Cross of Christ* (Downers Grove, IL: InterVarsity, 1986) 103; R. V. G. Tasker, *The Biblical Doctrine of the Wrath of God* (London: Tyndale, 1951) vii.

14. For more see Saint Anselm, *Cur Deus Homo* (trans. Sidney Norton Deane; Chicago: Open Court, 1903).

15. Stott, *The Cross of Christ*, 65.

16. Waldenström, *The Reconciliation*, 30–31.

appropriately expresses God's desire for humans to be reconciled, and God's enduring love for humanity fuels God's hatred of sin. Things could not be otherwise.

Within this view, Waldenström makes two distinctive points regarding God's wrath. First, God's love for humanity and his hatred of sin are constants. The cross does not change the depth of God's love for humanity because it is already perfect and unchanging. First John 3:16 attests that we know God's love because Jesus laid down his life for us. Such a love does not need to be restored because it was never lost, and this is and always was a great cause for celebration.[17] Likewise, God's wrath is neither satisfied nor appeased in Christ.[18] Scripture indicates that God's wrath is an expression of his hatred for all sin and unrighteousness. God will always be displeased with humans when they sin because it will always be part of God's righteous nature to be angry about sin.[19] Even while Christ died on the cross once and for all, as long as sin exists, God's wrath exists.

The purpose of the cross, then, is not to change God's wrath or God's love. It is to change *us*. Christ's atoning work on the cross enables humanity to perceive the depth of God's love. On this point, some have confused Waldenström with the moral demonstration view of Abelard.[20] Such a comparison is misguided because Waldenström makes clear that Christ's work on the cross is more than a demonstration.[21] It actually changes humanity by covering over sins, rendering persons "right" with God. Nor is the purpose to appease God through a kind of punishment. Against the notion that penalty is the focus of Christ's death, Waldenström cites Rom 5 and the parable of the Prodigal Son to argue that God's saving purpose is reconciliation, specifically to reconcile *humans* to God. As such, it is much more than a reprieve from punishment due for sins.[22] The power of the atonement, according to Waldenström, lies in God's self-giving love.

17. Ibid., 12.

18. Ibid., 21.

19. Ibid.

20. Peter Abelard (1079–1142) emphasized God's love at the heart of Christ's work on the cross. Moved by such a demonstration, human beings become repentant and accepting of God's love. Much of the power of the cross is based on the powerful example of Christ's love. Some theologies have taken the element of grace and mystical power out of the cross, attributing this to Abelard. Other scholars, however, argue that the lack of the supernatural work of the cross misrepresents Abelard. See Peter Abailard's "Exposition of the Epistle to the Romans," in *A Scholastic Miscellany: Anselm to Ockham* (ed. Eugene R. Fairweather; Louisville: John Knox, 1982) 276–87.

21. It is also misguided as a potential misrepresentation of Abelard. See the previous note.

22. Waldenström, *The Reconciliation*, 13–14.

Waldenström's second point is that God's wrath has an important eschatological dimension that cannot be overlooked. As I noted above, God's wrath remains as long as sin is a reality, and the cross does not diminish God's hatred of sin. Those who sin in the present are "children of wrath" (Eph 2:3), and God continues to bring wrath on those who disobey (Col 3:6). Scripture also warns of "the wrath to come" (Matt 3:7; Luke 3:7). The impending wrath of the Lamb comes in the form of judgment (Matt 25:31–46; Rom 2:5), will be executed by Jesus, the Lamb himself (Rev 6:16), and consists of God separating from himself all who have not repented and been renewed (Heb 6:6).[23] Because of Christ's atoning work, the possibility for righteousness is now ours, and it is a possibility for life.

Working from Rom 5, Waldenström sums up the eschatological trajectory of God's wrath as follows. In the past, while we were sinners, Christ died for the ungodly. Now in the present we are justified by the blood of Christ. Christ's blood has both reconciled us to God and begun a process whereby God continues to reconcile the world. In the future we will be saved from wrath not through Jesus' death but by his life. Paul writes, "much more surely, having been reconciled, will we be saved by his life" (Rom 5:10). By examining the whole trajectory of God's wrath Waldenström points us to the movement of God's action in saving history. In the language of the church: Christ has died! Christ is risen! Christ will come again! If we were to rephrase Christ's work in terms of our participation, we might say: we are buried with Christ, we rise with Christ, and we walk in newness of life. To remain "stuck" in any of these dramatic moments is to deny the complete and ongoing work of Christ on the cross.

Waldenström's work shows love, reconciliation, and life—not death and punishment—constituting the hope of the atonement. While he agrees with penal substitution's posture towards the depth of wrath within God's nature, Waldenström diverges strongly from the idea that Christ's death satisfied God's desire to punish human beings for their sin. Penal substitution views suffer from the categorical error of believing that Christ's death satisfied a penalty instead of serving as an offer of salvation. Within the story of salvation both God's wrath and God's love reveal God's desire to reconcile the world to himself. The consequences of sin are either that God's offer of salvation will be accepted and completed in a future time *or* that humans will be separated from God (and hence in some sense the penalty of sin still exists!). The atonement is for the sinner, not God, and the eschatological trajectory of God's wrath negates penalty as the primary purpose of Christ's death. God's wrath

---

23. Ibid., 24.

exists in the backdrop of his love and work of reconciliation, from which the atonement derives its power and purpose respectively.

God's Sacrifice

A second key issue in the penal substitution view is the substitutionary nature of Christ's death. Was Christ our substitute? Did he offer his own life so that humanity could be saved? On one level, believers would answer an emphatic *yes* to both questions. Central to the Christian faith is the fact that Christ died and rose in order that sinners might be saved. However, the *way* in which Christ's death atones for sins has been a theologically contested point. For example, did Jesus die *instead* of us or as our *representative*? How did he identify with humanity? Such questions relate to the sacrificial nature of Christ's death. A discussion of sacrifice moves the argument toward greater clarity, not only around what Jesus' death accomplished, but also around the relationship between repentance and forgiveness.

As with God's wrath, the place of sacrifice in the penal substitution view is, rightly, prominent. Specifically, penal substitution holds that the nature of Christ's sacrificial death is best defined by propitiation. For the purposes of clarity, the point of contention between penal substitution and its critics lies in the translation of the Greek word *hilastērion*.[24] Translators debate over the term "expiate"—meaning to make amends for a wrong, to forgive a sin or crime, or a sacrifice that removes sin—and the term "propitiate"—meaning to avert God's wrath or to remove God's anger by appeasing God's justice.[25] John Calvin, for instance, argued Christ's death is more than an act of *expiation*. Christ actually *propitiated* the wrath of the Father.[26] Other proponents of penal substitution argue with Calvin that Christ's death turns away God's wrath and that propitiation is critical for our salvation.[27]

Waldenström adheres to the language of propitiation, but not in the sense that Jesus' death is an offering that appeases God's wrath. Jesus does not *propitiate* God.

---

24. For a thorough and accessible discussion on propitiation and expiation, see Leon Morris's chapter "Propitiation" in his book *The Atonement: Its Meaning & Significance* (Downers Grove, IL: InterVarsity, 1983) 151–76.

25. There are actually three debated translations of *hilastērion*: propitiate, expiate, and mercy seat. For a technical discussion see Judith Gundry-Volf's entry "Expiation, Propitiation, Mercy Seat," in *Dictionary of Paul and His Letters* (eds. Gerald F. Hawthorne, Ralph P. Martin, and Daniel G. Reid; Downers Grove, IL: InterVarsity, 1993) 279–84.

26. Baxter, "The Cursed Beloved," 55.

27. Morris, *The Atonement*, 176; Schreiner, 94.

Jesus *makes propitiation* for the sins of the people. He defines Christ himself as the atoning offering whose life, death, and resurrection accomplish two things: 1) to blot out sin by cleansing or sanctifying sinners from their sins, and 2) to reconcile sinners to God. He bases this claim on the characteristics of ritual sacrifice in the Old and New Testaments.

The notion of sacrifice in Scripture is extremely complex, so I limit my comments on Waldenström to three of the more salient points. First, the purposes of sacrifice in the OT were primarily for atoning for sins and for expressing gratitude. In the latter case (some of which were bloody), persons offered sacrifices to thank God for help received, and the sacrifices signified expressions of peace.[28] In sacrifices offered for atonement Waldenström notes first that grave sins—such as sins against the Ten Commandments or those punishable by death—are not atoned for by sacrifice. Next, in cases where the sinner is poor, grain makes an acceptable offering, and no sacrifice is required (Lev 5:11). In another example, he notes that atonement is asked of a whole group of people for an unsolved murder, and the act of sacrificing a heifer marks their forgiveness (Deut 11:1–9).

Second, in each of the above examples of sacrifice the relationship between sin, punishment, and forgiveness is *never* a matter of simple exchange, transfer of guilt, and vicarious punishment (e.g., Lev 4:15, 24; 16:21). The complexity around atoning for sins is underscored in the sacrificial rite in the Day of Atonement. Here the OT reveals that the blood, or source of life, effects atonement. The priest sprinkles the animal's blood in the temple in order to cleanse the sanctuary from the sins of all the people (Lev 16:15–16). The atoning work blots out or covers over the sins of Israel. Next, the live goat is presented. The priest lays his hands on the goat's head, confesses all the sins of the people, and sets the goat free into the wilderness (Lev 16:20–22). The live goat, not the dead one, bears on itself all the sins of the people of Israel, for it is the blood of life that makes atonement (Lev 17:10–11).

Third, Christ's own atoning sacrifice in the NT, most obviously in the Letter to the Hebrews, takes the character of the priestly office. The priestly office of Christ belongs to the work of grace and takes both sin and God's desire to remove sin into account. The priestly role is one of mediation and representation. Christ is ordained by God to act on behalf of humanity and to represent them (Heb 5:1). The primary action is *offering*. The blood of Jesus as High Priest, as 1 John 1:7 and 9 says, cleanses and purifies us from all sin. Hebrews 9–10 brings us further into the priestly reality of the blood of Christ, for it is Christ's blood, in contrast to that of goats and

---

28. Waldenström, *The Reconciliation*, 45.

bulls, that cleanses us. Christ himself offers this perfect sacrificial blood which has the power to forgive. The writer of Hebrews thus declares, "How much more will the blood of Christ, who through the eternal Spirit offered himself without blemish to God, purify our conscience from the dead works to worship the living God!" (Heb 9:14). Christ is the mediator of the new covenant, the covenant of forgiveness, and the shedding of his blood serves not as penalty for sins but as purification for worship.

In penal substitution and Waldenström's views alike, substitution is not an inaccurate description of Christ's sacrificial death. However, substitution as a metaphor does not fully capture the work of Christ's death. While some, such as J. I. Packer, concede to little difference between substitution and representation,[29] let us examine their claims. "We identify with Christ against the practice of sin because we have already identified him as the one who took our place under the sentence of sin," according to J. I. Packer.[30] John Stott writes, "The notion of substitution is that one person takes the place of another, especially in order to bear his pain and so save him from it."[31]

The above descriptions fall into two errors. First, substitution is understood as vicarious punishment over vicarious purifying, even though the latter has great merit in Scripture. Waldenström, in fact, argues against vicarious punishment entirely, maintaining that *nowhere* is it written that God demands punishment to be endured. He cites the story of Nineveh as a pre-Christian example of God noting the Ninevites' repentance and changing his mind about the calamity he said he would bring upon them (Jon 3:10). He notes other examples of forgiveness offered without penalty (Sabbath law, Deut 15:1; the parable of the Unforgiving Servant, Matt 18:23–35; the sinful woman, Luke 7:36–50). Sins are sometimes expressed as debts; however, Waldenström, along with Jesus himself (Matt 6:12), maintains that debts are *forgiven*, not paid or punished.

Second, substitution as put forward by penal substitution is too exclusive. By "exclusive" I have in mind primarily the idea that humans are not participants in Christ's atoning work. Scot McKnight describes the scholarly discussion of the exclusive nature of the atonement as Christ dying and rising *instead* of us, nevertheless

---

29. J. I. Packer, "What Did the Cross Achieve? The Logic of Penal Substitution," *Tyndale Bulletin* 25 (1974) 3–45, see p. 17.

30. Ibid., 24.

31. Stott, *The Cross of Christ*, 136.

for our benefit.³² In contrast, inclusive representation is the idea that *we* die and rise with Christ.

Inclusive representation resonates with Morna Hooker's work on Paul's use of "interchange," and her explanation stresses the participatory nature of the cross. She argues that Christ acts as our representative and participates with us, not simply in our stead. Paul's statement in 1 Thess 5:10—"Christ died for us so that we might live"—is no simple exchange.³³ To the contrary, as Rom 5:12–19 shows, Christ is both a representative and inclusive figure through whose death and resurrection we *share* as we participate in Christ's experience of vindication and reversal.³⁴ Why is this so important and beyond minor discrepancies, as Packer might say, between "substitution" and "representation"? Reading Paul, Hooker exclaims that it is not enough for Christ to identify with humanity. Believers must also identify with Christ. They must be willing to share in Christ's death, as part of the offer of new life, and to make an act of "self-abnegation" similar to Christ's own.³⁵ This happens, Hooker writes, at baptism, but also "again and again throughout the Christian life, which is a continual process of reckoning oneself dead to sin and alive to God."³⁶

Though Waldenström uses the more general language of sacrifice in his work, his meaning intersects directly with Hooker's analysis of interchange. Specifically, Christ's death has the nature of an invitation to Christian living, it is participatory in nature, and that participation takes the form of repenting of sin and forgiving our brothers and sisters. In other words, Christians participate in Christ's work of reconciliation. Waldenström's biblical work on sacrifice leads us into the truth that Christ's reconciling work is not simply negative, i.e., sin is punished. Scripture tells of the positive dimension of sacrifice by which we are made pure.

The sacrificial context of the atonement pushes us to challenge our views of how believers participate in Christ's death. Waldenström's work emphasizes purification, reconciliation, and the priestly character of sacrifice. Within that context, confession is important as the acknowledgment of the barrier of sin and the power of God's forgiveness in overcoming that barrier. When persons participate in this

---

32. Scot McKnight, *A Community Called Atonement* (Nashville: Abingdon, 2007) 112.

33. Morna D. Hooker, "Interchange and Suffering" in *Suffering and Martyrdom in the New Testament* (eds. William Horbury and Brian McNeil; Cambridge: Cambridge University Press, 1981) 71.

34. Ibid., 70.

35. Ibid., 72.

36. Ibid., 73.

reconciling work—or die and rise with Christ on an ongoing basis, they enter into the reality that is the cross.

Be Ye Reconciled! The Church's Ministry of Repentance and Forgiveness

Thus far I have emphasized two critical points. First, penal substitution has made a "timely" error with regard to God's wrath, focusing on the death of Christ as appeasing God's wrath. While penal substitution has made important contributions regarding the significance of God's wrath and its relationship to God's holiness and human sin, penal substitution neglects the ongoing, eschatological quality of God's wrath, distorting the nature of penalty and the good news of Christ's death and resurrection. Second, penal substitution emphasizes the nature of Christ's substitution as Christ dying for us. While penal substitution has rightly emphasized that *Christ alone* can die the death that atones for human sin, Christians are nevertheless called to die and rise *with* Christ. The sacrificial moment of Christ's death is not one that takes our place so that we do not have to suffer. To the contrary, it is one that emphasizes the power of Christ's life to cover human sin and offer all the opportunity to participate in God's own work in the world.

Simply stated, penal substitution, with its merits, cannot be the end of the story. Sin still exists, we continue to be in need of forgiveness, and God is wrathful when his people erect barriers, estranging themselves from the reconciliatory work of the cross. Earlier, I commented that any theology of the atonement must address how God draws humans to himself, given the barrier of sin. I turn now to a description of the church's ministry of reconciliation in light of what we have learned from Waldenström and others.

First, the problem with punishment as symbolic of what happened on the cross draws us away from, rather than toward, a ministry of reconciliation. Punishment satisfies our desire for justice, at best, and revenge, at worst. If punishment is meted out, the victim can rest in some sense of satisfaction that the offender has been given her just desert. If punishment is received, the offender can rest in some sense that she has been redeemed—she owes nothing else to her victim. Punishment is easy; the bad guys lose, the good guys win, end of story, happily ever after. Everyone is off the hook. But is this the account in the gospel?

Waldenström has said no. Punishment cannot be the heart and soul of reconciliation because punishment does not lead to working out our sin. It does not lead to solidifying relationships with God or with one another. The biblical narrative describes the cross in terms of debts *forgiven*, not paid. More than a simple rhetorical word play, the distinction forces us to consider an economy of payment, which is closer to punishment versus forgiveness. How, if at all, do they differ?

Payment has the character of a completed economic cycle. When I decide to buy something and offer money for it, the item is given to me, and I am no longer in relationship to the seller because our business is concluded. Considering payment in the context of compensating for a wrongdoing toward another, it might look similar. If I were to drive too fast and rear-end the car in front of me, I would owe the driver a debt to cover the damage. Until I pay it, I am in relation to him, because he will presumably keep calling me for the money. The relationship is defined by something external, namely the debt. Upon payment, however, I am no longer under any obligation to continue the relationship. I have paid in full, and the cycle is completed. This is the nature of payment in economic practices, and its description points to the nature of the relationship between debtor and creditor.[37]

The above exchange is not as simple or transferable, however, in the economy of forgiveness. Take, for example, the sin of gossip. If I were to slander my Christian sister, and later note her pain and the wrongness of my actions and repent, I would have offered her something. However, even if we use the language that I, the "debtor," gave something to her, the "creditor," it cannot be said that I paid in full. I am still, in a sense, obligated or indebted to her well-being. Even were she to forgive me, there still exists an amount of hurt, pain, or remembrance—however great or slight—of my sin against her.

If we look to Christ's work on the cross for further insight, her forgiving me does the exact *opposite* of paying off a debt. In combination with my repentance, her forgiveness solidifies, expands, and deepens, rather than concludes, our relationship. Specifically, the relationship between sincere repentance and sincere forgiveness, while it cannot nullify the effects of sin, pulls the actors more deeply into Christian love, into the economy of the eschatological trajectory of Christ's work on the cross. However painfully, we are drawn together by being united with God in a relational bond that by the world's standards is highly unfeasible. Whereas in the economy of payment the relationship is defined by something outside of the relationship, the debt itself, in the economy of forgiveness the relationship is defined by a gift that is given precisely in order to *strengthen* the relationship.

---

37. For another interesting way to frame the discussion in the language of ransom and redemption, see Fredrick Holmgren, "The Concept of God as Redeemer in the Old Testament," *Covenant Quarterly* 19, no. 2 (1961) 9–18.

This description fits with Waldenström's view of God's wrath and of sacrifice. God's wrath has a clear eschatological trajectory. In other words, God's relationship with sin is not simply wrathful; God does something about it. He sends his Son as a mediator of sin, offering us an option beyond death, namely resurrection and eternal life. Nevertheless, the fact that we still await judgment points to the fact that sin is not finally over, that we still live in it, and that we will still be judged for it. God's hope is that in view of the cross, sinners repent of wrongdoing and forgive one another. This, in fact, is the church's ministry. It is the way God draws near to humanity and the way humanity also draws near to one another.

In his work on violence and memory Miroslav Volf poignantly writes of the gravity of the church's ministry of reconciliation.[38] His book takes place in the wake of a twenty-year enduring scar. His is a story of abuse in which he was the victim of months of military interrogations. In an effort to validate the human experience of sin and the desire for revenge, yet also to draw on the power of the cross, Volf raises these questions: How should a people who *love* remember the wrongdoer and the wrongdoing? How does the history of the wronged person's own sin figure into the memory of the wrongdoer? What effect does the death of Jesus Christ, who saved the ungodly, have on the wrongdoer? How should we remember sin, given that Christ atoned for it? What does it mean to remember a wrongdoing *now* in the framework of the promised life to come?

Volf's responses to these difficult questions echo Waldenström's understanding of God's wrath within an eschatological trajectory of judgment and hope and Christ's sacrificing work on the cross as a work that purifies us. In short, final reconciliation is God's work, and it includes judgment that is shaped by the atonement.

1) It is a judgment of grace (because it is executed in the name of Christ who dies for the sins of all). In judgment God in truth exposes the sin and transforms the sinner.

2) It is a social event. Judgment happens between people.

3) If the Last Judgment is to succeed as a transition to the world of love, each person will joyfully appropriate the results of the judgment. Wronged and wrongdoers will see themselves as Christ—the just Judge, full of mercy—sees them.

---

38. Miroslav Volf, *The End of Memory: Remembering Rightly in a Violent World* (Grand Rapids: Eerdmans, 2006).

This depiction of judgment is eschatological and recalls Matt 25. While reconciliation is God's work, it constitutes the heart of the church's ministry. We are called to practice repentance and forgiveness as they constitute justice, love, and reconciliation.

These things symbolize the heart of the cross, and if Christians take them seriously, it ought to shape our interpersonal relationships, both within and outside of the church, for it calls us truthfully to examine our lives and confess our wrongs to one another. It radically shapes our social relationships and the way that we think about immigrants, the sick, and, perhaps most especially, those in prison. How does our doctrine of the atonement enable us to draw near to these persons whom Christ names the least of these? These questions warrant far deeper study in light of our ministry of reconciliation. Finally, we rejoice at the way the atonement allows us to see God—both wrathful and loving, both Judge and Reconciler.

Conclusion: Happily Ever After

The atonement is rightly a doctrine about God repairing his relationship to humanity. However, this is not the end of the story, for we are given the ministry of reconciliation—a relationship-focused ministry that can *only* be redeemed in the shadow of the cross. The "once and for all" nature is not, now that Christ has died for our sins, that we can rest "happily ever after." The once and for all is that now we can work out our salvation with fear and trembling, now we can confess our sins and repent with courage, now we see the justice of forgiveness and are endowed with the grace to enact it, now we are invited to receive the ministry of reconciliation that Christ himself invites us into, and it is happy work. It is not the kind of life that fairy tales describe as "happily ever after." It is more like purgatory than paradise. Nevertheless, it is life symbolized by the cross. If there is any "happily ever after" in the Christian life, surely it is when the cross has, finally, worked itself out of a job, and we are reconciled one to another.

RESPONSE TO CLIFTON-SODERSTROM

Timothy L. Johnson

Clifton-Soderstrom's paper provides a good summary of P. P. Waldenström's view on the atonement. It provides treatment of the classic atonement frameworks and to the current literature on the subject. It underscores the significance of Waldenström's view, and I have little with which to disagree. Perhaps my best contribution can be in giving more context for understanding Waldenström and his importance.

My task here at North Park is Field Education, but I have had the rich opportunity of teaching denominational history in the Evangelical Covenant Church's Orientation program. This is a program through which many new Covenanters are introduced to essential elements of our denominational story. The influential role of P. P. Waldenström is one that our teaching team addresses at great length. Based on my work in teaching this history, I believe there is interesting congruence between the man himself and what he teaches as well as the time and place in which he lived and worked.

After being invited to participate in this symposium I saw the movie *Atonement* and found that it has striking relevance for our discussion. The movie dramatized well the plain fact that human beings are woefully inadequate at righting their own wrongs, and this makes for a desperately sad reality. Subsequently I learned from our Covenant colleague and former dean, Robert K. Johnston, who teaches Theology and Film at Fuller Theological Seminary, that he not only uses the movie *Atonement* but also ties it to the work of Waldenström as interpreted by Donald Frisk (another former dean) in his book *Covenant Affirmations* (Chicago: Covenant Publications, 1981). The point of all this is that theological work can be done even through popular culture and church meetings, which is demonstrated by Waldenström's own history. In addition to being a theologian Waldenström was a politician and a popularizer, both relevant to understanding his message on reconciliation in his time and place.

The Politician

Waldenström served for two decades in the Swedish parliament (The Rigstad). He served as the second president of the Swedish Covenant at a time of crisis (1904).

The leader who preceded him (Erik Jacob Ekman) was charged with being a universalist, so Waldenström, who was quite popular, was called upon to stabilize things for this new fellowship.

Waldenström displayed the capacity to relate across the theological spectrum. For example, he received an honorary doctorate at Yale Divinity School in 1889. He also established some significant rapport with the prominent revivalist Dwight L. Moody. (David M. Gustafson writes in "Dwight L. Moody and the Swedish Mission Friends" of their "mutual respect").

He exerted influence on both sides of the Atlantic. He was influential in the early development of the Mission Covenant (the name of the Evangelical Covenant Church in the beginning) both in Sweden (1878) and America (1885). He made three trips to America in 1889, 1901 and 1910.

Waldenström was able to span class differences as well as theological and geographic differences. He was a patrician by birth yet became a folk hero to the masses. He was the son of a physician, well-educated (having received a Doctor of Philosophy from the University of Uppsala in 1863), an ordained clergyman (1864), and a member of the governing elite, yet he became a leader of a lay movement.

The Popularizer

Waldenström wrote in a way that reached masses of people. At the age of twenty-four (1862) his allegory "Squire Adamson or Where Do You Live" was widely distributed and read in serial form. This work offered social critique particularly directed at the Lutheran State Church and had a significant impact on lay people.

He became editor of the influential religious paper *Pietisten* in 1868 upon the death of the previous editor C. O. Rosenius. This publication was one which shaped the masses and their theological thinking. In 1872 Waldenström published in *Pietisten* his significant reflections on the atonement. Although it was entitled "Sermon For The Twentieth Sunday After Trinity," it was never actually preached. Its thirty-three points shook the established church and registered with the hearts and minds of many people.

Evidence of Waldenström's popularity can be accessed when one googles his name on the internet. The Wikipedia entry for him includes a vivid picture of him rendered by prominent Swedish artist Carl Larsson in 1914. This would be roughly equivalent to an American preacher being the subject matter of a painting by Norman Rockwell at the height of his popularity. To this day there are scores of offices and living rooms of Covenanters that display an artistic rendering of Waldenström.

A question that emerges from this reflection is whether or not the academic community can find its way to validate or respect the role of the politician and the popularizer, who just happens also to be a theologian. As a parish pastor for twenty-five years, it could be said that much of what I did had to do with making matters clear to a broad audience as well as exerting political leadership to a congregational body. In the case of figures like Waldenström it might be said that he was not the first or the best at saying something, but he had the most access to the people, and he had a large impact. His teaching and preaching registered with masses of people. Atonement, after all, conveys the bridging of a gap or gulf or span. The role of a politician and a popularizer when properly exercised is to do that very thing.

There are a number of theological themes that are central in Clifton-Soderstrom's paper which intersect with these concepts. Words like reconciliation, representative, and mediator certainly connect to the Pauline use of the term "ambassador" as well as to the notion of politician. Clifton-Soderstrom points to a relational emphasis as well as the truth that Christ participates with us, and this parallels the popularizing task. Waldenström lived and worked in a time when most of the people were demoralized by an agrarian economy that was not working, by the angst of multitudes of their own migrating to the western hemisphere, and by state church doctrine and practice that seemed to devalue them.

All this was perhaps best summarized by a commemorative marker at Waldenström's home church. A plaque in Bethlehem Church in Gavle says of Waldenström "He gave our people a purer picture of God." Surely that is foundational for thinking of atonement.

THE SOCIAL DIMENSION OF ATONEMENT IN THE TORAH

Viktor Ber

In my treatment of atonement in the Torah I want to start with our current society. One of its prominent aspects would probably be the emphasis on the individual, so typical for the modern and postmodern West. This emphasis, of course, has had its historical and philosophical roots. Our western individualism also has had its counter-reactions, such as socialism (understood neutrally), national socialism, or communism.

Being a Czech and having spent my childhood in a communist regime, it was interesting to observe how a forced and unnatural emphasis on community (the actual word used was "collective") gradually led many to an even stronger and suspecting individualism. People would mostly take part in the official communal life only *pro forma*, or they avoided it altogether. People tried to retreat to their private lives, families, hobbies, etc. Formally many people were members of the communist party or other official organizations just in order to be able to get a better job or because of fear—sometimes real, sometimes just imagined. The changes in and after 1989 meant for people an opportunity to become individualistic without becoming politically incorrect or even suspicious to the state. Of course, the influx of the well-known "individualistic agenda of Western consumerism" soon followed, which the communist leaders had so much feared.

As a post-communist convert to Christianity, I lack personal experience with the life of the church before these important changes in my country. Certainly the church now offers an alternative way of life, and it did so during the communist years. The denominations in the Czech Republic are many and varied with different ideas of what "church as a body" means. The Brethren Evangelical Free Church,[1] to which I belong, does in general value the community. At the same time, our pietistic and revivalist roots lead us to emphasize personal experience with Christ, personal (individual) conversion, and personal spirituality. Consequently, some of my questions when approaching the grand theme of atonement were centered on

---

1. http://cb.cz/main/en/home.

individualism. Does our current general appreciation of individualism somehow affect our understanding of atonement? Systematic theories of atonement are not necessarily individualistic, but it seems so easy for us to understand them in such a way, especially satisfaction and legal theories. The problem seems to be between an individual and God.[2] Is this correct? The Old Testament's emphasis on the community in most of its parts seems to provide a natural correction of individualistic thinking. Christopher Wright wrote that "we need to see Old Testament language of atonement and sacrifice in much more than individual terms. It had social and even cosmic significance."[3] This is exactly what I want to analyze in several pentateuchal texts.

The key term for atonement in the Hebrew OT is the lexical root *KPR*. Of course, the theology of atonement can be studied in many other texts in which this root does not appear. However, to keep this paper to a reasonable size we will limit ourselves to texts where it can be found.

I will first present an overview of suggested meanings of *KPR* in biblical texts and then look at selected texts from the Torah, especially in Leviticus, where this term is found frequently. I also will analyze two non-cultic narrative texts in the Torah which I consider to be paradigmatic atonement texts. I will approach the texts with interest primarily in their poetic and rhetorical aspects. Constantly we will be raising the question of the social dimension of atonement in these biblical passages.

KPR in the Old Testament

The root *KPR* is found in different contexts and primarily the cultic texts of Leviticus. Its etymology and exact meaning are disputed both by philologists and theologians. At least three different approaches exist.[4]

The first understanding sees the basic meaning of the verb *KPR* as "to cover." Besides some comparative arguments it is based on a quotation from Jer 18:23 in

---

2. See e.g., the critique by S. S. Maimela, "The Atonement in the Context of Liberation Theology," *International Review of Mission* 75 (1986) 261–69.

3. C. J. H. Wright, "Atonement in the Old Testament," in *The Atonement Debate: Papers from the London Symposium on the Theology of Atonement* (eds. D. Tidball, D. Hilborn, and J. Thacker; Grand Rapids: Zondervan, 2008) 77. J. Goldingay also treats this in his *Israel's Faith* (vol. 2 of *Old Testament Theology*; Downers Grove, IL: InterVarsity, 2006) 528ff.

4. See the excursus on *KPR* in J. E. Hartley, *Leviticus* (Word Biblical Commentary; Nashville: Thomas Nelson, 1992) 63–66. A similar but more detailed introduction can be found in R. E. Averbeck, "כָּפַר (kāpar II)," in *New International Dictionary of Old Testament Theology and Exegesis* (ed. W. A. VanGemeren; Grand Rapids: Zondervan, 1997) 2.689–710.

Neh 4:5 [Hebrew, 3:37], where the verb *KSH*, "to cover," is used instead of *KPR*, the word used in Jeremiah. Some other texts are quoted in support of this view, e.g., the substantive *koper*, "pitch," in Gen 6:14 with the idea of pitch that *covers*. This view is reflected in translating the word *kapporet* in description of the ark of the covenant by such words as "the lid" or "the cover," which otherwise is translated as the "mercy seat."

The second understanding starts from the presumably related noun *koper*, meaning "a ransom" (e.g., Num 35:29–34 or Prov 16:14), or even "a bribe" (Gen 32:21). Given such an understanding, the verb *KPR* in the piel verbal stem is usually translated "propitiate," "reconcile," or "appease."

The third understanding is based mostly on the cultic usage of the verb *KPR*, and there the basic meaning is identified as "purge" or "purify." The biblical support comes from texts like Jer 18:23 with its synonymous parallelism of *KPR* and *MḤH* ("wipe out"). Grammatically the understanding of *KPR* as purification (removing uncleanness) is the same as expiation (removing the sin). Some scholars still want to distinguish these two, while others think there is no major difference.

The etymology and the basic meaning of the verb were once considered very important theologically. In his influential study on atonement C. H. Dodd in 1935 argued that at least the translators of the Bible from Hebrew to Greek did not understand the verb *KPR* (in the piel) in the sense of "propitiating the Deity" but rather as removal of guilt, sin, or impurity. The LXX translators did not understand the cult in terms of pacifying an angered Deity; rather it was seen as God's provision for disposing of people's sins.[5] The idea of a God who can or should be "pacified" may indeed sound rather primitive. On the other hand, the concept of propitiation keeps the whole problem in very personal terms between God and humans, as the relevant biblical texts suggest.

We will not specifically address this issue in the present paper. To many recent scholars the third of the three suggested views seems most attractive, at least for many cultic texts. However, these meanings are not necessarily mutually exclusive, as some admit.[6] In one of the central texts (Lev 16) these two ideas are clearly combined and dealt with together, as we shall see.

---

5. C. H. Dodd, *The Bible and the Greeks* (2 ed.; London: Hodder and Stoughton, 1954, first published in 1935) 93.

6. W. H. C. Propp, *Exodus 19–40: A New Translation with Introduction and Commentary* (Anchor Bible 2A; New York: Doubleday, 2006) 467. Hartley, *Leviticus*, 64, also comes to the conclusion that *KPR* both "removes pollution and . . . counteracts sin."

KPR in the Cultic Texts of Leviticus

The root *KPR* is mostly found in the cultic texts of Leviticus. Its very first occurrence raises questions and does not nicely fit in the above suggested theories of the meaning of *KPR*. In Lev 1:4 we find an instruction for bringing an offering (*qorbān*). This offering is not explicitly related either to the sin or to impurity.[7] Yet, right after the offering is accepted, the atonement (*KPR*) is granted to one who brought it. Usually the need of atonement in this type of offering is explained by *a priori* impurity or sinfulness of any person.[8] The mention of *KPR* here could alternatively be a way of introducing this important concept in Leviticus. Perhaps it could also mean that *KPR* is not so strictly tied to areas of sin or impurity. In this verse it follows the verb *RṢH*, "be accepted," perhaps "be graciously accepted." The overall atmosphere of the whole offering seems to be positive; *KPR* here could possibly mean something like "establish a positive relationship" with the emphasis on the fellowship and communion between God and the person bringing the offering.

KPR and the Sin/Purification-Offering (Leviticus 4)

Leviticus 4 refers to atonement in the context of so called "sin-offerings." However, since the noun for "sin" (*ḥaṭṭāʾt*) seems to be derived from the piel form of the verb *ḤṬʾ*, and since the piel form of the verb often means "to purge from sin," "to remove impurity," this offering should, according to some, rather be called the "purification offering."[9] In such a case the argument follows that *KPR* in this context means *the purification of the tent of the meeting* and its equipment, especially since the blood of the sacrifice is not applied towards persons but towards the objects, presumably to cleanse them from defilement from the sins of the people. At the same time it is clear that the real problem is not only the question of ritual purity but the question of forgiveness. The real (though possibly inadvertent) sin was at the beginning of the whole suggested situation (Lev 4:2, *ḤṬʾ*, Qal, "to sin") and this theme, i.e., "the sin which he has committed" (Lev 4:35) is remembered and forgiven (*SLḤ*) in the

---

7. Actually it is the only use of *KPR* in connection with the "whole offering" (*ʿōlāh*) besides Ezek 45:15, see Hartley, *Leviticus*, 19.

8. See e.g., G. J. Wenham, *The Book of Leviticus* (New International Commentary on the Old Testament; Grand Rapids: Eerdmans, 1979) 57: "Thus the burnt offering does not remove sin or change man's sinful nature, but it makes fellowship between sinful man and a holy God possible. It propitiates God's wrath against sin."

9. The most influential proponent of this opinion has been Jacob Milgrom, see e.g., his "Sin-Offering or Purification-Offering?" *Vetus Testamentum* 21 (1971) 237–39.

very end of this section. The structure of this chapter is quite clear. Leviticus 4:1–2 introduces the common theme, i.e., what to do in case of "inadvertent"[10] sins. A special procedure is prescribed for four different groups: the anointed priest, the whole congregation, a ruler, and anyone of the common people.

The first two cases are more serious and the whole procedure of *KPR* is more complicated. The blood of the sacrifice is brought "before the Lord" and is sprinkled "towards" or perhaps right "on" the veil of the sanctuary (Lev 4:6, 17). Also the value of the animal used for the offering must be relatively high (a young bull) when offered for the sin of the anointed priest and the congregation, while the ruler offers a he-goat and the commoner brings (only) a female goat.

What are the dynamics of social relationships expressed by the text's rhetorical components? The first imagined sinner is the "anointed priest," most likely the high priest (Lev 16:32). The prominent position of his case in the chapter suggests that this is the most serious situation. Immediately it is stated that the priest's sin means "bringing guilt on the people." It is interesting that, while the procedure for the offering in this first case is prescribed, the final formula promising or declaring *KPR* is missing. One suggestion has been to see in this omission the reason for the Day of Atonement (Lev 16),[11] which seems very likely. Leviticus 16 indeed assumes that there are certain sins to be atoned for and carried away. If this is so, we must also consider the question of guilt brought on the congregation by the high priest's sin. Does it also remain without full *KPR*? If so, then Lev 16 becomes the real center of Leviticus. Both the high priest and the congregation come before the Lord on the Day of Atonement in urgent need of atonement. The priest's sin has affected the congregation as well. The procedure in Lev 4:3–12 suspends the effects of the sin, but the full *KPR* takes place during the Day of Atonement.

The next case starts in Lev 4:13 and treats the sin of the community. The imagined situation is that the "whole congregation of Israel" sins, but the sin remains hidden. Yet the guilt is brought on the whole congregation. Despite the modern idea of strictly personal and individual responsibility, here the guilt is collective. The law is not at all interested in details like responsibility of small children, or e.g., whether

---

10. The meaning of the expression *bišgāgāh* and its translation have been much discussed. It seems two ideas are intermingled in it: the notion of "going in the wrong direction," "act wrongly," and the sense of an unpremeditated act, which, however, does not have to mean "not being aware of one's acts." See W. C. Kaiser, "The Book of Leviticus," in *The New Interpreter's Bible* (ed. L. E. Keck; Nashville: Abingdon, 1994) I.1033f; cf. Hartley, *Leviticus*, 55.

11. N. Kiuchi, *The Purification Offering in the Priestly Literature* (JSOT Supplement Series 56; Sheffield: Sheffield Academic Press, 1987) 125–28.

people possibly not personally involved in the sin are also considered guilty. The congregation is represented by the elders together with the priest. The priests as members of the community are also affected by the sin; therefore, they must not eat any of the animal. Its remains must also in this case be burnt outside the camp.[12] The priest does not cease to be a part of the community.

The procedures for the next two cases (a sin of a ruler and a sin of any common member of the community) show similar traits. The offering in each case can be relatively less expensive. The instruction to burn the remains of the animal outside the camp is missing, and the procedure is compared to the "peace offering" (Lev 4:26, 31). In the case of the offering for the sin of an individual the reference is made to the "pleasing odor to the Lord," similar to the peace offering (Lev 3:5) or the *qorbān* (Lev 1:9). The *KPR* is administered by a regular priest, not the "anointed priest."

Summary for the Sin-Offering

Leviticus 4 presents the institution of an offering as a way of solving usual and expected problems when the holy God dwells among humans. This set of instructions shows interest in *KPR* being available to the whole community in its social diversity. The priest has an important role in assisting in the atonement of all groups or individuals in the society; therefore, his sin creates an extremely critical situation which does not seem to be fully solved even by the procedure in this chapter. The second most serious danger comes when the whole community is collectively threatened by the sin. In such a situation the elders must represent the community and seek the atonement. Atonement for an offence must be sought by a "secular" ruler as well. However, it is equally important that even a common person in Israel continually takes care of his or her relationship with God through *KPR*.

The text implies mutual accountability of the members of the community when it says "the sin is made known to him" (Lev 4:23, 28). To identify a sin or a wrong deed is not strictly an individual responsibility of a given person. Neither is there a reason to think it was exclusively a priest's job. It is assumed that the holiness of the community is defended by all its members.

Leviticus 5:1–4 speaks of further potential problems and Lev 5:5–13 offers solutions to make *KPR* and obtain forgiveness. We will not go into detail here. The main point is that the sins or uncleanness have their social aspects (especially sins relating to providing testimony, giving an oath, etc.) and that atonement in such matters

---

12. Hartley, *Leviticus*, 63.

is in the interest of the whole society. The socially sensitive alternatives regarding the animal for the offering (or even the possibility to bring a flour offering) give a chance, but also set a duty, to the poorest in the society to look for *KPR*.

Atonement and Reparations

The set of instructions in Lev 5:14—6:7[Hebrew, 5:26] differs from previous cultic laws by requiring financial or material compensation in addition to the atonement ritual. Also, whereas in the preceding laws the *KPR* was made in the context of a *ḥaṭṭāʾt* ("sin-offering" or "purification offering"), now the offering is described as *ʾāšām*. Instead of the traditional translation "guilt offering," the expression "reparation offering" has been used recently to emphasize its distinct feature.[13]

This section is structured around two speeches of the Lord to Moses.[14] Both speeches show strong formal parallels. They are both introduced by the same introductory formula ("The Lord spoke to Moses"), in both speeches the sin is called a "breach of faith" (√*MʿL*), and in both cases the atonement (*KPR*) should be accompanied by compensation to the offended party.

Regarding the contents, whereas the first speech is concerned with sins against "the holy things of the Lord," the second instructs people how to make atonement in case of sin against the property of one's neighbor. Sins against the things of another person are by the parallel structure of this passage put on the same level with the sins against the things belonging to God. Deception, robbery, and similar attacks on another person's property are called "a breach of faith against the Lord" (Lev 6:2 [Hebrew, 5:21]). One reason why God is directly offended by such actions can relate to the fact that a false oath is involved, and so the name of the Lord is abused. The reason for strong condemnation of such behavior does not seem to stem from exclusively "cultic" concerns. The social aspect is also important, and "secular" sins like robbery or oppression (Lev 6:4 [Hebrew, 5:23])[15] equally belong in the category of "breach of faith."

The compensation in cases of social transgressions belongs to the offended person. The actual formulation of the instruction explicitly connects the restitution on the interpersonal level with bringing the offering to God so that they are conducted

---

13. Hartley, *Leviticus*, 75; J. H. Hayes, "Atonement in the Book of Leviticus," *Int* 52.1 (1998) 5–15, 10ff.

14. See Lev 5:14 and 6:1 [Hebrew, 5:20]. Lev 5:17–19 looks like a kind of a summary.

15. Hartley, *Leviticus*, 83. See also Exod 22:8[Hebrew, 7]ff.

on the same day (Lev 6:5 [Hebrew, 5:24]). Only then can *KPR* before the Lord be completed and the sinner is forgiven (6:7 [Hebrew, 5:26]).

In these cases of reparation offerings the necessity of making things right on both a cultic and a social level is of great importance. The two areas are interrelated. This is the characteristic feature of biblical law as can be observed in many biblical legal texts. This perspective is also present in the teaching of Jesus (Matt 5:23ff.).

The Day of Atonement

Although we have already encountered texts in Leviticus dealing with the question of atonement for the whole community (Lev 4:13ff.), Lev 16 is still a unique text in this regard. In descriptions as well as prescriptions of the ritual we can recognize two tracks. The first one sees the purpose of the atonement ritual in a removal of impurities, as the concluding formula for the first part of the ritual states: ". . . thus he shall make atonement for the holy place, because of the uncleannesses of the people of Israel, and because of their transgressions, all their sins; and so he shall do for the tent of meeting, which abides with them in the midst of their uncleannesses" (Lev 16:16, RSV).

So the main emphasis here is on the removal of impurities of the Israelites (see also Lev 16:19) through the use of the blood of the sacrificed animal. The Lord dwells among his people, but this inevitably means "among their uncleannesses" too. Such a situation calls for a solution, which is provided by the *KPR* ritual.

The second track is interested in removing the actual sins and transgressions of the people. The purpose of this line of thinking is expressed in Lev 16:34: ". . . that atonement may be made for the people of Israel once in the year because of all their sins" (RSV).

The sins are removed by the well-known ritual with the "goat for ʿăzāʾzēl" on whom "transgressions, sins, and iniquities" of the people are laid so that they can be carried away. The chapter makes use of the rich Hebrew terminology for sin (*pešaʿ*, *ʿāwōn*, *ḥaṭṭāʾt*). These expressions are used in the plural and refer collectively to the sins of "the children of Israel."

Both tracks, the removal of impurity and the removal of sins, are interconnected. Atonement (*KPR*) plays a role in both of them (Lev 16:16, 24, 30, 32 etc.). The connection between the two distinct tracks is clear from Lev 16:16, where the impurities of Israelites (specifically their impurities which became attached to the sanctuary) are put on the same level with their "transgressions and sins." If the consequence of the sin is death, the same is valid for the impurity of the people because it directly threatens the purity of God's dwelling among his people (Lev 15:31). Also, the reference to the death of Aaron's sons in the very beginning of Lev 16 shows the question of purity as the matter of life or death. This idea is probably rather strange to people today. Various explanations of this concept in the OT have been offered, e.g., the purity–impurity opposition as reflecting the general opposition of life and death, the opposition of order and chaos, etc. This concept is, however, very important for its social dimension. Impurity is considered a danger for the society, which cannot be easily dealt with. Impurity tends to spread. Somehow it is able to get from one person to another (Lev 15:5ff.); it can even contaminate the most holy places (Lev 15:31). Therefore, a "contaminated" person must be excluded from the community at least for a certain period of time (Lev 13:21, 26, 31, 54). Still, *it seems the priestly writers could not imagine how the impurity might possibly be limited strictly to affected individuals and how impurity could be definitely stopped.* There was atonement for individuals after being "decontaminated," but the ritual in Lev 16 shows that at least once a year the whole community stood before the Lord in the need of purification and atonement.

What social dynamics can we observe during the Day of Atonement as described in Lev 16? Great attention is given to Aaron the high priest, to whom most of the directions are addressed, but it gradually becomes clear that the whole Israelite community is the main beneficiary of the ritual. Even though the chapter starts with ritual cleansing of Aaron and his house, the first half of the chapter comes to a climax with the revelation that it is *mainly the impurities and sins of the people* that are atoned for (Lev 16:16, 19).

The scapegoat ritual (16:20ff.) takes care of the sins of the Israelites as a community. This is a collective treatment of sin; it relates to the individuals only as they are part of the whole group. The final paragraph (Lev 16:29–34) underscores this understanding through a change in the rhetorical focus. Suddenly the whole community is being directly addressed, not only Moses or Aaron. Until now it was not clear what the role of the people in the ritual was. The people were absent as their impurities and sins did not allow them to take any active role in the atonement (16:17). At the end of the section their role is revealed; they are "to humble themselves" and keep the day as "the Sabbath of solemn rest."[16]

So in contrast to any individualistic idea of atonement, the text in Lev 16 shows the Day of Atonement as a huge event for the whole community, during which

---

16. The verb ʿŠQ, "oppress," suggests a situation in which power is abused by a ruler or an authority, see 1 Sam 12:3.

they—not as individuals but as the whole people—can receive purification and have their sins removed. The importance of this day is retained in the Jewish tradition, including the strong emphasis on the community. Before Yom Kippur a Jewish believer should seek forgiveness from his neighbors.

Two Paradigmatic Atonement Narratives

Two very special texts are different from the cultic instructions studied so far. The hero in the first story is the eponymous father of Israel. The main human character in the second is the founder of the religion of the people of Israel. Interestingly both of them become involved in *KPR*, though each in a different way.

Jacob, Esau, the Face of God, and *KPR* (Genesis 32–33)

Genesis 32:20[Hebrew, 21] is the first moment in the pentateuchal narrative where the verb *KPR* in the piel is used. The main character is the patriarch Jacob, so it is very tempting to read the story from his life as Israel's theological reflection regarding her own identity.

The story is well known, so we can immediately go to the function of *KPR* in the narrative. It appears embedded in Jacob's speech in instructions regarding words to be reproduced by Jacob's servants to Esau. In the structure of the narrative this *KPR* comes as an explanation of Jacob's preceding actions. By sending the gifts Jacob wants Esau to see him as one trying to get *KPR*: "atonement" or perhaps "reconciliation". This narrative theme is continued in Gen 33 in which the brothers finally meet face to face and the renewal of their relationship is demonstrated.

The narrative of the two brothers is strangely interrupted by the popular pericope about Jacob's wrestling by the brook Jabbok. The commentators note that this is not a real interruption. Jacob's "wrestling" with his brother Esau and with the Unknown by the brook Jabbok are interconnected through the poetic features of the text. The word "face" is one of the key terms. Jacob wants first to "atone/appease [*KPR*] the face" of Esau in order to be able "to see his face" afterwards (Gen 32:20[Hebrew, 21]). The narrator does not allow this motif to fade out. In Gen 33:10 Jacob confirms that he indeed does see his brother's face and that to see it "is like seeing the face of God." Precisely God's face was what Jacob saw (or at least he came to the conclusion that he saw it) the previous night, so he called the place of the wrestling *Peniel*, "Face of God." What does this observation mean for our study of atonement?

First, *KPR* is again a matter of life or death; it is the only way to survive. Jacob is aware of the danger (Gen 32:11 [Hebrew, 12]) and *KPR* is his hope (Gen 32:20 [Hebrew, 21]).

Second, *KPR* does not appear to be a mere judicial solution of a problem. At least at this point in the narrative the desired result is not mere material compensation, though it seems to have been offered and eventually accepted (Gen 33:8–11). What Jacob really says he wants to achieve is to *see his brother's face*, and he expects from Esau "raising of his face." Jacob wants to be accepted by Esau. This is what happens in Gen 33:4. In light of the results, *KPR* seems to be not only a legal settling of a case but rather a means of renewing relationship and bringing it into the condition of šālôm.[17]

Third, the original conflict between Jacob and Esau and Jacob's subsequent desire of "atonement" are presented in terms of interpersonal human relationships. The abrupt intervention of the mysterious man changes this perspective as the person is identified by Jacob and indirectly by the Unknown himself as God. So wrestling with God is an important moment in the story of Jacob and Esau. The theologian behind this narrative by its specific arrangement suggests that real *KPR* in interpersonal relationships is only possible through "wrestling with God face to face." It is an analogical way of thinking about the theology of "reparation offerings" encountered in Lev 5:14ff. There, on the contrary, access to God was conditioned by previous or simultaneous "putting things right" with one's neighbor.

Fourth, yet another perspective can be offered by viewing Jacob and Esau as representatives of their eponymous nations. In such a perspective Israel is described as one who must seek peaceful cohabitation with "brother Esau." The wrestling with God removes from Israel fear of a potentially stronger neighbor. Though Israel may be weaker or even "struck by God," Israel can achieve such a peaceful relationship with his "brother" Esau–Edom—or maybe precisely because of being struck.

KPR as Intercession and Parley (Exodus 32–34)

This text too can be called paradigmatic. It brings the reader into the moment of Israel's "great fall" just after they were created as a new nation and after they accepted God's covenant. It is the first case of atonement (*KPR*) directed towards God in the

---

17. Also in Lev 23:27f. reference is probably made back to Lev 16, where the community is again instructed to "humble themselves" and to "make atonement" (*KPR*) before the Lord.

pentateuchal narrative.[18] Even after draconic execution by the Levites in an attempt to purge the community, Moses thinks something more is needed. He decides to ascend the mountain again in order to *KPR* the Lord (Exod 32:30). Since the priesthood is not yet available, perhaps also due to Aaron's failure, Moses attempts to make atonement by confessing the people's sin and by asking the Lord to forgive the sin ("to carry the sin"). Should God's response be negative, Moses asks to be blotted out of the book the Lord is writing. God's answer is ambiguous. The Lord does not accept the idea of Moses being blotted out together with the sinful nation; only one who sinned will be erased from the book. There is still some hope for the people. Moses' leadership will continue, the Lord's angel will lead as well, but the punishment will come, and indeed, some plague comes right away (Exod 32:35).

Therefore the question remains. How successful was Moses in "making atonement"? The theme is re-opened in the next chapter (Exod 33) as certain parallels with Exod 32 show. The idea of the Lord's angel/messenger is taken up again, though this time clearly as a negative alternative to the presence of God himself. Moses again tries to put forward conditions: "If thy presence will not go with me, do not carry us up from here" (RSV). The parley continues in Exod 33. The prominent characteristic of the dialog is a sense of growing intimacy in the relationship between Moses and God, exactly in the moment when such intimacy is not available to the Israelite community. The Lord talks to Moses directly (Exod 33:9), even "face to face, as a man speaks to his friend." Moses confidently presents himself to God as one who has found God's grace (Exod 33:12, 13), and in Exod 33:16 he tries to include the whole people in that grace. God does not object, but in his explicit confirmation of grace speaks only of Moses (33:17). Moses again in Exod 34:9 calls upon God's grace not only for himself, but also for the sake of the people.

God seems to accept this tone of speech and its intimacy. The Lord knows Moses "by name" as Moses himself declares and the Lord confirms (Exod 33:12, 17). The Lord also tells Moses that he is going to proclaim his name before Moses (33:19), i.e., reveal his real identity. The next logical step in this process is the only one possible, seeing the real "face" of the partner (or, as Moses puts it, "seeing your glory"). Why is this so important for Moses exactly at this point in the narrative plot? Seeing God's face probably means a guarantee of mutual understanding in this hotly debated issue of full reconciliation between God and Israel. God's solution

---

18. The word (*šālôm*) is not actually used in the narrative. Also, some disharmonic tones are still present. What does Esau mean by offering a company of his (armed) servants? Why does Jacob tell Esau that he would follow him to Seir and then goes rather to Succoth?

goes in two directions. First, Moses is not totally refused, despite his unheard of request to see God's glory. He will be able to see it, albeit in a limited way. Second, the Lord keeps the door open for his own freedom and sovereignty when "making atonement" through Moses with his people. Just as his glory is not revealed fully, so in the atonement an aspect of unpredictability remains. The same openness sounds in God's self-revelation in the tautological formulation in Exod 33:19 and also in God's dialectic exegesis of his own name in Exod 34:6f.

In this awesome passage the biblical narrator is not scared of strong anthropomorphisms ("face to face," the picture of God "walking" around Moses, covering him with his "hands" to be able to see only "the back" of the Lord), although it might create small inconsistencies. For example, Moses talks to God face to face, but at the same time is told he cannot see God's face. The anthropomorphisms help to see the dialog as a social interaction between two people, actually between two friends. Only after the trust has been established, Moses can raise his request again, and the atonement can be finished (Exod 39:9). The result of the finished atonement should be forgiveness (*SLH*) of the "iniquity and sin" of the Israelites, God's presence with his people, and the renewal of Israel's identity as God's special inheritance (*NHL*).

God's answer in Exod 34:10–27 shows that "making atonement" has been finished. The covenant is fully renewed by the miraculous "creation" of a new relationship of God with Israel (Exod 34:10). In this speech God makes reference to main portions of the biblical law so far presented in Exodus. This probably means that the complete covenant is being offered again. The verbatim fulfillment of God's instruction for building the sanctuary serves the same purpose. What was broken by Israel's sin is being made new. The Lord's glory finally fills the sanctuary in Exod 34, and with this the main concern of Moses (God's presence) is solved.

To summarize, *KPR* seems to mean at least three things in this narrative. First, it takes place through a mediator (Moses). It is a classic example of intercessory ministry. Such ministry is only possible when based on deep solidarity, here demonstrated in Moses' attitude towards sinful people. His offer to be erased from the book was not accepted by God as relevant, but still it shows the depth of Moses' identification with the people. Second, Moses' ministry of atonement is based on his ability to boldly interact with God on behalf of the people. Third, the immediate goal of making atonement is "forgiveness of sin" for the whole community, but the expectations are higher. The atonement should be more than mere pardon of a death sentence. Actually the idea of punishment is perhaps not quite abandoned by God. Still, the result of atonement must be God's presence among his people. This idea of atonement goes way beyond its mere legal understanding and also beyond mere appeasement of a strong and mighty opponent.

In this regard this event of atonement is similar to that of Jacob and Esau. In both cases the narrative shows the resulting situation as a *renewal of fellowship*.

Summary and Perspectives

The purpose of this paper has been to present an interpretation of atonement texts in the Torah with special interest in the social dimensions of atonement. From Lev 4 in the context of *sin-offerings* (or *purification-offerings*), we have seen that the cultic law is very concerned about atonement being available to various groups in the society: the whole community, a ruler, or any individual. The high priest has a special role in making atonement, especially when the whole community is concerned. Therefore, an extremely serious problem was created by the high priest's sin. A ritual was prescribed for such a situation, but the question of atonement for the high priest remained open. I believe one can perceive in Lev 4 a sense of mutual and communal responsibility for making atonement (*KPR*) which can be defined as *removing obstacles that prevent full fellowship of an individual or the whole community with God*.

Leviticus 5:14—6:7 [Hebrew, 5:26] provides instructions for the *guilt offering*. This ritual is characteristic by a requirement to provide compensation to God, in a case of sin against God's holy things, or to a person, in a case of sin against things of another person. The compensation is a necessary part of the process of atonement, and the compensation to a person is put on the same level with the compensation to God.

Leviticus 16 is a central cultic text for atonement in the Torah. It describes and prescribes how first the high priest and then the whole community can find atonement. It connects two important areas in which Israel must seek atonement, the areas of sin and of purity. Especially the metaphor of purity has important social aspects.

The story of Jacob and Esau shows how deeply God gets involved in matters of "reconciliation" or "atonement" in human relationships. This is expressed prominently by the way God identifies with the whole situation of the two brothers through his wrestling with Jacob. Also Jacob knows that "to make atonement" with his brother and see his face will be "like seeing the face of God."

The narrative of Moses' encounter with God shows how the ministry of courageous intercession can play a crucial role in the process of atonement. In both narrative texts (and perhaps also in the cultic use of *KPR* in Lev 1:4) we argued that the atonement is not mere "appeasement" or "non-punishment," but actually a renewal of fellowship and communion.

These atonement texts from the Torah offer significant instruction for the life of the church. They suggest we should stop placing so much attention on atonement as relating only to the individual. The atonement is not only the matter of one's personal sin being "carried to ʿăzāʾzēl. The sins of the whole community must be taken away. Dealing sensitively and publicly with the question of sin and also with forgiveness and reconciliation are required.

We should also rethink the metaphors of purity and impurity in the context of the church. Impurity and defilement are social problems and make sense only as such. Impurity in the Torah is an invisible enemy. Defilement is a phenomenon that a person cannot avoid by individually adhering to ethical standards. One simply gets polluted by dwelling "in the midst of a people of unclean lips" (Isa 6:5).

The social dimension of atonement leads us to think about the church's mission as well. Authentic interest in one's personal atonement and in atonement for the church leads us to think of the outsiders. The church constantly purified is a great miracle of God, but the church is called to participate in purification of the world through mission and sacraments. Related to this is the church's intercessory ministry, which should also be reconsidered in light of Moses' example.

RESPONSE TO BER

Jeremy J. Wynne

Viktor Ber has revisited a critique of Western individualism that is, at first glance, well-worn. At the same time, this message remains a difficult one for us to hear and so continues to be both poignant and eminently relevant. In particular, I appreciate Ber's personal comments—his willingness to share not only his experiences surrounding the great political events of 1989 but also his sense for the lingering overemphasis within his own church upon faith as *personal* experience. Certainly we know something in the United States about the weaknesses (and perhaps too the strengths) of individualism. Still, Ber's story, and especially his perspective on the "forced and unnatural" character of certain social-*isms*, is an arresting one. In response, my first word to him is one of thanks for a very thoughtful paper.

As all good papers do, Ber's opens up several worthwhile avenues for inquiry. I would like to commend two questions as particularly important. First, I wonder whether there are resources in Leviticus (or perhaps Genesis or Exodus) which would enable a deeper and more theologically serviceable way of conceiving the wholeness of the faith community than is possible through an appeal to the category of "the social." This latter category is not up to the challenge of supporting the weight of biblical discourse about atonement. Is this, for example, a general concept? Do we already understand what is social *prior* to reading and hearing Scripture? It is undeniable that the OT presents human life as in some sense irreducibly *social*. As Ber has pointed out, life is conceived in these books as existing in a web of relationships, mutual dependences, and obligations one to another. The sin or impurity of individuals threatens or compromises the entire community, exposing everyone to death. The requirement for atonement thus implies, as Ber has stressed, a "mutual accountability," and this corresponds to the effects of atonement which are received as benefitting "the whole Israelite community." This point is further reinforced by his consideration of Gen 32–33 and Exod 32–34. His thesis that the narrative or dramatic shape of human life in Scripture reveals the nature of reconciliation is both simple and brilliant.

What, specifically, can we say about the *ontology* operating below the surface of these various divine commands and reconciliation narratives? This is a much more complex question. While full articulation may require a distinctly NT vocabulary, the questions themselves are prompted in the Old. My concern is for that which unites the people of God, for that which constitutes inclusion among the people of the covenant. What precisely does it mean to *be* together? What is the ontological force, for example, of the "growing intimacy" between God and Moses which Ber references? In our less reflective moments we might describe God's people—and I assume that this includes the church—in ways which suggest that we ourselves devise and produce this unity. We might invoke a life of shared commitments. One of these commitments, in fact, might be to a critique of individualism, which, however deeply we feel to be a genuinely Christian conviction, might turn out to be merely a negative reaction, a movement toward the other end of an abstract polarity. The temptation toward this kind of reasoning is at least suggested when Ber proposes that a view of atonement and sacrifice that bears "social and even cosmic significance" provides "a natural correction" to individualism. I do not think such abstractions are often intentional, but I do believe the argument leaves us in a predicament. Thus my first question: does Leviticus (with the help of Genesis and Exodus) in fact provide one with the ontology needed in order to say well that God's people are *given* as "a society," and that this gift is the product of *God's* reconciling work? Might we be better prepared theologically to approach the people of God as a "corporate" unity?

Second, to what extent are the effects of atonement in Leviticus—the reconciliation of the sinful and the purification of the impure—made *morally intelligible*? I would suggest that a strong focus on "the social" dimension of atonement, developed strictly from within the Pentateuch, has the effect of highlighting a gap between God's promise to purify and reconcile his people and a realistic account of the sufficiency of this work in his people's lives. In reading this essay I found myself asking about the connection between the shedding of animal blood and the wiping out of the sins of the community. How do we speak rightly of a transference of guilt if what is *right* does not permit, at least in any ordinary sense, judgment upon a substitute or representative? We may find in our readings of Lev 4, 5, and 16 that there is a demonstrable fittingness between sacrifice and atonement, but atonement theories are intended to develop and elucidate the inner logic of this effect. Thus we will inevitably ask about the inner logic of this transference. Is it strictly a function of God's will? The narrative of Exodus seems to offer little help on this matter. In fact, it may pose other equally difficult questions focused on the similar gap between Yahweh's just railing against the people's idolatry at Sinai and his wonderfully sudden and unmerited re-institution of the covenant. The concern is not mine alone. One prominent OT scholar has proposed that these two moments in God's life simply cannot be thought together. Much to the contrary, this scholar suggests, God's life displays a "profound and durable incongruity," such that Yahweh's presence to Israel is "marked by an open-ended, unresolved two-sidedness."[1]

Were I myself to propose one potential answer to both concerns, I would say the OT and NT alike suggest a finality to the work of the Messiah, to the life, death, and resurrection of the Lord Jesus. Just as Ber does in his passages, so too in the NT one can trace the deployment of the atonement lexicon, observing especially the connection between *kippur* and *hilastērion* in Rom 3:25 and in Heb 9:5. These passages are distinct in suggesting that the sacrifice of Jesus Christ is qualitatively different. It is less God's *coup de grâce*, a death blow that finally secures God's ongoing determination to put down human rebellion. Rather, it is an act undertaken once and for all and is the very proof and demonstration of God's righteousness, the effectiveness of which depends upon a genuine incarnation of the eternal Son. That is one compelling way to respond to the questions I have raised. There certainly may be others.

In any case, you will notice that each of the questions I have asked arises only where one attempts to forestall a canonical reading of God's drama of reconciliation and redemption. In the final analysis an articulation of atonement (or a focus upon one aspect of the atonement, such as its "social" dimension) will be more adequate when it is worked out with direct or indirect reference to God's "plan for the fullness of time" (Eph 1:10) and its center in the cross of Christ. Akin to the spatial metaphors discussed at this conference, perhaps this is the irreducibly temporal or historical character of atonement. I am not in any sense unsympathetic to that first pass through Scripture that Brevard Childs has commended as part of his own intercanonical project. Here the aim is to read texts, like Leviticus, in their particularity and richness and allow them first to convey the message of reconciliation in their own terms.[2] This, then, is the reasoning behind my second question for Ber. If we forestall knowledge of the cross and attempt to hear Leviticus, at least for a moment, as one witness to the period of open-endedness during which "God passes over sins" (Rom 3:25), can we say anything about the *moral intelligibility* of the connection between atoning sacrifice and its effects or about the inner logic of the God's unfolding work?

---

1. Walter Brueggemann, *The Book of Exodus* (Nashville: Abingdon, 1995) 947, 951.
2. Brevard S. Childs, "Toward Recovering Theological Exegesis," *Ex Auditu* 16 (2000) 121–29.

"TO THOSE WHO WERE DISTANT AND THOSE WHO WERE NEAR": ATONEMENT, IDENTITY, AND IDENTIFICATION

Brian Bantum

"Atonement is history." (Karl Barth)

The doctrine of atonement expresses a pattern of relationship, the interaction between God and humanity. At its heart the doctrine of atonement is a consideration of the one who atones and those who are atoned for. In considering the effects of Christ's work on humanity, Barth's invocation, "atonement is history" draws together not only the effects of Christ's work but those who participate within it. In this way atonement is fundamentally a consideration of who Christ is and who we were, are, and will be. To suggest "atonement is history" is to suggest atonement is a claim of Christian identity.

In the modern world (but particularly in the last fifty years) identity has emerged as an increasingly complicated and politicized area of reflection. Most often identity is associated with questions of race, ethnicity, and gender, but it is not often directly correlated to the doctrinal claims of Christian reflection. While identity may not have been traditionally the explicit center of Christian reflection upon Christ's work, the doctrine of atonement seeks to address a fundamental question, "Who are we?" The language of *who* is particularly important because oftentimes the doctrine of the atonement is cast in terms of status, in terms of *what*. That is, Christ's work is discussed in relationship to the status it confers upon a person or persons. Humanity is innocent, or justified, for instance. Whereas the question, "What are you?" engenders a status, the question "Who are you?" requires a more complicated narration of location, relationships, and hopes. The question "Who are you?" is a question of history. History, in this sense, is an exercise of identity, a recollecting of those realities, events, and relationships that have forged themselves together in the particularity of a person or people and guides how they organize their lives together. Here Barth's clarification of the claim, "atonement is history" is instructive. He writes, "But the atonement is the very special history of God with man, the very special history of man with God."[1] The atonement concerns identity insofar as it attempts to narrate the particularities of the relationship between God and humanity and thus articulate who humanity is.[2] In this respect the claim concerning atonement is not only about humanity's relationship with God, but about an identity with God that echoes and becomes present within human interrelationships. This intersection of Christ's atoning work with the shape of our lives with one another is a theme consistent throughout Scripture and is particularly evident in Eph 2.

This essay will outline how atonement can be understood as an articulation of identity and will focus on two prevalent ways atonement has been expressed in Christian reflection, namely satisfaction and deification. As well, I will provide a consideration of how atonement in Levitical law expands these traditions of reflection and begins to open a horizon of Christian identity in a rapidly changing and violent twenty-first century. To this end I will explore how Eph 2 expresses Christ's work, but more particularly how humanity's condition and subsequent redemption is described in distinct but related ways in Eph 2. In Ephesians Paul[3] articulates the effect of Christ's work upon humanity in terms of identity. The particularity of Jews and Gentiles allows an understanding of atonement and the Christian life to inhabit the challenges of difference and violence in our contemporary world.

I will begin with a brief discussion of how two distinct traditions have drawn upon Eph 2 in discussing atonement. Drawing from these descriptions I will highlight the underlying concerns of each view as well as how these views of atonement reflect a certain construct of human identity. Lastly, I will outline the interconnections between the conceptions of atonement in Eph 2 and a similar rhythm of atonement described in Lev 16 where the restoration of Israel required the sins of the people to be placed upon a goat and sent into the wilderness far from the gates of the city.

---

1. Karl Barth, *Church Dogmatics* IV.1 (trans. G. W. Bromily; New York: T. & T. Clark, 1956, 2003) 157.

2. The question "who" does not exclude the question "what." Rather, the question "who" expands the implications and contextual significance of the "what."

3. Here I am not making an explicit claim for Pauline authorship of Ephesians. Throughout this essay I will speak of Paul as the writer, primarily to maintain the nature of letters being written by a particular person to a particular people. I do this cognizant of the complicated claims of authorship at stake in all of the biblical narratives. "Paul" in this regard, can refer to Paul himself or to an author in the Pauline tradition. In either case, the interaction between a writer and a body of people that that writer has in mind is important, and it is this dynamic I am trying to maintain.

Interpretations of Atonement and Ephesians

Atonement can be broadly characterized as Christ's work, the restoration of humanity, and in particular the sacrificial death of Christ upon the cross.[4] Within this broad framework Christian reflection has characterized both the human condition and, relatedly, the nature of Christ's atoning work in various ways. Two prevalent means of describing Christ's atoning work have been satisfaction and deification.[5] Both of these emphases can be seen as echoes of themes in Eph 2. The first corresponds to an emphasis upon humanity's disobedience, its guilt, and its subjection to punishment. The second framework can be seen as interpreting Christ's atoning work as participatory, where Christ's work becomes a mode of presence in the world and in the believer.[6] Anselm of Canterbury provided the earliest systematic articulation of disobedience and sacrifice in *Cur Deus Homo* (Why God Became Man). Anselm's strong emphasis upon the justice of God and the proper ordering of relationship between humanity and God can be seen in Eph 2:1 and 3 where humanity was described as "you who were dead, objects of wrath." Anselm's conception of the atonement came to be understood as a satisfaction model of atonement that greatly influenced Western theological reflection.[7]

The fundamental connection between death and atonement is certainly not isolated to Christ's work as satisfaction. Yet, the account of atonement as satisfaction in particular intones Christ's redemptive work within a narrative of legal transgression and disobedience, the fundamental disorienting of human fidelity. This legal

---

4. Of course it should be noted that any distinction between Christ's person and Christ's work is ultimately illusory. See Dietrich Bonhoeffer, *Christ the Center* (New York: Harper & Row, 1960).

5. Satisfaction and deification are not intended to encapsulate all traditions of thought about Christ's work. They are intended to be representative of two significant branches of reflection which are among a diversity of conclusions and expressions.

6. I have intentionally avoided classifying these approaches as Western, Eastern, Catholic, Orthodox, or Protestant, cognizant of the fact that these two emphases can be found in all of these traditions in various ways. I do think it is fair to say that these represent two predominant emphases in Christian reflection that shape subsequent assumptions about sin, discipleship, etc.

7. New Testament scholar Markus Barth outlines these two emphases while considering whether the reconciliatory power of Christ's work is centered upon the cross or in the incarnation. While M. Barth himself favors an interpretation of this language as sacrificial, his observation highlights how this chapter's conception of the atonement is complex, to say the least. See Markus Barth, *Ephesians, Translation and Commentary on Chapters 1–3 and 4–6* (AB; Garden City, N.Y.: Doubleday, 1974) I.302–4. For an excellent summary of how Anselm's view of atonement has been inflected in Western theological tradition and its relationship to violence, see Lisa Sowle Cahill, "Quaestio Disputata—The Atonement Paradigm: Does It Still Have Explanatory Value?" *Theological Studies* 68.2 (2007) 418.

framework was particularly acute in the Middle Ages and the theology of Anselm of Canterbury. In his description of why God became man, Anselm highlights humanity's impasse, "God cannot remit a sin unpunished, without recompense, that is, without the voluntary paying off of a debt, and that a sinner cannot, without this, attain to a state of blessedness, not even the state which was his before he sinned."[8] Anselm's emphasis upon the necessity of sacrifice to restore a relationship, to "satisfy" the debt of honor is understood most clearly within the framework of fidelity between landowners and those who served the landowners. The system of honor undergirded the entire feudal system and thus became a means of interpreting God's salvific economy.

Underlying a satisfaction theory of atonement is the prevailing assumption of humanity's incapacity or fundamental inability to bridge the gap that emerged from humanity's refusal to honor God. Anselm describes both the state of humanity and its fall within a legal framework. The gap between humanity and God is characterized not only as sin but more specifically as sin that would subject humanity to punishment and death as consequence of its failure properly to honor God. In the midst of humanity's status as violators, humanity is redeemed by God's mercy which satisfies humanity's debt with God's own Son.

Drawing from Eph 2, similar characterizations of humanity's transgressions are described by Protestant Reformers and Catholic theologians alike. Speaking of humanity's fundamental sin and subjection to judgment, Martin Luther commented on Eph 2:3, "You may be worried that it is hard to defend the mercy and equity of God in damning the undeserving, that is, ungodly persons, who, being born in ungodliness, can by no means avoid being ungodly, and staying so, and being damned, but are compelled by natural necessity to sin and perish."[9] Luther's reading of Ephesians demonstrates the emphasis upon humanity's unworthiness and utterly desperate condition.[10] The legal status Anselm outlines becomes in Luther an ontological state; punishment and death become synonymous with humanity.

---

8. Anselm of Canterbury, "Cur deus homo," in *Anselm of Canterbury: The Major Works* (eds. Brian Davies and Gillian Evans; New York: Oxford University Press, 1998) Book 1.19, p. 302.

9. Martin Luther, "Bondage of the Will" in *Martin Luther: Selections from his Writings*, edited by John Dillenberger (New York: Anchor Books, 1962) 200.

10. Thomas Aquinas provides a more nuanced account of Ephesians to and the distinction between the state of the Jew and the Gentile and their conditions of judgment before God. See Thomas Aquinas *Commentary on St. Paul's Epistle to the Ephesians*, Lecture 2, p. 89–117. Nonetheless, Aquinas also seems to emphasize the necessity of sacrifice in the atoning work of Christ, but with a slightly different effect upon Jews and Gentiles.

Sinfulness as a fundamental condition of humanity lies at the heart of both Protestant and Catholic conceptions of the human condition. Ephesians 2 begins with a description of those under judgment, with those who "were dead, objects of wrath." The opening verses of Eph 2 demonstrate how views of atonement such as satisfaction and others that emphasize humanity's subjection to punishment are centered upon a conception of humanity as fundamentally disobedient. Anselm would speak of this disobedience as an abrogation of proper order between God and humanity, while Calvin would take the language of "nature" in v. 3 to speak of human nature ontologically.[11] In this way Eph 2 displays the struggle of Christians to discern the shape and depth of humanity's sinfulness and the offence against God. Whether this offence is a disordering, a violation of one's fundamental orientation towards God, or a sinfulness bound to one's nature, these views bind humanity to punishment, a punishment that must be meted out in order to restore humanity and somehow protect God's justice.

While some traditions have expressed atonement in relationship to judgment and wrath, a second tradition of thought is also prevalent in Christian thought. The tradition of theosis or deification is a way of describing humanity, its sinfulness, and its redemption in terms of participation. Here humanity is conceived as bent towards God, in communion with God. Seventh century theologian Maximus the Confessor comments on the words of Eph 2:7, "in order that in the coming ages he might show the incomparable riches of his grace, expressed in his kindness to us in Christ Jesus." From this passage Maximus highlights not mercy from wrath but the aim of the incarnation. He writes, "Since, therefore, the ages predetermined in God's purpose for the realization of his becoming human have reached their end for us, and God has undertaken and in fact achieved his own perfect incarnation, the other 'ages'—those which are to come about for the realization of the mystical and ineffable deification of humanity—must follow henceforth."[12] Rather than highlighting humanity's subjugation to death, Maximus interprets humanity's nature in light of the incarnation.[13]

---

11. See Jean Calvin, *Institutes of Christian Religion* (eds. John Thomas McNeill and Ford Lewis Battles; Library of Christian Classics, vols. 20–21; Philadelphia: Westminster, 1960, 2006) 4.16.17, p. 1340.

12. Maximus the Confessor, "Questions—To Thalassius" in *The Essential Writings of Christian Mysticism* (ed. Bernard McGinn; New York: Modern Library, 2006) 409.

13. Again, the differences between satisfaction and deification are intended to highlight a difference of emphasis, not to interpret the two as contradicting systems. Both the reality of sin and death as well as humanity's participation with God are present in both traditions of interpretation. While both tradi-

This emphasis is reflected slightly differently in Origen's commentary on Ephesians where the question of humanity's nature is addressed more directly. Origen suggests humanity is subject to wrath, not because of its nature, but because of its trespasses.[14] The distinction Origen makes is connected to the nature of the human body that Christ takes on in the incarnation. If the body is by nature subject to wrath, why redeem it? But, if the body is good and subject to death because of its acts, Christ's work in that body takes on a different significance. Origen distinguishes between what it means to be human and what it means to be sinful. What Maximus and Origen both highlight is a consideration of atonement as restoring humanity in the face of its *acts*. In this view Mary's significance, for instance, lies not in an escape from death but from a profound union with God. The height of humanity's union with God is personified in Christ, and thus the incarnation makes living into one's true humanity possible. Christ's death is a completion of the Word's submersion into humanity. Atonement conceived as theosis does not suppose that humanity will be the same as Christ. The emphasis of recreation is an incorporation of the human being into this communion whose very distance draws in death. Atonement signifies a "bringing near," a proper contemplation, in which humanity's refusal of God and resultant movement towards non-being becomes re-oriented towards God, making life with God possible again.

While these descriptions of satisfaction and deification have only been cursory, the differences in emphasis are clear. Each tradition echoes an aspect of Eph 2, articulating the difficulty of human sin and conversely a vision of human thriving. Within the economy of satisfaction, human thriving is narrated in relationship to the perfection of order, of proper relationship of a vassal to a lord, of a citizen to the state. As such the notion of identity becomes articulated in terms of a proper status within those relationships. One is justified or innocent. One's relationship to God is articulated in terms of one's status before God, in terms of their *whatness*, so to speak, that is grounded in an assumption of humanity's fundamental difference from God.

In contrast, deification articulates human identity in terms of communion, in terms of movement within this relationship. This dynamic relationship, this partici-

---

tions draw on these themes, they do so with differing emphases that are important in considering how identity is being conceived in these moments.

14. Origen, "Commentary on Ephesians," in *The Commentaries of Origen and Jerome on St. Paul's Epistle to the Ephesians* (trans. and ed. Ronald E. Heine; Oxford Early Christian Studies; Oxford: Oxford University Press, 2002) 122–24.

pation within God's own life also describes humanity within this economy. A construct of identity within this vision of the atonement outlines humanity's likeness to God and articulates humanity's possibilities in its movement towards God. It also demonstrates that humanity more broadly is fundamentally relational.

While these two traditions of theological reflection can be seen as themes within Eph 2 and have contributed vitally to how the church understands Christ's work, have we too quickly universalized Eph 2:1–10, especially in regarding humanity in general as "children of wrath?" When Paul refers to the "circumcised" in 2:11 or to the reconciliation of "near" and "far" in Eph 2:13, are these the first implicit mention of Jews in Eph 2? More directly, what is the constitution of the "old" entities that are brought together in the "new man" Christ? In what ways does deification account for the transformation of relationships among those who are different? Have both Eastern and Western interpreters of Ephesians fully grasped the claims of the "new man?" How do these accounts of atonement (and any account of atonement for that matter) render absent the distinction between Jews and Gentiles in their respective descriptions of Christ's work? Is the difference between God and humanity the only difference that matters?

In considering Eph 2, is it possible to consider atonement as an identity that corresponds to a particular politic—who can be killed and who cannot, who has access and who does not? By considering Eph 2 as expressing two distinct aspects of atonement—from within Israel's own life and outside of Israel's covenantal life, Christ's preaching to those who are near and those who are far represents a confluence of two distinct aspects of atonement becoming present in Christ's body and thus in Christ's people. The "new man" is not the cessation of differences, but the necessity of these differences becoming present in one body (the church) that opens humanity to a possibility of peace that struggles with difference and does not wash over it, even while these differences are subjected to the possibility of change.

A consideration of how Ephesians articulates atonement from within a Levitical rhythm provides insight on the fundamental difference between humanity and God distinct to satisfaction (and the West) and on the dynamic relationality of deification (the East). Neither emphasis is allowed to be abstracted from the particularities of human living with which the atonement is irrevocably bound. That is, to consider the atonement from a perspective that universalizes the human condition ignores the particularity of Jesus' body and his identity as a Jew. Also, it bypasses the patterns of difference Jesus negotiated and redeemed in his life and ministry. To examine the

Levitical rhythms of Ephesians is to begin to outline the politics of the atonement and the possibilities of identity for any person who claims the name Christian.

Atonement of Those Far and Near

As Paul describes Christ's preaching to those who were far and those who were near, he describes the atonement not in terms of status but in terms of distance. As such, the atonement is not about status alone, nor participation alone, but a transformation of identity, a transformation of those who were dead to those who are living. Put differently, the interconnection between Christ's person and work makes possible human personhood and work.

Ephesians 2 describes the atoning work of Christ in two distinct ways that intersect in Christ's body. In 2:1 Paul addresses "you who were dead through the trespasses and sins," and in v. 11 he addresses "you Gentiles by birth, called 'the uncircumcision.'" A consideration of how Paul articulates the Ephesians' condition, and thus the nature of their corresponding presence within the Christian community, is important for understanding the varied meanings of atonement within Christian and Jewish reflection. Also, Paul's description of atonement expresses how the atoned for become participants in visions of life and identity, important for all Christian self-reflection. Here I want briefly to consider the differing portraits of atonement presented in Eph 2. These two descriptions can be loosely identified as the *disobedient* and the *separate*. Paul's description of atonement can be understood in clearer relief when we consider his varying depictions of who is atoned for and what their conditions were prior to Christ's work.

The Disobedient

Paul writes, "You were dead through the trespasses and sins in which you once lived, following the course of this world, following the ruler of the power of the air, the spirit that is now at work among those who are disobedient" (Eph 2:1–2). The human condition was one of disobedience and death, which made humans justifiably "objects of wrath" (Eph 2:3). In the midst of this condition Paul points to the atonement, to the "but God" (Eph 2:4) that "covers over"[15] human disobedience so that we are "made alive together with Christ—by grace you have been saved—and raised

---

15. I will be drawing from a number of descriptions of atonement highlighted by Walter Brueggeman in *Reverberations of Faith: A Theological Handbook of Old Testament Themes* (Louisville, KY: Westminster John Knox, 2002).

us up with him in the heavenly places in Christ Jesus" (Eph 2:5–6). The condition of the disobedient is characterized within an existing relationship, the bounds of which have been violated or transgressed. While Israel is not explicitly invoked in these early passages, the latter half of the chapter describes the "the uncircumcised" which could be understood to be a contrasting identifier to those who were previously referred to as "you" in 2:1. For both the far and the near Paul's invocation of transgressions bears within it a deeply covenantal rhythm.

The "you" referred to in v. 1 makes an explicit contrast between those who are in the world and those who are being spoken to. Paul continues, "All of us lived among them in the passions of our flesh, following the desires of flesh and senses, and we were by nature children of wrath, like everyone else" (v. 3). While Paul is making a claim concerning human nature and all humanity's capacity for refusing the God of Israel, Paul is also highlighting that there are a certain people who are somehow set apart from those who follow the cravings of their sinful nature. Because of this, the death of these people is a death due to their transgressions, to their disobedience and refusal to abide within the confines of their covenantal relationship with YHWH. Thus the identity of the "you" of vv. 1–5 is articulated within a covenantal grammar that is both highlighting the disobedience of a certain people and also distinguishing Israel from other peoples of the world. Atonement in this context can be understood within the overarching drama of YHWH and Israel, culminating within the person and work of Christ. In the community of Ephesus, Paul is suggesting that in Christ this drama between YHWH and Israel now also includes the Ephesians.

The nature of atonement within this context is an articulation of mercy, of redemption within the person of Christ that allows those dead in transgressions to be alive in Christ (2:6). Paul's description of the mechanics of Christ's atoning work is less specific here, but its context within the covenantal (or legal) framework of Israel is crucial. Christ comes to those whose lives were defined by their disobedience and extends mercy to them. The importance of atonement taking place within a context of Israel's disobedience highlights atonement, not as reinstating a status of "obedient," but drawing Israel once again into the relationship that this covenant established in the first place. They are people "created in Christ Jesus for good works, which God prepared beforehand to be our way of life" (Eph 2:10).

Atonement is found within a relationship and more particularly a historical relationship. That is, Paul is pointing to atonement articulated within the grammar of Israel's covenant with YHWH. Jon Levenson, professor of Jewish Studies, highlights the fundamentally relational character of Israel's covenant with YHWH upon Mt.

Sinai. The covenantal life of Israel was the ground of its own existence as a people.[16] Paul places the context of atonement or redemption for Israel within the tension of Israel-world-YHWH that constitutes their very existence. Israel's movement toward the world is intrinsically a movement away from YHWH such that a work of atonement or reconciliation must recalibrate a proper tension within Israel's own life and correspondingly inhabit the rhythm of Israel's existence in the world. Without this reconciliation they were a people "dead in their transgressions" (2:5a), and as such Israel's life could not correspond to the "good works, which God prepared in advance for us to do" (2:10).

In this respect, atonement in the opening pericope of 2:1–10 places an understanding of the human condition within the covenantal structure of Israel's own creation and obedience (or disobedience). Read in this way, atonement can be understood as a reordering of the relationship in which the Creator and the created, but more particularly Israel as a people created by God, become properly oriented toward their Maker. This reordering of relationship is not isolated to Israel and YHWH, but the particularity of atonement within this historical, embodied relationship cannot be overlooked and can be seen more clearly in how atonement is characterized by Paul as a separation rather than disobedience in 2:11–13. The covenantal reality of Israel reverberates within the life of Gentiles, but it is most directly understood, not in terms of explicit covenantal disobedience, but in terms of fundamental distance.

The Separate

"[R]emember that at that time you were without Christ . . ." writes Paul in 2:12. Addressing the readers of the letter, Paul begins to highlight the significance of Christ's work as addressing something more than disobedience. Paul expresses Christ's work in relationship to the uncircumcised, not only as mercy, but primarily as inclusion, as nearness, as participation. Paul continues his exhortation to the Gentiles in Ephesus to recall their former life when they were "excluded from citizenship in Israel and foreigners to the covenants of the promise, without hope and without God in the world" (2:12). The characterization of the Gentile's condition is not one of disobedience but one of not having heard, of distance, and alienation.

---

16. Jon D. Levenson, *Sinai and Zion: An Entry into the Jewish Bible* (New York: HarperOne, 1987) 26.

The atoning work of Christ in this moment is described in terms of participation and nearness rather than redemption from punishment and wrath. For these Gentiles, "in Christ Jesus you who once were far away have been brought near through the blood of Christ" (2:13). The condition of the Gentiles described by Paul is fundamentally related to the covenantal identity of Israel, but Paul's description of their atonement renders their position within this redemptive process in particular way. "Dead according to transgressions" is not the same as being "without God in the world." These two related but distinct ways of describing humanity's condition in need of Christ's atoning work begin to highlight how in Christ human particularity becomes present in Christ and reconstituted through his life and thus within the church.

Outlining the differing aspects of atonement and the distinct parts that are sutured together in Christ's person and work allows us to see the power of Paul's concluding remarks regarding Christ's reconciliatory work: "For he himself is our peace, who has made the two one and has destroyed the barrier, the dividing wall of hostility" (2:14). Paul's reference is twofold. In one respect Christ's work crosses over the gap between God and humanity, but at the same time Paul is also drawing upon the two distinctive aspects of Christ's work that overcame disobedience and distance. In this overcoming Jesus knits two particular peoples within himself and thus the atoning work of Christ creates something new among those peoples.

In this way Eph 2 demonstrates atonement as a recreation, but a recreation of two distinct aspects of human sinfulness. In one respect Christ extends mercy to the disobedient from within the rhythm of Israel's covenantal life. At the same time Christ extends that covenant beyond Jewish identity, drawing those who are far near to himself and making the two peoples into one. In spite of this, Christian reflection has not articulated atonement in terms of identity and certainly not in terms of reconciliation with one another. Why is this the case?

The allusion to nearness is amplified when considered in relationship to Israel's Day of Atonement as described in Lev 16. On the Day of Atonement Aaron was commanded to sacrifice a bull for a sin offering and a ram for a burnt offering (Lev 16:3). Similarly, Aaron was to bring two goats to the entrance of the Tent of Meeting and there cast lots. Leviticus 16: 9–10 describes the scene: ". . . one lot for the Lord and the other for the scapegoat. Aaron shall bring the goat whose lot falls to the Lord and sacrifice it for a sin offering. But the goat chosen by the lot as the scapegoat shall be used for making atonement by sending it into the desert as a scapegoat." The liturgy moves between three atoning moments, Aaron (and Aaron's family), the community of Israel, and the wilderness (those outside). The atoning work exercised by Aaron is the mediation of God's mercy from within the community and within the covenantal life that gave birth to the community.

The Day of Atonement serves to bring peace in the ongoing relationship between Israel and YHWH. The atoning sacrifices of the bull, the ram, and the goat of the Lord express the identity of Israel as belonging to God and thus are expressions of Israel's history and possibilities. In this way the sacrifices are not merely about death but about the fundamental relationship that constitutes Israel's very history and identity. In this way the covenant is about history or as Levenson suggests, "It is an orientation toward history, a 'feeling' that history points to something transcendent which prepares the ground for an image of relationship that is drawn from the historical sphere."[17] The Day of Atonement is an expression not only of Israel's transgressions but a testament to their relationship to a God who renders certain acts good and others bad.

The interpretation of Israel's existence is narrated through a covenantal self-understanding that renders such sacrifices necessary and further narrates Israel's day to day life within their own lands. The Day of Atonement does not "reset" Israel's guilt or innocence, establish one's status as "not guilty," but rather the Day of Atonement expresses Israel's identity as belonging to YHWH, as subject to a particular mode of life with one another and with the world because of this identity. The atonement is an act that works from *within* a particular relationship and the parameters of that relationship that have been established within the covenant.

Atonement in the opening pericope of Eph 2 begins to highlight this inner movement of atonement. It shows, when "God raised us up and with Christ" (Eph 2: 6), that Christ's work is *re*storing, *re*ordering, and *re*newing in the midst of a people's association with the world, with those who are "outside."[18] The atonement takes place within a people who have been given explicit boundaries and the means

---

17. Levenson, *Sinai and Zion*, 41.

18. The "you" and the "we" referred to in Eph 2:1–10 is a curious intermingling of Jewish and Gentile identity which makes difficult determining to whom the author refers and whether he is included. My interpretation of this passage relies on Paul's later dichotomy between those far and near. Paul seems to be making a clear delineation between Jews and Gentiles that are subsequently reconciled in Christ's one body being made into something new. This reconciliation would suggest a more marked differentiation at some previous point in the text. I am identifying this differentiation between 2:1–10 and 2:11–13, suggesting that Paul has in mind two distinct aspects of Christ's atoning work among Jews and Gentiles that become present and efficacious for all in Christ's body.

of participating within the life of God which they have violated and transgressed, which is the reason an atoning was required.[19]

At the heart of later theological reflection that came to be known as a satisfaction theory of atonement, God's honor was violated because the ordering of the relationship had become misshapen. The debt humanity owes to God is this: "All the will of the rational creature ought to be subject to the will of God."[20] While the justice of God must be maintained, what is nonetheless clear is that God's justice is concerned with the maintenance of a relationship, a covenantal rhythm within the lives of those who believe.

In the midst of this reconciling movement within the covenantal life of Israel and YHWH, Paul broadens the implication of Christ's life towards Gentiles, exhorting those who "were separate from Christ, excluded from citizenship in Israel and foreigners to the covenants of promise, without hope, without God in the world" (Eph 2:12). Christ's atoning work becomes a work intrinsic to Israel's life and presses the covenantal identity of Israel completely into the world.

Drawing again from the liturgy of the Day of Atonement in Lev 16, the second goat brought to the Tent of Meeting was not sacrificed for the sins of the community. Instead,

> When Aaron has finished making the atonement for the Most Holy Place, the Tent of Meeting and the altar, he shall bring forward the live goat. He is to lay both hands on the head of the live goat and confess over it all the wickedness and rebellion of the Israelites—all their sins—and put them on the goat's head. He shall send the goat away into the desert in the care of a man appointed for the task. The goat will carry on itself all their sins to a solitary place; and the man shall release it in the desert. (Lev 16: 20–22)

The Day of Atonement described in Leviticus thus was not only a practice reconstituting a relationship within Israel's community, but in this case it hardened the boundaries between Jewish and Gentile identity. Those in the wilderness, beyond the walls of the community, were analogous to the wickedness that prevented Israel from inhabiting its personhood as elect.

---

19. Interestingly Thomas Aquinas notes the way Ephesians delineates between Jews and Gentiles, highlighting the Gentiles' sin as bound to both their devotion of the world as well as the demons of the world whom they worshipped. Aquinas goes on to suggest that the Jews themselves were guilty of devotion to the world, but not because of the demons of the world. Aquinas suggests that both Gentiles and Jews are subject to wrath, but with slight differences. It is difficult to tell whether Thomas meant to suggest this as a slight towards Jews or if this was merely a textual observation.

20. Anselm, *Cur deus homo*, Book 1. 11, p. 283.

Yet, in Ephesians we see the atoning work of Christ not only becoming an exercise of Israelite identity, but now extending itself beyond the figurative Tent of Meeting to include those "who were far away." The covenantal rhythm of Israel does not cease beyond the confines of the community but, like the scapegoat, is brought into the wilderness. Here the sins of the community are not heaped upon those who are rendered non-being by virtue of their status as Gentiles, but rather the Tent of Meeting, the very presence of God, is extended into the wilderness. The wilderness becomes included within the tabernacle where God meets God's children.

Taken as a whole, Eph 2 displays Christ's body as the goat as sin offering and as scapegoat. Jesus is the one who is within and the one who is outside. The conflation of these two poles does not diminish the covenant but articulates how the world exists within the covenant. Those who were excluded, separate, and foreigners to the covenant now are present within; they are citizens. In the midst of this transformation of the Gentile from exclusion to inclusion, however, there is a mutual transformation. That is, Jewish identity is not left unaffected, rendered innocent in the midst of Christ's obedience.

Atonement in Paul's view is not only the transformation of one's condition, from guilty to innocent or foreigner to alien, but more profoundly the suturing of these peoples into a new people. The idea of a new people is, of course, fraught with danger and challenges. Such dangers have been tragically frequent in Christian reflection and practice broadly construed as supercessionism, the claim that the new covenant is the disestablishment of Israel as God's chosen people. These anti-Semitic claims have ranged from violent to dismissive, but in all of them a fundamental difference between Jews and Gentiles is articulated. In both of these moments Christian reflection has presumed Jesus' body to be fully Gentile rather than the reconciliation of Jews to Gentiles within a Jewish body.

Ephesians 2 points us to a vision of atonement that occurs *within* Christ's body, as exercising a mutual transformation wherein the Gentile body becomes present within Jesus' Jewish body. Salvation is not escape from punishment or entry into relationship with God alone. Rather salvation or atonement is fundamentally a mode of personhood, an identity. That is, in Christ's identification with humanity, with his presence among Jews and his ministry to Gentiles, Jesus *creates* from those who abide within his body. For the one atoned for, the atonement becomes, not solely a proper standing before an equal measure of justice, but a fundamental aspect of personhood that is exercised, lived into and out of.

The peace that is offered to those near and to those far away becomes a possibility only within a corresponding and present relationship to the one who was far or near. To say it more directly, if atonement is about identity, identity is about who are near or far to us. Paul draws the reader of Eph 2 into an echo of the covenantal rhythm that constituted Israel's own identity. The Day of the Atonement was about a reconciliation of Israel's personhood, drawing the community into who it was called to be even as it distinguished itself more profoundly as distinct from those in the wilderness. However, in Ephesians Paul draws the wilderness into the community and the community into the wilderness. Christ's identification with humanity is with those who are both near and far, the sin offering and the scapegoat.

The consequence of this radical identification becomes the instantiation of a new identity within those who become bound to this man who is bound to humanity. Paul exhorts the Ephesians that "[Christ's] purpose was to create in himself one new man out of the two, thus making peace, and in this one body to reconcile both of them to God through the cross, by which he put to death their hostility" (Eph 2:15b–16). The significance of Christ's new body is not the erasure of difference but the permanent binding of one people to another.

The image of reconciliation here must not be confined to social interactions. It includes a fundamental transformation of identity that is born in the union of divinity and humanity. That is, Paul layers the creation of a new people upon Jesus as a vision of new humanity. Images such as "the dividing wall of hostility" apply not only to Jew and Gentile but also to the fundamental conflict between God and humanity, a divide that necessitated Israel's personhood/existence in the first place. Identity in Christ in this way suggests a personhood that is both bound to God but also is bound to a people who were understood to be radically other.

Thus Christ's personhood reconstitutes identity in relationship to those within and those without and in the midst of this movement these new people become a "whole building . . . joined together . . . a holy temple in the Lord" (Eph 2:21). In Christ's atoning work identities become transformed, but they are not only transformed. They are relocated and transfigured. Such an identity is not the transcendence of difference but a cohabiting, a conjoining.[21]

---

21. I want to nuance slightly the conclusions of some interpreters of Ephesians such as Andrew T. Lincoln who suggests "there is no escaping the conclusion that Eph 2 depicts the Church in terms of a new third identity, one which transcends the old ethnic and religious identities of Jew and Gentile" (see Andrew T. Lincoln, *Ephesians* [WBC 42; Dallas: Word, 1990], 163). New Testament scholar Love Sechrest offers a more nuanced approach to the creation of a third race suggesting "Christians suspend the bonds of allegiance to their birth even as they preserve the memory of having been born Gentiles

Atonement, Peace, and Identity

Ephesians 2 has long been invoked as a passage of reconciliation that points to the cessation of hostility and division between groups in conflict. The consideration of Eph 2 in light of how it conceives the atoning work of Christ in respect to these two groups of people, as well as how this reconciliation echoes the covenantal rhythms of Jewish life, opens up both a more problematic and a promising image of what reconciliation might look like and why a doctrine of atonement is so central to this process.

While Christ's atoning work serves to expiate humanity's sinful condition and turn humanity from a state of disobedience to obedience, the atonement does all of these through a fundamental transformation of identity. The atonement is Christ's identification with humanity such that humanity's identity is irrevocably tied to Jesus' body, not only to his body but to his people. In his body two are made one. In this way the atonement becomes a confession of emplacement and cultural transition where those who participate in this new personhood must begin to discern a new pattern of life together, struggling to find faithfulness in the midst of differences that do not merely vanish when rising from the baptismal pool or leaving one's homeland.

Ephesians 2 points us to an understanding of atonement wherein the patterns of everyday life can no longer be thought of apart from those who are different and yet eternally present to us because we are both in Christ. Thus atonement is not about similarity of belief but about lives bound together. The question of how Gentiles were to be included among those who followed Christ displays the difficulty Christ's work created among his believers and among Jews in particular. Those who were considered outside of the promises for so long were now being called to participate. They were no longer a people destined to dwell with the iniquities of Israel but now were participants in the promise, citizens. In this way the atonement signifies not the eradication of difference, but the difficult binding of these differences into a new personhood.

---

who were 'aliens from the commonwealth of Israel and strangers to the covenant of promise' (Eph 2:12)" (see Love Sechrest, *A Former Jew: Paul and the Dialectics of Race* [New York: T. & T. Clark, 2009] 231). M. Barth suggests the new man created in this moment is an eschatological person. For Barth, Jews and Gentiles are "the matter out of which he creates the new man [consisting of] Jews and Gentiles who had both been 'dead in sins' and 'hostile' to one another and God. Thus the new creation is not an annihilation or replacement of the first creation but the glorification of God's work. . . . This historic distinction remains true and recognized even within their communion." (M. Barth, *Ephesians*, I.310)

The subsequent life of the church would come to inhabit these deeply covenantal rhythms of washing (baptism), diet, and sacrifice (Eucharist) but in such a way that declared how difference was perpetually present within Christ's body. Atonement is in this way the perpetual unfolding of Christ's history with us, of Christ's history towards us, and of our history in him. To claim atonement is history is to make a claim that the humanity's condition of guilt was not a state of being, but a mode of life, caught up in the realities of every day. As such who we believed ourselves to be was constantly declared in the major and minor decisions of our lives together. To suggest atonement is history is to likewise suggest that humanity's justification is not an abstract declaration of innocence, but a fundamental remaking of who we are and who we are with.

Considering atonement from this perspective might lead us to our Jewish neighbors, imploring them to recognize Christ. Perhaps this consideration of atonement will allow us to consider how benign the church's claims have been for those who deem themselves atoned for, how limited our view of eternal salvation really is when we consider discipleship only to mean a shift in our viewing habits, attitudes toward sexual promiscuity, or doctrinal affirmations. Is it possible that Paul in Eph 2 is beginning to imagine something more, a death more complete and a rebirth more radical?

AN EVANGELICAL FEMINIST PERSPECTIVE ON TRADITIONAL ATONEMENT MODELS[1]

Linda D. Peacore

Is the Cross Good News For Women?

The resurgence of interest in the subject of atonement, evidenced by the many recent publications on the topic prompts recall of my own interest in the subject which first surfaced over fifteen years ago. The occasion was my encounter with a now classic feminist attack on traditional atonement theology from Joanne Carlson Brown and Rebecca Parker, who claimed, "Christianity is an abusive theology that glorifies suffering."[2] These words were not easy to ignore. Brown and Parker's observation troubled me, not simply because a harsh critique had been leveled against the core of Christian faith, but also because such a view is common within feminist theology. The fundamental objection from the perspective of many feminist theologians is that the cross of Christ is not good news or redemptive because the traditional metaphors for understanding Jesus' death are steeped in violence and offer an offensive view of God as one who inflicts suffering on an innocent son. In their opinion traditional understandings of atonement should be rejected. Despite this critique, the hope emerged for me then and remains today to find a way to take feminist theological priorities seriously without discarding the traditional atonement imagery that has been at the core of biblical and Christian tradition.

Any effort to understand feminist theology[3] must include an exploration of the category of women's experience, attempting to understand how it is defined within

---

1. Much of my research on this topic was a critical part of my doctoral thesis, now published under the title *The Role of Women's Experience in Feminist Theologies of Atonement* (Princeton Theological Monograph Series; Eugene, OR: Pickwick, 2010).

2. Joanne Carlson Brown and Rebecca Parker, "For God So Loved the World?" in *Christianity, Patriarchy and Abuse: A Feminist Critique* (eds. Joanne Carlson Brown and Carole R. Bohn; Cleveland: Pilgrim, 1989) 26.

3. Some prefer to speak of feminist "theologies" rather than "theology." We will use the singular form of the word in this essay, although it is understood that it by no means reflects a unified feminist theology. As in all types of theology, there is variety within the broader categories.

feminist theology and how it is used in theological method. As we will see, women's experience plays a crucial role in feminist theology, including feminist views of atonement. One must ask: what *is* women's experience and *how* does it affect feminist theologies of atonement? Our contention is that the stress on women's experience within feminist theologies of atonement leads to a subjective understanding of Christ's work on the cross without giving adequate attention to the objective elements. While rightly demonstrating the importance of women's perspectives in theological doctrine, specifically in the area of soteriology, such approaches in the end fail to give an account of justification that provides real redemption for women and men.

The Category of Women's Experience

Feminist theology's first significant focus on women's experience is most often attributed to an influential piece written by Valerie Saiving in 1960 entitled "The Human Situation." From the viewpoint of feminine experience, Saiving criticizes the tendency in theology to identify sin with self-assertion and love with selflessness.[4] She argues that although men and women share common experiences, women's sin cannot be characterized as will-to-power, as sin so often is, because such an account is based primarily on masculine experience, thus, portraying the human condition from an exclusively male point of view. For Saiving women's sin is more aptly described in terms of underdevelopment or negation of the self.[5] Whether or not one agrees with her conclusions regarding sin, Saiving's timely article drew theology's attention to the significant role of experience in theology and demonstrated that to some degree experience, male or female, affects all theological reflection.

Like other liberation theologies, feminist theology affirms the important point that all theology is the construction of particular persons and faith communities and that the voices of those on the periphery of traditional theological dialogue are necessary for our understanding of God. Likewise, we recognize that experience is a necessary element of theological reflection, and in particular we value the perspectives of those traditionally at the margins of theology. However, in terms of feminist theology, the category of experience has limitations. First, there is the inherent problem of defining it. What exactly is women's experience? Diverse meanings describe

---

4. Valerie Saiving, "Human Situation: A Feminine View," in *Womanspirit Rising: A Feminist Reader in Religion* (2d ed.; eds. Carol P. Christ and Judith Plaskow; San Francisco: Harper & Row, 1992) 25–26.

5. Ibid., 37.

women's experience as religious or spiritual, bodily, or sociopolitical. Arguably the most significant of these for feminist theologians is related to sociopolitical aspects of women's experience, especially women's experience of oppression. This notion of women's experience is defined by women's struggle against patriarchy and is an aspect of all feminist theology either implicitly or explicitly.

While oppression is a consistent theme for speaking of women's experience, the category still eludes precise definition. In contrast, however, its use within feminist theology is fairly consistent in that women's experience functions as a source and norm for theological reflection. Experience provides the raw material for theology in addition to the means by which other sources are incorporated and/or excluded. Most feminist theologians understand the constraints of claiming women's experience as the *only* source and, therefore, identify other theological sources as well, such as pragmatic concerns, ecological insights, and Christian tradition. Nevertheless, experience has a normative function in feminist theology, determining which material will make an appropriate contribution to feminist theological discourse and which will not. Although many within feminist theology question the content and use of the category, it is agreed that women's experience must be retained as a crucial element of theology for fear that without it the influence of women's identity will be lost.

It is necessary to consider the role of women's experience in feminist theology since it provides the framework from which feminist theologies of atonement are shaped. Closer analysis is needed of the impact of women's experience on the doctrine of atonement. Attention will be given to the charge of "divine child abuse," to Rosemary Radford Ruether's view of liberated humanity, and to a womanist perspective on redemption.

Feminist Interpretations of Atonement

Divine Child Abuse

A noted feminist response to traditional atonement models describes them as divine child abuse—that the death of an innocent son, either at the hands of or by permission of the father—is an example of child abuse that perpetuates systems of abuse within the Christian tradition. Johanna van Wijk-Bos summarizes this general critique as follows:

> An angry male god wills and accepts the death of his only son as a substitute for the death of the ones who deserved god's anger. In the words of

some critics this understanding parades divine child abuse as salvific and then lauds the child who suffers 'without even raising a voice' as the hope of the world. This conviction moreover communicates the message that suffering is redemptive.[6]

Many of the concerns raised by feminist theologians within this perspective are related to issues of authority and the role of suffering. Traditional views, they argue, project a wrong picture of authority whereby the enemies of God are reconciled to each other through Jesus' death. They claim that such approaches to atonement portray humanity as under the bondage of sin, requiring the ransom of Jesus' death. Sin causes humanity to be at a deficit, so Jesus, as the pure sacrifice that is able to cleanse humanity of sin, pays the debt on its behalf. Furthermore, this position supports the notion that the human race is dependent upon the father to restore it. Even if the father simply allows his son's punishment (rather than actually inflicts the punishment), another's suffering has atoned for the children's flaws and is the sacrifice that makes a way to new life. Ultimately, such theologies of atonement communicate that it is good to sacrifice ourselves, coinciding with a view of Jesus as being obedient to the Father. Feminist critics of this approach contend that the Christian tradition has not challenged this central problem of atonement doctrine, that is, Jesus' suffering and death and God the Father's responsibility for it. They question the necessity of Jesus' suffering and why it should be commended to the Christian disciple at all.[7]

Rosemary Radford Ruether

Rather than offering a pointed critique of traditional atonement models, feminist theologian Rosemary Radford Ruether comes at the issue from a different angle. She asks whether christological symbols have been used to enforce male dominance and whether the person of Jesus of Nazareth can be a positive model of redemptive humanity for feminist theology.[8] Unlike other feminist theologians who have developed an extended critique of specific atonement models, Ruether outlines what she considers to be the patriarchalization of Christology over the first five centuries

---

6. Johanna W. H. Van Wijk-Bos, "Shadow of a Mighty Rock," unpublished paper for the American Academy of Religion Annual Meeting, (New Orleans, November 1995) 5. In addition to Brown and Parker, feminist theologian Rita Nakashima Brock also offers this type of critique of traditional atonement models. See her *Journeys by Heart: A Christology of Erotic Power* (New York: Crossroad, 1988).

7. Brown and Parker, "For God So Loved the World?" 4.

8. Rosemary Radford Ruether, *Sexism and God-Talk: Towards a Feminist Theology* (London: SCM, 1983) 114.

in which the early Christian church was transformed from a marginal sect within first-century Judaism into the imperial religion of the Christian Roman Empire. Fundamentally for Ruether, Jesus renews the prophetic vision by proclaiming a reversal of the system of religious status, where the Word of God does not validate the existing social and religious hierarchy but speaks on behalf of the marginalized. Ruether understands Jesus as one practicing a new reality of social relations, demonstrated by his use of the familiar *Abba* for God and how he speaks of the Messiah as a servant rather than a king. For Ruether, Jesus manifests the *kenosis of patriarchy*, the announcement of the new humanity through a lifestyle that discards hierarchical privilege and speaks on behalf of the lowly.[9] In Ruether's Christology Christ is to be understood as a paradigm of liberated humanity, where Jesus saves us by modeling authentic, liberated humanity, rescuing us from sinful distorted relationality and challenging us to save others. All who live with this sense of liberation are offered redemption and can continue Christ's identity as redemptive humanity going ahead of us.

Delores Williams' Womanist View

Critique of traditional atonement theology also comes from womanist theology.[10] Based on the historic experience of black women, particularly in terms of surrogacy,[11] Delores Williams argues that black women need to construct a Christian understanding of redemption that is more meaningful for them. Not unlike Ruether, she finds resources in the Synoptic Gospel accounts of Jesus, understanding Jesus as providing a *ministerial* vision for right relations. In this framework the cross represents humanity's attempt to kill the vision which Jesus brought. However, his death is not the last word, but rather the resurrection is the victory of his *ministerial* vision over the evil that tried to annihilate it. In order to respond meaningfully to black women's historic experience of surrogacy oppression, a model for redemption

---

9. Ibid., 137.

10. Because neither black nor feminist theology could articulate the distinct ways in which black women experience God, the academic discipline of womanist theology evolved, appropriating Alice Walker's definition of *womanist*.

11. Williams identifies black women's oppression in surrogacy roles, such as in the areas of nurturance (mammies), field labor, and sexuality. Delores S. Williams, "Black Women's Surrogacy Experience and the Christian Notion of Redemption," in *After Patriarchy: Feminist Transformations of the World Religions* (ed. Paul Knitter; Maryknoll, NY: Orbis, 1991) 2.

can have nothing to do with a surrogate or substitute role that Jesus played.[12] For Williams redemption has to do with God, through Jesus, giving humankind a *ministerial* vision as a resource for ethical thought and practice. Jesus conquered sin in his life through his ministry of teaching, healing, and casting out demons.

Williams is not alone in her stress upon experience and is one example among many of people who give the category a crucial role in theological method. Regardless of their final conclusions, feminist theologians, white and non-white, enlist a form of women's experience to determine the content of atonement doctrine. They focus on those aspects of the tradition which will not offend the experience of women. Due to women's experience of oppression, including physical abuse and domination, feminist theologians are understandably suspicious of parts of the biblical narrative and Christian tradition that contain elements of violence and oppression. However, by excluding the violence and suffering related to Jesus' death we are left with an atonement theology that emphasizes Jesus' life over his death and resurrection. The source of redemption becomes Jesus' life and ministry only. Such an understanding is in contrast to traditional theories, in particular the three primary models of atonement: a satisfaction theory developed by Anselm, the *Christus Victor* model expounded by Aulén, and a moral influence position often attributed to Abelard. It is to those that we turn.

Challenging Traditional Atonement Models

An Anselmian/satisfaction view of atonement considers sin to create so great a debt to God that humanity cannot pay and that only by the death of God's unique Son could God receive satisfaction. The feminist critique understands God's desire for justice and God's desire to love as in conflict in this view. This approach, they argue, seems to endorse suffering. God's Son submits to a sacrificial death out of overwhelming love for God and the world. Consequently, if suffering is sanctioned as an experience that frees others, the faithful disciple will endure suffering in the conviction that her pain will free another she loves. For these feminist theologians, "The image of God the father demanding and carrying out the suffering and death of his own son has sustained a culture of abuse and led to the abandonment of victims of abuse and oppression."[13] Related to this critique of satisfaction models is the

---

12. Delores S. Williams, *Sisters in the Wilderness: The Challenge of Womanist God-Talk* (Maryknoll, NY: Orbis, 1993) 165.

13. Ibid., 9.

condemnation of sacrifice and how these images are evoked in liturgies, hymns, and the piety of the church in ways that are potentially harmful to women.

Although there are multiple layers of critique of classical atonement models, it is the Anselmian/satisfaction model which most often comes under attack from feminists for several reasons. These include a focus upon punishment rather than healing and the influence of feudal or forensic imagery related to Anselm's cultural context. However, the main point of contention is related to the objective aspect of atonement characterized by this model and how it promotes abuse. Many acknowledge the abusive edge that is part of this approach, but some wonder if a satisfaction model of the cross actually fosters abuse or if aspects of the Christian (Reformed) tradition encourage abusive practices.[14] Saying that atonement theology is often used abusively is different from saying it is always and necessarily abusive.[15] It is possible that the feminist critique of this atonement model fails to address the complexity of the matter, i.e., how a culture of abuse develops from such atonement imagery and why and how the church sustains abusive relationships.

The *Christus Victor* model comes under fire from feminist theologians because it claims that suffering is a prelude to triumph and that suffering itself is an illusion. The theme of *Christus Victor* is divine conflict in which Christ fights against the evil powers of the world and in victory over them reconciles the world to God. Feminist theologians would reason that a believer who is influenced by this view will be persuaded to endure suffering as a prelude to new life. In the *Christus Victor* model God is pictured as working through suffering and, therefore, pain is perceived as a gift in which God provides guidance and purpose. They ask whether such an approach may lead some women to accept pain and suffering, particularly as the partners of abusive spouses, with the hope of obtaining some kind of glory in their suffering. Not surprisingly, from this point of view, a *Christus Victor* theology will have devastating effects on human life because, as feminist theologians argue, victimization never leads to triumph. In fact, they see the *Christus Victor* theory of atonement as defaming all those who suffer because it trivializes tragedy.[16] It seems that we are again confronted with the question of how a model of redemption is itself harmful

---

14. Richard J. Mouw, response to Johanna W. H. Van Wijk-Bos, "The Shadow of a Mighty Rock," unpublished paper for the American Academy of Religion Annual Meeting (New Orleans, November 1995) 4–6.

15. Leanne Van Dyk, "Do Theories of Atonement Foster Abuse?" *Dialog* 35.1 (1996) 24.

16. Ibid., 7.

to women and/or whether the exercise of such models in the life of the church elicits suffering.

What has often been considered a moral influence theory of atonement related to Peter Abelard is also questioned by feminist theologians. They understand Abelard as challenging the satisfaction theory, conceiving the barrier between humanity and God not to be in God but in human beings. Human beings need to be persuaded to believe faithfully in God's overwhelming mercy and to see Jesus' willingness to die for them as evidence of God's love. Abelard believes that in recognizing our loved condition we will commit ourselves to God in gratitude and obedience. Feminist theologians argue that this approach portrays the suffering victim as one whose suffering has the power to confront us with our guilt and call us to a new decision. Such suffering is portrayed as powerful enough to move us to repentance, and this is problematic for certain groups who are historically victimized. For feminist theologians critical of this view, Abelard's model is more than simply moral persuasion.

It is intriguing that even Abelard comes under attack from feminist theologians despite an atonement model which is more often considered subjective rather than objective. If feminist atonement models tend to favor a subjective emphasis, would not Abelard have some appeal? Moving away from a rigid satisfaction model, Abelard saw the love of God as the means and motive for redemption and that Christ's death is not a debt paid to either God or the devil.[17] His view of atonement sees Christ's death as drawing us away from love of self into deeper relationship with God. Redemption is the spiritual transformation of sinners effected through Christ's life and death.[18] In this sense Abelard's is a subjective theory of atonement because the objective event of Christ's death is not something that necessarily changes the human standing before God. Abelard's emphasis is on how this event alters the subjective experience of the believer. Because he does not do away with the objective event altogether but sees it as affecting the believer in a different way than the objective views, feminist theologians resist this model as well.

The consistent condemnation of these traditional models of atonement leads some feminist theologians to reject any form of Christianity that includes atonement: "We must do away with the atonement, this idea of a blood sin upon the whole human race which can be washed away only by the blood of the lamb."[19] For them,

---

17. J. G. Sikes, *Peter Abailard* (Cambridge: Cambridge University Press, 1932) 207.

18. Richard E. Weingart, *Logic of Divine Love: A Critical Analysis of the Soteriology of Peter Abailard* (Oxford: Clarendon, 1970) 210.

19. Joanne Carlson Brown, "Divine Child Abuse?" *Daughters of Sarah* 18.3 (1992) 28; and Brown

women should only remain in the Christian tradition if it condemns suffering; there should be no glorification of suffering. They advocate new interpretations of salvation, presenting Jesus as one who lived a life in opposition to unjust, oppressive cultures and who was unjustly put to death by humans who chose to reject his way of life. In their view, the resurrection is not enough to redeem the travesty of Jesus' suffering. To know God is to do justice; therefore, God does not need to be appeased or demand sacrifice. As a result of the influence of the category of women's experience, particularly their experience of oppression, the objective aspects of traditional models are rejected and what remains is basically an example model of atonement.

Sin and Redemption

What else besides the role of experience contributes to the neglect of an objective element in feminist approaches to atonement? The answer may be found in the relationship between sin and redemption. As noted above, Valerie Saiving, and Judith Plaskow after her, provided an important feminist perspective on sin, identifying the predominant definition of sin as one developed exclusively in terms of pride, a view, they argue, that fails to portray women's experience of sin. Therefore, feminist theologians frequently discuss sin in terms of relationality, that there is a disconnectedness with others and oneself. This is an existential concept related to the notion of estrangement whereby redemption becomes that which reunites what is estranged so that women find their authentic selves, no longer alienated from themselves, the creation, and others. Atonement theology developed within this understanding of sin leads to a view in which redemption is something that occurs in human existence rather than between God and humanity or in cosmic terms. This emphasis in feminist atonement theologies is a result of the role of women's experience which provides the content for accounts of sin and salvation. Salvation is understood as that which addresses women's experience of oppression under patriarchy, utilizing concepts like liberation, justice, and healing. To some extent feminist theology has gotten it right. Women (and men) need healing from their experience of patriarchy. Human beings are estranged from themselves, one another, and the world, and atonement brings a change in these relationships. Therefore, even some aspects of traditional atonement theology—the human predicament as one of estrangement and loss of potential—would resonate with the feminist understanding.

---

and Parker, "For God So Loved the World?" 26.

However, the fall and sin produce an estrangement the extent of which feminist theologians seem unaware. Feminist views acknowledge fractured relations, but fail to identify their source. They are grounded upon particular views of sin and redemption that are defined by the category of women's experience and are not determined by an understanding of our relationship to God. Consequently, feminist atonement models lack an objective element and a recognition of the need for forgiveness as an experience that leads toward change in ourselves, others, and the world.[20] Experience is conceived from a human point of view rather than informed by God's role in our relationships. Sin, understood from the perspective of our broken relationship with God, is a social phenomenon which then affects all levels of relationships.[21] Alienation from God leads to alienation from ourselves and others. Feminist theologians perceptively reveal the pervasiveness of fractured relationships within humanity and the world, but they do not fully account for the reason or acknowledge the necessity of reconciliation with God as the condition for reconciliation between people and creation. In order to have a subjective element of atonement there must also be the objective. The cross creates redeemed forms of experience by virtue of changing our relationship to God. Atonement depends upon the historical moment of Christ's death, though we must be careful not to lock it into one time and space.[22] From a Trinitarian perspective we see that through the Holy Spirit, the objective event has subjective effect in the experience of forgiveness and empowerment to live a life of love. It is an act of God and also an experience of human beings.[23]

Because the feminist accounts of atonement do not account for the relationship between the objective and subjective aspects, Jesus is presented as a paradigm or model that saves us by modeling authentic, liberated life with the community continuing his example. Put another way, in these perspectives Jesus is a model of how we should live in opposition to oppression; therefore, the life of Jesus is stressed over his death and resurrection. The theological significance of Jesus is transferred from his death to his life, thus severing the relationship between such a life and the possible death it risks. If one lives according to Jesus' vision, then is not suffering and pain a potential outcome?

---

20. H. R. Mackintosh, *The Christian Experience of Forgiveness* (London: Nisbet, 1927) 152.

21. Eberhard Jüngel, *Justification: The Heart of the Christian Faith* (trans. by Jeffrey F. Cayzer; Edinburgh: T. & T. Clark, 2001) 129.

22. Paul S. Fiddes, *Past Event and Present Salvation* (London: Darton, Longman & Todd, 1989) 4.

23. Mackintosh, *Christian Experience of Forgiveness*, 153.

A theology of atonement based on the life of Jesus must account for his life, death, and resurrection, for these are part of a whole. Without that we lose the connection between the objective and subjective elements of redemption. A subjective view offers an important dimension to atonement theology, but an objective element is also essential. A proper understanding of atonement should incorporate both subjective and objective elements, otherwise we risk misunderstanding what has been accomplished through Christ's cross for us. The strength of an objective theory of atonement is that it expresses the once-for-allness of the cross of Jesus. However, it does not integrate the human response to God and the healing of human personality here and now, which is a strength of a subjective approach. A view that emphasizes the objective aspect puts the focus upon a past event and may contribute toward passivity in Christian believers. Alternatively, a Christian life influenced more by a subjective perspective would be characterized by an effort to experience personally God's grace and to model Christ's love in the world. While this is necessary, confidence in what God has already done in and for us may be lacking, leading to an emphasis upon human action rather than the divine work of reconciliation. Therefore, we see that the objective and subjective elements are essential and interrelated. Reconciliation to God confronts us as objective for it is the act and pronouncement of God while also being subjective as an experience of human beings that leads to spiritual transformation.

An Example Model of Atonement

Many feminist theologians would not perceive the lack of an objective element in atonement theology as a defect. In fact, there is a direct attempt to bypass an objective component and focus entirely on the subjective. If the objective aspect is rooted in the violent death of an innocent son made as a sacrifice to a divine Father, then surely feminists have no misgivings about stressing the subjective effects of atonement. As a result, we are left with feminist models of atonement that are fundamentally defined by Jesus' example. Such an approach exposes three basic deficiencies: it ignores its dependence on other models, it overestimates human ability to follow Jesus' example, and it fails to show how imitating Jesus is redemptive.

If our understanding of Jesus' life is primarily gained through the biblical witness, it would seem that Scripture is the most significant resource for learning about atonement, and yet feminist theologians are ambivalent about granting the Bible authority in the development of theological doctrine. For instance, feminist theologians like Brown and Parker do not use Scripture as a source for their atonement theology at all, while others like Ruether make an effort to recover particular biblical elements such as the Synoptic accounts of Jesus' life and the OT prophetic tradition. Regardless of their distinct approaches, most Christian feminist theologians seem convinced that biblical texts must be engaged at some level and that the influence of the historical context upon atonement metaphors is also a factor. Therefore, from their perspective, a wide range of biblical, traditional, and innovative metaphors may be used to express salvation.[24] Within most feminist theology, the biblical text is not considered the *sole* source and may be critically appropriated for atonement theology along with other elements such as the sociopolitical context, the sacrificial metaphor, and eschatological hope.[25]

While we may be in basic agreement with a theological method that incorporates a variety of sources, if most Christian feminist theologians accept that the biblical text has a place in feminist theology, one would expect that the variety of atonement metaphors in the Bible would be considered in more detail as part of feminist theologies of atonement. As evidenced by the predominant feminist views, there is a striking neglect of several biblical models: sacrifice, ransom, release, transformation, and reconciliation.[26] Feminist theologies of atonement emphasize Jesus' life, but any consideration of his life as a model for all who struggle against oppression would seem to require engagement with other biblical models in order truly to comprehend Jesus' life and mission. For instance, if Jesus understood his life as having atoning efficacy (Mark 10:45) or that he came to fulfill the role of the Suffering Servant (Isa 53), then there is a multidimensional understanding of Jesus as example that feminist theologians have not taken into account.

Another difficulty with an example model of atonement is that it fails to deal with the reality that human beings are unable to follow the example of Jesus Christ. Most feminist understandings of sin and the subjective focus of their atonement models do not sufficiently take into consideration the depth of human sin and how,

---

24. For instance, the metaphor of "healing" is more likely to be predominant in the contemporary context. See Leanne Van Dyk, "Vision and Imagination in Atonement Doctrine," *Theology Today* 50.1 (April 1993) 11.

25. Thelma Megill-Cobbler, "Women and the Cross: Atonement in Rosemary Radford Ruether and Dorothee Soelle," (Ph.D. dissertation, Princeton Theological Seminary, 1992) 410.

26. There are multiple verses that represent these general understandings, not least among them being the OT sacrificial system. The categorization of these should be somewhat flexible since some passages could work equally well under one type of metaphor as another. A sampling of such passages would include Lev 25:47–55; Matt 26:28; Mark 10:45; Luke 4:18–19; John 5:24; Acts 20:28; Rom 3:24f, 4:25, 6:2, 8:35f; 1 Cor 5:7; Eph 2:18; Heb 9:12; 1 John 2:2.

ultimately, redemption by following an example is no redemption at all. As we have seen, a feminist view of sin that is defined by estrangement and lack of relationality results in a notion of salvation that is meant to address this alienation. Atonement is understood as a new way of life for humanity, and Jesus' life is a vision that guides us and announces a transformative mission against the sin of oppression. To some degree, this view of redemption is true. And yet, such an approach fails to address the seriousness of sin because it is the very state of the human condition that keeps us from following Christ's example.

Noting that women have been oppressors as well as oppressed, some white feminists and feminists of color have raised concerns about example models of atonement. This is one area where women's experience reveals that sin is not experienced by all women the same.[27] Womanists recognize that the use of the category of women's experience as defined by white feminists is in danger of oppressing women of color just as patriarchy has historically oppressed women. The oppression of minority women by white women reveals the importance of an objective dimension of atonement.[28] Although the nature of women's sin may be conditioned by their particular social and historical experience, they do function under the conditions of the fall, as all human beings do. Women are capable of sin! Women are not simply innocent victims, and no conversion of their minds or some intrinsic goodness can free them from the implications of sin.[29]

Related to this problem is the basic lack of redemption that such a model of atonement provides. Embedded in feminist views of atonement is the belief that human beings are somehow able to transform the negative and oppressive structures of our world. We have argued that the liberation presented in an example model of atonement consistently falls short of delivering the transformation it promises and inspires due to an overly subjective understanding of atonement that results in an insufficient doctrine of human sin. As long as sin is understood either strictly in terms of patriarchy or in relational disconnectedness, and redemption is found by following Jesus as a paradigm for liberated humanity, we will continue to struggle on our own to live as liberated people. Sin is radical rebellion, and genuine reconcilia-

---

27. Susan Brooks Thistlethwaite, *Sex, Race and God: Christian Feminism in Black and White* (London: Geoffrey Chapman, 1990) 87.

28. Megill-Cobbler, "Women and the Cross," 412.

29. Angela West, *Deadly Innocence: Feminist Theology and the Mythology of Sin* (London: Cassell, 1990) 36.

tion can only come from the side of the divine.[30] When we fail to follow Jesus' model adequately, where is our redemption to be found?

Feminist theologians are challenged to reconsider the Christian tradition and its rich resources for understanding and experiencing genuine liberation. Certainly it is reasonable that one theory or another will be more meaningful to particular groups at particular times; however, should some biblical models have a standardizing influence that transcends our experience? The primary understanding of women's experience used in feminist atonement theologies contains an appropriate rejection of oppression, yet it leads to theories of atonement that neglect much of the Christian tradition and biblical metaphors because of their perceived oppressive content. In excluding the violence and suffering of Jesus' death from any model of atonement, feminist theologians place more emphasis upon Jesus' life which accounts for a type of example model that we allege lacks genuine transformation of individuals and the world. What results is that feminist theologians approach the Gospel stories with the aim of drawing attention away from Jesus' crucifixion and find meaning for the cross in other metaphors and symbols. The cross is removed from the context of the unity of Jesus' life, work, death, resurrection, and ascension.[31]

From an evangelical perspective there are serious problems with such a feminist approach to atonement. This is perhaps rather uncontroversial since we are working under the presupposition that the whole of Scripture is authoritative for theological doctrine and that Christian tradition and the role of experience are valuable, though lesser, resources for theological method. Nevertheless, a commitment to feminist concerns and to the message of the Bible should persuade us to take seriously the feminist contribution. As liberation theologies have rightly shown, within the history of Christian theology there are voices on the margins that have not been heard. Therefore, we need to identify the benefits the feminist approach has for theological reflection.

---

30. Kathryn Greene-McCreight, "Gender, Sin and Grace: Feminist Theologies Meet Karl Barth's Hamartiology," *Scottish Journal of Theology* 50:4 (1997) 431–32.

31. Kathryn Greene-McCreight, *Feminist Reconstructions of Christian Doctrine: Narrative Analysis and Appraisal* (New York: Oxford University Press, 2000) 74. Greene-McCreight argues for a narrative reading of Scripture in line with William Christian, George Lindbeck, and Hans Frei. Such an approach to Scripture would avoid the segregation of Jesus' life from his death and resurrection which we find in much feminist theology.

Contributions of Feminist Models

It may seem obvious but is worth repeating. The role of experience in feminist theology (and all theologies of liberation for that matter) is a crucial reminder that experience is an important part of theological reflection. The aim of feminist theology is not so much to reinstate the role of experience as to correct a bias in the type of experience that shapes theological reflection.[32] Feminist theologians have reminded us that there is no pure perspective from which we may construct theology and that the whole theological process is deepened when experience is included, providing layers of meaning previously unexplored.

This valuing of women's experience within the doctrine of atonement leads to a useful reevaluation of violent imagery. The feminist critique of traditional atonement models related to the penal substitutionary view, in addition to the imagery of violence and suffering, draws attention to the manner in which Christian doctrine may endorse an image of a vengeful God who sacrificed his Son in order to pay the penalty for sin which God himself required. The feminist critique identifies how these models of atonement have been interpreted and promoted in the church and ways in which this perpetuates and devalues women's experience. The feminist challenge to atonement theology underscores the function of Christian doctrine and how it relates to interaction between women and men as well as our understanding of God. In this regard, the feminist critique is helpful and necessary.

Another strength of feminist theologies of atonement is that they highlight the need for a subjective element in any account of salvation. Retaining a subjective element of atonement is critical to a proper understanding of Christ's death and is faithful to Scripture. Salvation in the Bible is depicted in terms of a past event that has implications for our final outcome. Equally it is also portrayed through the example of Jesus' encounters with the sick, lonely, and demon-possessed as a present reality and part of God's desire to change the immediate, physical existence of people. A subjective emphasis illustrates the need to contextualize the gospel; theology must be able to speak to us in our present context. Because feminist theologians are determined to have theology correspond to the contemporary experience of women, their paradigms for redemption relate to experience, thus contributing to theology's ongoing relevance. In our desire to emphasize the need for an objective element in atonement models, we might take a cue from the feminist approach

---

32. Monika Hellwig, *Whose Experience Counts in Theological Reflection?* (Milwaukee: Marquette University Press, 1982) 11.

and work to maintain the subjective aspect as an important and crucial part of any atonement theology.

Feminist Theologies of Atonement Fall Short

Despite such benefits of a feminist approach to atonement, there remain significant drawbacks. First among these is the role of women's experience, including efforts to define the content of women's experience and determine its use in theological method. In light of the fact that there is not one definition of women's experience that is representative or acceptable to all women, feminist theologians are faced with a dilemma. On the one hand, in an effort to preserve the political power of the category of women's experience, they attempt to construct a universal norm that will not fall into essentialism. On the other hand, their desire to be more inclusive results in an emphasis on particularities, which may lead to relativism. This tension also relates to how experience functions within theology. We recognize the importance of context or experience while at the same time realizing that it is not solely determinative. Within the interchange between experience and theories of atonement, a particular model may force new meaning on our metaphors that we had not imagined.

We have seen how the category of women's experience, its content and use, contributes to feminist theologies of atonement that stress the subjective elements of atonement and reject those aspects that include violence and oppression (i.e., traditional substitutionary and satisfaction metaphors). However, even though the feminist approach is considered more subjective, it actually fails to provide the transformative experience that is part of a proper subjective approach. The primary reason for this is that the feminist approach does not provide an adequate account of the effects of sin. Feminist theologians are too optimistic about human ability to follow Jesus' example and to transform oppressive structures and systems. Racism is a crucial reminder that things are not as they should be and, indeed, not as they should be among women as well. Recognizing that the traditional understanding of the fall has often been used against women, feminist theologians avoid discussing it and the notion of original sin associated with it. This leads to neglect of an objective element in atonement theories since there is no perceived need for something that will actually change our standing before God.

Unfortunately, by rejecting some doctrines due to their deleterious effects as they have functioned in the Christian tradition, feminist theologians have essentially thrown out the baby with the bath water. If our objective reality remains unchanged, then how can our subjective experience truly be transformed? Certainly there are theological reasons for making Jesus an example; however, if sin is bondage then an example is not enough to save us. We need redemption.[33] Therefore, we assert that feminist views of atonement do not provide a redemption that brings genuine liberation or healing and wonder if feminist theology has too quickly dismissed traditional atonement metaphors. Is there a way forward for an evangelical feminist who desires to remain grounded within the biblical tradition *and* uphold an understanding of women's experience? A possible answer might begin first with the category of women's experience—continuing to use women's experience as a significant theological resource, but defining it within an understanding of its limitations. It is possible for the category to be incorporated in our theological method in such a way that gives due weight to women's experience as well as other valued theological sources like Scripture and tradition.

Keeping that in mind, we can develop atonement models that integrate the subjective and objective elements.[34] In order to avoid an overemphasis upon either the objective or subjective element we must be informed by a Trinitarian perspective. There is no efficacy in atonement unless in Jesus God is present, and there is no subjective effect unless the Holy Spirit is the means by which we experience forgiveness and are empowered to live in the love of God. Atonement depends upon both the historical moment of Christ's death and the ongoing work of the Holy Spirit. The work of reconciliation has been done by God. God has initiated our reconciliation and achieved it. This act is not confined to the past because Christians experience this grace in their present lives. By experiencing the objective and subjective aspects of Christ's reconciling work we are able to respond with both gratitude and responsibility.

In the spirit of feminist theological method, let us consider the tension between objective and subjective elements of atonement in the context of women's experience. Imagine a Christian woman who has suffered harmful sexual abuse as a child. She accepts what Christ has accomplished on the cross, knowing that she has been made clean and free from the burden of sin. And yet, she continues to live with the remnants of this traumatic experience in her daily life. She tries to function as one

---

33. Colin E. Gunton, *The Actuality of Atonement: A Study of Metaphor, Rationality and the Christian Tradition* (Grand Rapids: Eerdmans, 1989) 158–59.

34. Here we have help from the tradition. For one example, see Bruce D. Marshall, "Justification as Declaration and Deification," *International Journal of Systematic Theology* 4.1 (March 2002). Marshall sees Luther as a good test case for pursing the question of how justification as objective and subjective (declaration and transformation) might fit together, arguing that in Luther's Trinitarian framework God's decision to forgive us and God's decision to transform us are one and the same act (26).

who knows God's grace through Christ's redeeming work of atonement while at the same time being aware of how she is shaped by sin. She lives in the "now and not yet" of redemption. Herein lies the need for an objective and subjective element in any understanding of atonement. We find freedom and hope in the sure knowledge of the saving event of Jesus' death on the cross, and we gain strength and encouragement in our experience of the ongoing work of redemption in our lives by the Spirit.

Conclusion: A Richer Understanding of Atonement

Though it is right to talk about sin as disconnectedness, estrangement, and alienation, most feminist theologies of atonement fail to adequately address our deepest need, the necessity for an objective change in our very being which allows us to experience genuine transformation. While Anselm may have a rather quantitative way of putting things, his view draws attention to the fact that "the human condition is too enmeshed in evil to be able to be restored by its own agency."[35] It is an issue of the actuality of atonement—whether the real evil of the real world is faced and healed. The reality of sin is great in our lives and in our world. We need models of atonement that provide genuine redemption and we have determined that the feminist views fall short. Is it because of women's experience? Is it the category itself or the use of it in theological method? Is it the failure to take sin more seriously? Is it a lack of balance between objective and subjective models? Or is it the lack of a Trinitarian understanding of God's saving action?

Unfortunately, these questions may fall on deaf ears. Most feminist theologians are not concerned about the issues raised above: balance between objective and subjective elements of atonement, a thorough understanding of sin, or a Trinitarian framework for atonement theories. Because Scripture and tradition are read through the lens of women's experience, these will remain peripheral issues for many feminist theologians. Nevertheless, we maintain that feminist theologies of atonement and the critique of traditional models therein are relevant to our contemporary context with its stress on experience. We must take experience seriously as an important element in theological method, and a variety of factors should contribute to our understanding of that experience, including communal and individual, race, class, and gender distinctions. We need to hear these voices in conversation with Scripture and tradition. Along with this will be an effort to attend to and respect one

---

35. Gunton, *Actuality of Atonement*, 159.

another's atonement models.[36] The biblical witness provides multiple metaphors for atonement, and a mature Christian community should not limit itself to one or even a few images but is encouraged to grow into a "full-orbed vision."[37]

These many models for understanding the cross are not in competition with one another. Rather, they provide the means for communicating the complex mystery of Jesus' death, with specific models speaking loudly in one generation and more quietly in the next. The richest understanding of atonement might actually be found in the interaction of these longstanding, traditional models with contemporary perspectives on the tradition.[38] Perhaps that is the task which lies ahead. For those who value an evangelical feminist approach to atonement theology, we have begun to identify the ways in which a feminist model of atonement might be reconstructed, keeping in mind our wish for a model of redemption that is rooted in Scripture, takes seriously women's experience, and offers genuine liberation from the oppression that has so often characterized it.

---

36. This should include for feminist theologians those models that contain suffering, such as many Asian women value in their understanding of Christ's work.

37. John Driver, *Understanding the Atonement for the Mission of the Church* (Scottdale, PA: Herald, 1986) 246–47.

38. This is not to deny that there are theologians working to develop theological approaches that engage Christian tradition. See Greene-McCreight, *Feminist Reconstructions,* and Serene Jones, *Feminist Theory and Christian Theology: Cartographies of Grace* (Minneapolis: Fortress, 2000). Both place feminist perspectives in conversation with historical theology. Deanna Thompson's *Crossing the Divide: Luther, Feminism, and the Cross* (Minneapolis: Fortress, 2004) is an example of a constructive feminist conversation with Luther's theology of the cross.

RESPONSE TO PEACORE

Jo Ann Deasy

As a feminist who is part of the Evangelical community, I want to thank Dr. Peacore for her attempt to bring into dialogue these two theological traditions as they relate to various approaches to the atonement. As her paper highlights, she has taken on a daunting task, one that is steeped in complexity, but, as she states at the beginning of the paper, provides the hope of finding a "way to take feminist theological priorities seriously without discarding the traditional atonement imagery that has been at the core of biblical and Christian tradition."

Her paper primarily focuses on one aspect of her theological project: that of deconstructing feminist theology and feminist approaches to the atonement from an Evangelical perspective. She focuses on feminist theologians who have taken issue with the themes of violence and suffering present in traditional atonement theories, as seen in the three examples provided: those who posit the "divine child abuse" position, the work of Rosemary Radford Ruether, and the work of womanist, Delores Williams. Given the breadth of theological approaches that include women's experience as one of their primary sources (for example womanists, mujeristas and some minjung theologians) as well as the diversity within feminist theology, Peacore's paper might have been strengthened by articulating a clear focus on a single theme rather than attempting such a broad critique. By painting such broad strokes, she was often not able to present the various approaches with enough complexity to allow for meaningful dialogue.

Peacore focuses her critique of feminist approaches to the atonement on three key areas: their use of women's experience, their emphasis on the subjective aspects of the atonement, and their understanding of sin. I would like to push our discussion in each of these areas a step further by providing a few observations and questions.

Peacore rightly critiques the essentializing of women's experience that forms the foundation of much feminist theology. As Jacquelyn Grant and Susan Thistlethwaite highlighted in their works *White Women's Christ and Black Women's Jesus* and *Sex, Race, and God* almost twenty years ago, early feminist works failed to take into account differences in women's experiences due to race and class. More recent feminist theologians, such as Rebecca Chopp and Mary McClintock Fulkerson, have moved to discourse analysis as a way of recognizing the diversity present in the category of women's experience. Peacore seems to suggest, however, that because of the inherent problem of defining women's experience, the category of women's experience has limitations in theological method. I would argue, however, that rather than serving as a limitation, attention to the variety of women's experiences only serves to enrich our theological dialogue. It pushes feminist theology to consider the intersection of categories of race, class, and gender in the construction of identity and the construction of theology.

Even with its limitations, Peacore recognizes "that experience is a necessary element of theological reflection and, in particular, the value of perspectives from those traditionally at the margins of theology." What is unclear to me, however, is how Peacore uses the category of experience in her own theological method. Perhaps, since her focus was on the deconstruction of feminist approaches to the atonement, she did not feel that she had space in this paper adequately to critique traditional approaches to the atonement for their failure to address the needs of women and other marginalized people. If all theology is constructed in a particular context, it seems that an adequate dialogue between feminist and traditional approaches to the atonement would need to consider, not just the contemporary context of feminists, but the historical contexts, particularly in regards to their approaches to women, of Anselm, Aulén, and Abelard.

Perhaps Peacore's central critique of feminists' approach to the atonement is their emphasis on the subjective aspects of the atonement. Peacore argues that such an approach is insufficient and that "in order to have a subjective element of the atonement there must also be the objective." While I do not necessarily disagree with Peacore's argument, I would suggest that the language of subjective and objective is problematic from a feminist perspective. Historically "subjective" views of the atonement emphasized the changes effected in human beings. "Objective" views of the atonement emphasized the changes effected in God. However, the language of "objective" as a category of the atonement would be problematic to feminist theologians who argue that all truth is constructed. The language of "objectivity" in atonement theory can become confused with an objective view of truth that fails to take into account the power dynamics that were in play in the construction of such theologies in the first place. One must wonder if this masking of power dynamics is not often at the heart of feminist contentions with atonement theories. Objective approaches to the atonement often fail to take into account the different implications their theories will have on people in power and people who are oppressed, on the perpetrator and on the victim. There is a lack of connection between agency in the atoning work of Christ and agency or lack of agency present in the suffering of humanity.

The third area of critique for Peacore is the feminist understanding of sin and redemption. Peacore observes that feminist theologians seem unaware of the extent of estrangement produced by sin and the fall. I would perhaps argue that a much more nuanced discussion of sin is necessary for a true understanding of feminist approaches to sin and redemption. Feminist theology, for the most part, was developed precisely as a response to the effect of sin in this world. Perhaps one might argue that feminists do not focus sufficient attention on the more ontological notions of sin, but they certainly recognize the estrangement and violence present in our world as a result of sin. Peacore's paper would have been strengthened by a more careful discussion of the various aspects of sin in this world including the individual, the corporate, the systemic, and the ontological.

This is highlighted in the example she gave near the end of her paper when she asked us to imagine a Christian woman who had suffered sexual abuse as a child. Peacore writes that "she accepts what Christ has accomplished on the cross, knowing that she has been made clean and free from the burden of sin. And yet, she continues to live with the remnants of this traumatic experience in her daily life. She tries to function as one who knows God's grace through Christ's redeeming work of atonement while at the same time being aware of how she is shaped by sin." Peacore argues that such an experience highlights the need for both an objective and a subjective element in any understanding of the atonement. This young woman can find freedom in "the sure knowledge of the saving event of Jesus' death on the cross" and can "gain strength and encouragement" as she experiences "the ongoing work of redemption in our lives by the Spirit."

While I am sure this is not what Peacore intended in her example, at first glance it appears as if Peacore is equating this young woman's experience of sexual abuse with some personal sin in her life for which she needs to atone. Peacore may simply be talking about the need for this woman to atone for her inherently sinful human nature. However, a victim of abuse will often interpret such a statement to reaffirm her conviction that she herself has sinned in the process of being abused. I am not talking about the sinful actions that might result from her being malformed through an abusive experience. The woman herself will bear the sin of another, the sin of the one who abused her, the sin of the community that did not protect her, the sin of a society that for centuries treated women as objects. The woman herself will bear the sins of the world and take them on as her own. She will attempt to atone for a sin that is not hers, a task that is more than any one human being can accomplish. If we intend our theories of the atonement to provide hope to both the victims and the abusers, the oppressors and the oppressed, we must consider sin from all angles and present a view of the atonement that both forgives us from our own sin and cleanses us from the sin of others.

A majority of Peacore's work focuses on the deconstruction of feminist views of the atonement, but she does so out of the hope of reconstructing a model that takes feminist theological priorities seriously. I agree with Peacore that we must take feminist concerns seriously. We must hear the concern that feminists raise about the potential connection between violent images of God, especially as present in the atonement, and the violence in our world and in the church that is so often directed at those without position or power. If we are truly committed to taking feminist theological priorities seriously, then we must move to this next constructive step. Still, Peacore's suggestion that we must move towards a more Trinitarian perspective on the atonement has significant possibilities, and I look forward to hearing in her next paper how those ideas develop.

SAVING BODIES: ANAGOGICAL TRANSPOSITION IN ST. GREGORY OF NYSSA'S COMMENTARY ON THE SONG OF SONGS[1]

Hans Boersma

Whatever the precise reason Olympias, the pious deaconesss of Constantinople, requested that St. Gregory of Nyssa expound for her the Song of Songs, she can hardly have been oblivious to the paradoxical character of the situation. Having been widowed several years earlier after only a very brief marriage and still only in her early or mid-twenties, she refused Emperor Theodosius's request that she marry his Spanish relative Elpidius. Olympias reacted to the Emperor's suggestion with the comment: "If my King had desired me to live with a male He would not have taken away my first husband. But He knew that I cannot make a husband happy, so He liberated him from the bond and me likewise from the most bothersome yoke, and He freed me from subjection to a man, while He laid on me the gentle yoke of chastity."[2] Olympias's attitude incurred Theodosius's wrath, but he eventually came around, and Olympias was widely rumoured to have remained a virgin throughout her life. The wealthy deaconess was no stranger to the ascetic life of renunciation, and it is quite likely that she expected Gregory's exposition on the Song of Songs to assist her, as well as other Christians in Constantinople, in the life of virtue.[3] Certainly she

---

1. I want to express my appreciation to Markus Bockmuehl and Ron Dart for their comments on a draft of this paper and to Mark Husbands for his helpful response to my presentation.

2. In *Palladius: Dialogue on the Life of St John Chrysostom* (ed. Robert T. Meyer; Ancient Christian Writers 45; New York: Newman, 1985) 114 (no. 17). For background information on Gregory's homilies, I rely on J. B. Cahill, "The Date and Setting of Gregory of Nyssa's Commentary on the Song of Songs," *JTS* 32 (1981) 447–60.

3. Gregory demurs that although he eagerly takes up Olympias's request, she herself hardly needs the commentary: "The reason I accept your proposal with alacrity is not that I may be of assistance to you in the conduct of your life—for I am confident that the eye of your soul is clean of any passionate or indecent thought and that by means of these divine words it gazes without hindrance on the undefiled Beauty—but rather that some direction may be given to more fleshly folk for the sake of the spiritual and immaterial welfare of their souls" (*Gregory of Nyssa: Homilies on the Song of Songs* [trans. and ed. Richard A. Norris; Writings from the Greco-Roman World 13; Atlanta: Society of Biblical Literature, n.d.] 13; hereafter referred to as *Homilies*). This manuscript remains as yet unpublished; I am grateful to the series editor, Prof. David Konstan, for providing me with a copy of this new critical edition. In

must have realized that Gregory was not about to present her with a literal interpretation of the Song of Songs. The mystical theologian from Nyssa consciously took his stance in the tradition of Origen, the Alexandrian interpreter, and while some fourth-century preachers from the Antiochian tradition may have been inclined to a more literal reading, Gregory was known not to have any sympathies for what to his mind was far too narrow an approach to the interpretation of Scripture.

Olympias was not alone in her recognition of the paradox inherent in the fact that she, an ascetic widow (and perhaps a virgin), would request a commentary on a biblical book that more than any other appealed to fleshly desires and passions. For Gregory himself such paradox lay at the heart both of his understanding of the Song of Songs and of his view of salvation, which, as we will see, he considered closely related to each other. Thus, Gregory comments in the first of his fifteen homilies: "[W]hat could be more incredible [*paradoxoteron*] than to make human nature itself the purifier of its own passions, teaching and legislating impassibility [*apatheian*] by words one reckons to be tinctured with passion [*empathōn*]?"[4] Gregory goes on to explain that Solomon "so deals with the soul that she looks upon purity by means of instruments that seem inconsistent with it and uses the language of passion to render thought that is undefiled."[5] Thus, whereas the Septuagint had modestly restricted itself to the language of *agapē*, Gregory in his commentary goes beyond this and introduces the language of *erōs*, thus accentuating the paradox. Clearly aware of the audacious character of his undertaking, the bishop comments: "Therefore since it is Wisdom who speaks, *love* her as much as you are able, with your whole heart and strength; *desire* [*epithymēson*] her as much as you can. To these words I am bold to add, *Be in love* [*erasthēti*], for this passion [*pathos*], when directed toward things incorporeal, is blameless and impassible [*apathes*], as Wisdom says in Proverbs when she bids us to be in love [*erōta*] with the divine Beauty."[6] Gregory is speaking of an erotic love that we may describe with the paradoxical expression "dispassionate passion."[7]

---

each reference to the *Homilies*, the first number will indicate the number of the homily, which is then followed by the page number.

4. *Homilies* 1, 31.

5. *Homilies* 1, 31.

6. *Homilies* 1, 25.

7. Jean Daniélou has retrieved the significance of *erōs* for Gregory of Nyssa, highlighting that it is consistent with *agapē* and really constitutes *agapē*'s most intense form, which carries the soul beyond herself toward God, on whom she dependently relies (*Platonisme et théologie mystique: Doctrine spirituelle de Saint Grégoire de Nysse* (rev. ed.; Théologie 2 [Paris: Aubier, 1944] 199-208).

The paradox is more than an interesting peculiarity; it points to what Gregory is convinced is the Song's ultimate concern, salvation itself. In his first homily, Gregory contrasts salvation through fear [*dia phobou*] of punishment in hell with salvation through love [*dia tēs agapēs*] of God himself rather than merely of his rewards: "For by what is written there, the soul is in a certain manner led as a bride toward an incorporeal and spiritual and undefiled marriage with God. For he 'who wills all to be saved and to come to the knowledge of truth' (1 Tim 2:4) manifests in this work the blessed and most perfect way of salvation—I mean that which comes though love."[8] For Gregory, salvation comes through love, and it is a love that can be daringly expressed in the nuptial language of the Song of Songs. The sensuous words and images of the biblical text cannot be discarded; it is through erotic desire that God brings about salvation. For Gregory the sometimes sensuous body of the text is an indispensible means of salvation precisely inasmuch as it paradoxically opens up the way into the goodness and beauty of God himself.[9]

According to Gregory of Nyssa, then, God saves us through bodily means. However, this should not be taken to mean that Gregory's ultimate focus is on earthly or material bodies—whether bodily texts of passion (such as the Song of Songs) or bodily acts of pleasure (as represented in the surface level of the text). To focus on the body itself—whether the obvious, surface-level meaning of the text or the bodily passions—would be precisely to discard in rationalist fashion the paradoxical character of Gregory's "dispassionate passion" and to ignore the fact that for Gregory both biblical exegesis and the process of salvation involve a profound transposition (*metastasis*).[10] This transposition implies that, although bodily means are indispens-

---

8. *Homilies* 1, 15–17. 1 Tim 2:4 is a key text for Gregory; he uses it five more times in his homilies: *Homilies* 1, 35; 4, 143 (2x); 7, 227; 10, 321. God's desire that all be saved is connected, on Gregory's understanding, to the final restoration of all things (*apokatastasis*). Cf. Morwenna Ludlow, *Universal Salvation: Eschatology in the Thought of Gregory of Nyssa and Karl Rahner* (Oxford: Oxford University Press, 2000).

9. The Song's physical descriptions of the Bridegroom's beauty led to speculation about God's "heavenly body" both in Tannaitic literature and elsewhere. See Markus Bockmuehl, "'The Form of God' (Phil 2:6) Variations on a Theme of Jewish Mysticism," *JTS* 48 (1997) 1–23, at 17–19.

10. Cf. Gregory's comment that Paul "says that the movement [*metastasin*] from corporeal to intelligible realities is a turning toward the Lord and the removal of a veil (2 Cor 3:16)" (*Homilies* Preface, 5). Similarly, Gregory comments that the soul must learn to "turn passion into impassibility" (*Homilies* 1, 29). Bart vanden Auweele rightly comments: "Elle se comprend davantage comme une traduction que comme l'abolition de la lettre" ("L'Écriture sous le mode du désir: Réflexions sur le statut de l'Écriture dans les *Homélies sur le Cantique des cantiques*," in *Grégoire de Nysse: La Bible dans la construction de son discours: Actes du Colloque de Paris, 9–10 février 2007*, ed. Matthieu and Hélène Grelier, Collection des Etudes Augustiniennes, Série Antiquité, 184 [Paris: Institut d'Études Augustiniennes, 2008] 275–83, at

able for salvation, to remain strictly with the body would mean, ironically, to lose sight of the intended transposition and thereby to lose the purpose of salvation.

In the light of contemporary Gregory of Nyssa research it is important to make the point that salvation involves an anagogical transposition away from bodily text and bodily desire—the Greek term *anagōgē* means "leading upward." Recent Gregory research has tended to highlight the embodied character of human existence.[11] Again, it is not my intention to dispute the fact that for Gregory we are saved through bodily means. Nonetheless, some contemporary re-readings of Gregory decisively misinterpret Gregory's understanding of salvation, rendering it overly this-worldly by wrongly insisting on the centrality of this-worldly bodily and emotional realities. For instance, Mark Hart has argued that Gregory's encomium on virginity in his early treatise *De virginitate* should not be taken at face value but serves as a rhetorical ploy.[12] Gregory, in Hart's view, has a relatively low view of celibacy: it really is meant for the weak, for those who are unable to control their sexual passions. The truly wholesome life, on Hart's reading of Gregory, is that of marriage. This reading seems to me almost to turn Gregory's understanding on its head.[13]

---

281). Cf. also Richard A. Norris's comment: "[A]n exegesis involving 'transposition' is seen as necessary because (1) the text at hand gives an account of perceptible realities, but (2) the reality it ultimately concerns is of the intelligible order. It is the gap between these that 'allegory' bridges" ("Introduction: Gregory of Nyssa and His Fifteen Homilies on the Song of Songs," in *Homilies*, xlii–xliii).

11. In addition to the three authors discussed below, the reader may also consult Jeremy William Bergstrom, "Embodiment in Gregory of Nyssa: His Anthropology and Ideal Ascetic Struggle" (Th.M. thesis, St. Vladimir's Orthodox Theological Seminary, 2008); Sarah Coakley, *Powers and Submissions: Spirituality, Philosophy and Gender* (Malden, Mass.: Blackwell, 2002) 127–29; idem, "Re-Thinking Gregory of Nyssa: Introduction—Gender, Trinitarian Analogies, and the Pedagogy of the *Song*," *Modern Theology* 18 (2002) 431–43; Verna E. Harrison, "Gender, Generation, and Virginity in Cappadocian Theology," *JTS* 47 (1997) 38–68; idem, "A Gender Reversal in Gregory of Nyssa's First Homily on the Song of Songs," *StPatr* 27 (1993) 34–38; idem, "Male and Female in Cappadocian Theology," *JTS* 14 (1990) 441–71; Martin Laird, "The Fountain of His Lips: Desire and Divine Union in Gregory of Nyssa's *Homilies on the Song of Songs*," *Spiritus* 7 (2007) 40–57; idem, "Under Solomon's Tutelage: The Education of Desire in the *Homilies on the Song of Songs*," *Modern Theology* 18 (2002) 507–25; Morwenna Ludlow, *Gregory of Nyssa: Ancient and (Post)modern* (Oxford: Oxford University Press, 2007); idem, "Gregory of Nyssa and the Body: Do Recent Readings Ignore a Development in His Thought?" *StPatr* 41 (2006) 369–74.

12. GNO VIII/1, 247–343; ET: *Saint Gregory of Nyssa: Ascetical Works* (trans. Virginia Woods Callahan; The Fathers of the Church 58; 1967, reprint, Washington, D. C.: Catholic University of America Press, 1999) 1–75.

13. Mark D. Hart, "Gregory of Nyssa's Ironic Praise of the Celibate Life," *Heythrop Journal* 33 (1992) 1–19. Cf. also idem, "Marriage, Celibacy, and the Life of Virtue: An Interpretation of Gregory of Nyssa's *De Virginitate*" (Ph.D. diss., Boston College, 1987); idem, "Reconciliation of Body and Soul: Gregory of Nyssa's Deeper Theology of Marriage," *TS* 51 (1990) 450–67. Hart's insistence that celibacy is a

Rowan Williams, while not focusing on the body or sexuality per se, similarly downplays the "otherworldly" character of Gregory's theology by rehabilitating the role of grief (*lypē*) over the loss of loved ones.[14] By means of a detailed re-reading of *De anima et resurrectione*, Williams maintains that because this dialogue presents Macrina as accepting of her younger brother Gregory's grief, Gregory must regard grief as a positive human passion, a form of desire (*epithymia*) that can lead the soul's rationality (*logos*) in its search for truth and beauty. The result, according to Williams, is a dynamic and positive appraisal of the human passions and of grief in particular. William ignores, however, the leading role that human reason has in Gregory's thought; the passions are not supposed to dominate. For Gregory, the human passion of grief does not serve in a positive fashion at all. Grief is, as Warren Smith rightly argues, a *frustrated* desire that paralyzes the soul.[15] While grief over the loss of loved ones may seem appropriate to most Christians today, Gregory's Platonic and Stoic surroundings made him regard this temporal, earthly life as a mode of existence that death enabled us to transcend. Death, in other words, is for Gregory

---

concession to human weakness misinterprets Gregory at several levels. Most importantly, he misreads the role that weakness plays in Gregory's argument. On my reading, Gregory believes that if we are realistic about our carnal weaknesses, we may use such weakness as an occasion to learn to practice eschatological virginity already today. In addition, as Karras points out, (1) while Hart takes Gregory's critical comments about celibacy at face value, he inconsistently takes the bishop's criticism of marriage as ironic; and (2) Hart ignores that for Gregory the eschaton is a return to a prelapsarian non-biological state without food, sleep, sex, sickness, decay, and death; marriage, while not intrinsically evil, is for Gregory the first step into a postlapsarian, biological state. See Valerie A. Karras, "A Re-evaluation of Marriage, Celibacy, and Irony in Gregory of Nyssa's *On Virginity*," *JECS* 13 (2005) 111–21.

14. Rowan Williams, "Macrina's Deathbed Revisited: Gregory of Nyssa on Mind and Passion," in *Christian Faith and Greek Philosophy in Late Antiquity: Essays in Tribute to George Christopher Stead* (ed. Lionel R. Wickham and Caroline P. Bammel with Erica C. D. Hunter; Supplements to Vigiliae Christianae 19; Leiden: Brill, 1993) 227–46.

15. J. Warren Smith, "Macrina, Tamer of Horses and Healer of Souls: Grief and the Therapy of Hope in Gregory of Nyssa's *De anima et resurrectione*," *JTS* 52 (2001) 37–60; idem, *Passion and Paradise: Human and Divine Emotion in the Thought of Gregory of Nyssa* (New York: Herder & Herder, Crossroad, 2004) 15–17, 97–98. In addition, Williams overlooks Gregory's other writings on death, which clearly display his negative views of grief. See especially Gregory's *De mortuis* (GNO IX, 28–68; ET Richard McCambly, http://www.sage.edu/faculty/salomd/nyssa/mort.html) and his *Oratio consolatoria in Pulcheriam* (GNO IX, 461–72; ET Casimir McCambly, http://www.sage.edu/faculty/salomd/nyssa/). Cf. Ulrike Gantz, *Gregor von Nyssa: Oratio consolatoria in Pulcheriam*, Chrêsis: Die Methode der Kirchenväter im Umgang mit der antiken Kultur, 6 (Basel: Schwabe, 1999); Robert C. Gregg, *Consolation Philosophy: Greek and Christian Paideia in Basil and the Two Gregories* (Patristic Monograph Series 3; Cambridge, Mass.: Philadelphia Patristic Foundation, 1975); Monique Alexandre, "Le *De mortuis* de Grégoire de Nysse," *StPatr* 10 (1970) 35–43.

one of the key moments of advancement in the anagogical ascent to a higher level of participation in the life of God.

Finally, John Behr has argued against the familiar interpretation of Gregory having a low view of sexuality. He disputes the view that Gregory believed sexuality to have originated after the fall. Behr insists that for Gregory sexual intercourse was God's good gift already before the fall. This interpretation—remarkable in the light of all preceding Gregory scholarship—wrongly moves from Gregory's positive evaluation of embodiment to an insistence that the sexual passions of human beings are constitutive of their very identity, which of course implies that the passions are not subject to anagogical transposition into something of much greater and more ultimate concern.[16]

These new readings of Gregory, while amenable to a contemporary western mindset that tends to react sharply against premodern views of salvation due to its alleged dualism between body and soul and its concomitant supposedly low view of embodiment and sexuality, does not do justice to Gregory's overall position. It is true that one finds in the Cappadocian mystic a remarkably integrated anthropology. It is also true, as we will see, that Gregory has a positive view of the human body and that desire is something God uses to bring about human participation in his own goodness and beauty. We must keep in mind, however, the centrality of anagogy in Gregory's approach. Readings such as those of Hart, Williams, and Behr render a sanitized Cappadocian, whose theology is strikingly accommodating to our modern and postmodern views of the body and of sexuality.

---

16. John Behr, "The Rational Animal: A Rereading of Gregory of Nyssa's *De hominis opificio*," *JECS* 7 (1999) 219–47. Behr's views center on how to interpret Chapters XVI, XVII, and XXII of *De hominis opificio*. Behr's views do not stand careful scrutiny of the text. First, Gregory maintains that the eschaton is a restoration of paradise. Since there will be no marriage in heaven (Luke 20:35–36) Gregory believes there was no marriage (or sexuality) in paradise. Second, Gregory believes that although God created gendered human existence prior to the fall, he did so *because* he foreknew the fall. Gendered existence was God's way of making provision for procreation after the fall. Third, by means of allegorical exegesis, Gregory argues here that there was no physical nutrition in paradise: Wisdom, or the Good, was the "tree of life." This is in line with Gregory's fascinating exegesis of the two paradisal trees in his commentary on the Song of Songs (*Homilies* 12, 366–71). For an excellent refutation of Behr's idiosyncratic position, see J. Warren Smith, "The Body of Paradise and the Body of the Resurrection: Gender and the Angelic Life in Gregory of Nyssa's *De hominis opificio*," *HTR* 92 (2006) 207–28. Sutcliffe's 1931 article on paradise in Gregory may also serve as a rebuttal of Behr's reading. Sutcliffe shows that for Gregory paradise is not an earthly reality at all, but is a "supramundane region" without food, biological functions, and marriage; as a result, Gregory allegorizes the account of Gen 2–3. See E. F. Sutcliffe, "St. Gregory of Nyssa and Paradise," *Ecclesiastical Review*, NS 4 (1931) 337–51.

In this essay, I will argue that both the transposition of the human body (and the bodily senses) through deification in Christ and the transposition of the textual body from obvious to hidden meaning imply for Gregory an anagogical ascent from the material to the spiritual realm. Furthermore, these two transpositions are closely intertwined. The reader of the Song of Songs is only able to transpose the textual body of Scripture to the extent that his erotic desires are reoriented in Christ, and it is only an allegorical or anagogical interpretation of the Song of Songs that redirects the reader's desires from "brutish, irrational passions" to "incorporeal and spiritual and undefiled marriage with God."[17] Gregory, I will argue, believes that only by recognizing the significance of this twofold anagogical ascent will we be able to do justice to the saving role of Christ as the new bodily garment and to the church as the body of Christ. This essay is about saving bodies: trying to save the bodily senses and the textual body of Scripture without anagogical transposition renders us unable to recognize sufficiently the saving bodies of Christ (our bodily garment) and of the church (the body of Christ). This seems to be St. Gregory of Nyssa's view, and it is my belief that there is a great deal we can continue to learn from this rather "otherworldly" perspective.

First, I will discuss Gregory's understanding of sense perception (Section I, "Bodily Senses"). I will make clear that Gregory operates with a clear distinction between bodily sense perception and spiritual sense perception. Although both are God's gift and the two are interconnected, Gregory's concern with anagogy means that he prizes the latter above the former. Second, I will turn to Gregory's understanding of interpretation (Section II, "Bodily Text"). Here, I will discuss Gregory's defence of allegory as well as his use of such exegesis in connection with the Song of Songs. Gregory regards the text of Scripture as the divinely given means for participation in the divine life. Third, I will discuss what this participation looks like as we put on the Lord Jesus Christ by training the virtues (Section III, "Bodily Garments"). Gregory is deeply concerned with the life of virtue—not, it turns out, because he is a moralist, but because the life of virtue is itself a participation in the divine life and as such constitutes salvation.

Two caveats are in order, however, before I proceed. The first caveat has to do with the relationship between Gregory's understanding of salvation and traditional atonement models, such as Christus Victor, moral influence, and penal substitution. At first blush, this paper may seem only tangentially related to the theme of atonement. Indeed, this paper hardly discusses the traditional atonement models.

---

17. *Homilies* 1, 15.

There is a theological reason, however, for the lack of focus on these models. I do not dispute that Gregory regards Christ's life as a model of some kind in order to restore the image of God in human beings, nor do I mean to deny that a certain kind of exchange or substitution does occur in Gregory's writings, including his commentary on the Song of Songs. This paper will touch on both of these aspects. But scouring Gregory's writings to try and fit them in such predetermined frameworks would obscure the pattern (*akolouthia*) of Gregory's own line of thinking, a pattern that is of great importance to him.[18] Gregory's view of salvation simply cannot easily be slotted into one or more of the frameworks that make up our common theologies of atonement. This means that if we are to discuss atonement in Gregory we need to bracket our familiar models in order to determine what in his theology allows for at-one-ment. The answer to this question, which will become clear especially in the third section of the paper, is that Gregory believes it is Christ's uniting himself to our human nature that enables our participation in God's life; we come to God and are deified by being united to the universal human nature of Christ. In other words, it is the incarnation and our being united to Christ's humanity that atones and saves. This so-called "physical" approach to the atonement means that other categories are relegated to the background and perhaps need to be reconfigured (although that is a task beyond the confines of this paper).

The second caveat is that by focusing on only one of Gregory's writings I cannot provide a complete picture of his soteriology. Although St. Gregory is obviously convinced that the Song of Songs is meant to lead to salvation, the homilies focus on the relationship of the individual soul and the church (the bride) with Christ (the Bridegroom). This means that, although the objective work of Christ does enter into the picture, the subjective pole of salvation is much more prominent. Elsewhere in his writings Gregory does pay more attention to what we might want to call the "mechanics" of the atonement, or to what it is about the incarnation—and about Christ's person and work more broadly regarded—that enables us to reach salvation.[19] To

---

18. For the centrality of *akolouthia* in Gregory's thought, see Juan Antonio Gil-Tamayo, "*Akolouthia*," in *The Brill Dictionary of Gregory of Nyssa* (ed. Lucas Francisco Mateo-Seco and Guilio Maspero; trans. Seth Cherney; Supplements to Vigiliae Christianae 99; Leiden: Brill, 2010) 14–20; Paulos Mar Gregorios, *Cosmic Man: The Divine Presence: The Theology of St. Gregory of Nyssa (ca 330 to 395 A.D.)* (1980, reprint, New York: Paragon, 1988) 47–63; Jean Daniélou, "Akolouthia chez Grégoire de Nysse," *Recherches de Science Religieuse* 27 (1953) 219–49.

19. I am thinking, for example, of Gregory's *Oratio catechetica* (GNO III/4; ET: *The Catechetical Oration of St. Gregory of Nyssa* [ed. J. H. Srawley; Early Church Classics; London: Society for Promoting Christian Knowledge, 1917]). Cf. the following overviews: Lucas Francisco Mateo-Seco, "Soteriology," in *Brill Dictionary*, 694–99; Andrew Klager, "Passive Sacramentalism and Ontological Soteriology in

some extent, therefore, this essay offers a one-sided account. Still, in his other works Gregory tends to be concerned mostly with the human involvement in the process of salvation, and mystical writings such as the homilies on the Songs give us genuine insight, therefore, into what Gregory felt was central to a Christian understanding of salvation.

Bodily Senses

The notion that the five bodily senses corresponded and referred to spiritual senses originated with Origen and the Alexandrian tradition.[20] The doctrine of the spiritual senses subsequently made its way into St. Augustine's theology and thus became a mainstay in Western spirituality.[21] Although Gregory took a relatively independent stance vis-à-vis Origen, rejecting controversial teachings such as the pre-existence of the soul, the Alexandrian's commentary on the Song of Songs did impact Gregory's homilies. In fact, the influence is such that Gregory mentions Origen's commentary in his preface.[22] The doctrine of the spiritual senses is something that Gregory inherited from Origen's work and puts to pervasive use in his own commentary on the Song of Songs.[23] The numerous descriptions of sense perception throughout the

---

Hans Denck Gregory of Nyssa," *Direction* 35 (2006) 268–78; A. S. Dunstone, *The Atonement in Gregory of Nyssa* (London: Tyndale, 1964).

20. See *Origen, Spirit and Fire: A Thematic Anthology of His Writings* (ed. Hans Urs von Balthasar; trans. Robert J. Daly; 1984, reprint, Washington: Catholic University of America Press, 2001) 218–57.

21. Cf. Carol Harrison, "Senses, Spiritual," in *Augustine through the Ages: An Encyclopedia* (ed. Alan D. Fitzgerald; Grand Rapids: Eerdmans, 1999) 767–68.

22. *Homilies* Preface, 11: "If, however, we are eager, even after Origen has addressed himself lovingly and laboriously to the study of this book, to commit our own work to writing, let no one who has before his eyes the saying of the divine apostle to the effect that 'each one will receive his own reward in proportion to his labor' (1 Cor 3:8) lay a charge against us. As far as I am concerned, this work was not put together for the sake of display." For discussions dealing both with Origen's and Gregory's commentaries on the Song of Songs, see Mark W. Elliott, *The Song of Songs and Christology in the Early Church* (Studies and Texts in Antiquity and Christianity 7; Tübingen: Mohr Siebeck, 2000) 15–18, 24–29; Andrew Louth, "Eros and Mysticism: Early Christian Interpretation of the Song of Songs," in *Jung and the Monotheisms: Judaism, Christianity and Islam* (ed. Joel Ryce-Menuhin; London: Routledge, 1994) 241–54; Richard A. Norris, "The Soul Takes Flight: Gregory of Nyssa and the Song of Songs," *Anglican Theological Review* 80 (1998) 517–32.

23. Cf. Frances Young's comment: "Perhaps the most striking thing about Gregory's exegesis of the Song is his emphasis on spiritual senses. He believes, not unlike Origen, that there is a correspondence between the motions and movements of the soul and the sense organs of the body, and it is soon apparent that this undergirds his positive embracing of the discourse of sexuality to describe the soul's advance towards God and response to the divine allure. The whole point is that our earthly response to

Song of Songs provide Gregory with a good deal of opportunity to describe salvation as a process of anagogy or ascent. As we will see, Gregory regards the various bodily sensations that he finds described in the Song not as literal descriptions of physical pleasure but instead as references to spiritual perception. A spiritual transposition is required to interpret properly the biblical allusions to physical perception and to the pleasure that it yields.

Gregory first comments on the spiritual senses when he discusses Song 1:2 ("Let him kiss me with the kisses of his mouth, for your breasts are better than wine, and the smell of your perfumed ointments is better than all spices.")[24] Gregory interprets the Bridegroom's kisses as identical to the milk that flows from his breasts: by kissing the bride, the Lord touches the soul, while from his breasts—that is to say, from his heart—he nourishes the soul with divine teaching. The bride's desire for the Groom's mouth stands for the virginal soul's thirsting for the fountain of truth, in accordance with John 7:37 ("If any one thirsts, let him come to me and drink"). The result of this teaching of the truth of Christ is that the soul comes to share in the virtues of God, the odours of the divine perfumes mentioned in the text.[25]

Since the Song itself thus mentions the senses of touch, taste, and smell, Gregory uses the opportunity to discuss the doctrine of the spiritual senses:

> We also learn, in an incidental way, another truth through the philosophical wisdom of this book, that there is in us a dual activity of perception, the one bodily, the other more divine—just as Proverbs somewhere says, "You will find a divine mode of perception." For there is a certain analogy between the sense organs of the body and the operations of the soul. And it is this that we learn from the words before us. For both wine and milk are discerned by the sense of taste, but when they are intelligible things, the power of the soul that grasps them is an intellectual power. And a kiss comes about through the sense of touch, for in a kiss lips touch each other. There is also, though, a "touch" that belongs to the soul, one that makes contact with the Word and is actuated by an incorporeal and intelligible touching, just as someone said, "Our hands have touched concerning the Word of life" (1 John 1:1). In the same way, too, the scent of the divine perfumes is not a scent in the nostrils but pertains to a certain intelligible

---

beauty gives us a taste of what it would mean to transcend surface appearance and discern the Lord as the object of beauty *par excellence*" ("Sexuality and Devotion: Mystical Readings of the Song of Songs," *Theology & Sexuality* 14 [2001] 90–96, at 96).

24. For the Song of Songs I am following Norris's translation (see footnote 3); for other biblical passages I am using the RSV.

25. *Homilies* 1, 34–41.

and immaterial faculty that inhales the sweet smell of Christ by sucking in the Spirit. Thus the sequel of the virgin's request in the prologue says: *Your breasts are better than wine, and the fragrance of your perfumed ointments is better than all spices.*[26]

Gregory speaks in this passage of an analogy (*analogia*) between sense organs of the body and operations of the soul.[27] The latter enable us to take in the divine teaching (through taste and touch) and to participate in the virtues of God (through smell).

In Homily 6 St. Gregory again finds occasion to elaborate on his understanding of the five spiritual senses, since Song 3:7 mentions "sixty mighty men" standing around Solomon's bed: "Behold Solomon's bed: sixty mighty men surround it out of the mighty men of Israel." Convinced that the number of soldiers mentioned here must have a spiritual meaning, Gregory notes that five multiplied by twelve gives the number sixty, and he concludes from this that each of the twelve tribes must have five armed warriors guarding the royal bed.[28] Although on this interpretation of the number sixty, the text may seem to suggest five warriors from each tribe, Gregory explains that, really, there is only one man from each tribe:

> Now is it not plain that these five warriors are the one human being, with each of its senses deploying the weapon proper to it for the consternation of its enemies? The eye's sword is to look across and through everything toward the Lord, and to contemplate what is right, and not to be defiled by any unseemly sight. Hearing's weapon, similarly, is hearkening to the divine teachings and refusal to take in vain talk. In this way it is also possible to arm taste and touch and smell with the word of self-control, protecting each of the senses in the appropriate manner. So come terror and amazement upon the dark enemies, whose plot against souls finds its opportunity in darkness and at night.[29]

Gregory's rendering of the spiritual senses is clearly moral in character. Spiritual sight looks to the Lord instead of anything unclean. Spiritual hearing listens to divine precepts rather than to vain words. Spiritual tastes, touch, and smell protect our

---

26. *Homilies* 1, 35–37.

27. Richard T. Lawson highlights the fact that Gregory's homilies regard all speech of God as analogous in character ("'A Guide for the More Fleshly-Minded': Gregory of Nyssa on Erotic and Spiritual Desire" [M.S.T. thesis, School of Theology of the University of the South, 2009] 31–46).

28. *Homilies* 6, 207.

29. *Homilies* 6, 209.

temperance. Since the text seems to have the twelve tribes in view, Gregory explains that this signifies the entire church. The one bed refers to the unity of all who find rest and so are saved. After all, the Lord comments in his parable that "the door is now shut, and my children are with me in bed" (Luke 11:7). The Lord's mentioning of children must, according to Gregory, refer to those who have reached the state of dispassion (*to apathes*). Whether one has never experienced passion (children) or has driven away passion (warriors), either way, one has found true happiness. Thus, Gregory concludes his homily by commenting that in such persons "there is found the child, or warrior, or true Israelite who has come to blessedness: the Israelite who with a pure heart sees God; the warrior who stands guard in invulnerability and purity over the royal bed—that is, his own heart; the child taking rest upon the blessed bed, in Christ Jesus our Lord, To whom be glory to the ages of ages. Amen."[30]

We should not miss the strong sense of duality on which Gregory's understanding of the senses is based. His theology of the spiritual senses displays the paradoxical character that he believes lies at the heart of the Song of Songs. God uses the material senses of the body to fortify the life of virtue and so to give us a share in his impassibility (*apatheia*). This means for Gregory that in an important sense the spiritual is opposed to the material and that salvation lies in the perfection of the former. In Homily 6 Gregory divides all of reality into two categories. On the one hand, the intelligible and nonmaterial has neither limit nor bound; on the other hand, the perceptible and material is limited and determined by quantity and quality. Gregory then subdivides the spiritual between the uncreated or First Cause, which is immutable, and the created, which changes for the better by being enhanced in perfection and in participation in that which transcends it.[31] Likewise, in Homily 11, when commenting on the beloved putting his hand through the opening and the bride's belly crying out for him (Song 5:4), Gregory explains that the human soul has two natures: "One of them is incorporeal and intelligent and pure, while the other is corporeal and material and nonrational."[32] He immediately follows up on this by mentioning the need for anagogical transposition: "When, therefore, cleansed as soon as possible of her inclination toward a gross and earthly life, the soul looks up with the help of virtue toward what is akin to her and closer to the divine."[33]

30. *Homilies* 6, 211.

31. *Homilies* 6, 185–87.

32. *Homilies* 6, 353.

33. *Homilies* 6, 353. Cf. *Homilies* 12, 365: "For in us there is a dual nature. The one is fine and intelligent and light, while the other is coarse and material and heavy. Hence it is inevitable that in each of

Thus, through the interpretation of Scripture and through participation in divine virtues, the soul experiences a transposition away from the sensible or material and toward the intelligible and spiritual.[34] Salvation, for Gregory, implies ascent from the sensible to the intelligible, from the material to the spiritual. We can only properly understand Gregory's theology of salvation if we do justice to this twofold character of human nature. For Gregory, salvation itself is the anagogical transposition from the one to the other.[35]

It should not surprise that when St. Gregory looks for a place in the text that might legitimately expound this salvific transposition, he lingers on images of sleep and death. Since both these states imply inactivity of the bodily senses, Gregory interprets descriptions of sleep and death in the Song as indicative of the transposition from bodily to spiritual perception. For instance, when Gregory reads, "I sleep, but my heart is awake" (Song 5:2), he explains, "This sleep, though, is a stranger and alien to the ordinary course of nature. For in the usual sort of sleep, the sleeper is not awake, nor does one who is waking sleep: rather, sleep and wakefulness both come to an end in each other—they alternate in withdrawal from each other and come to each person by turns."[36] Mentioning each of the five senses, Gregory insists that sleep is an image of death since there "is no activity of seeing, or of hearing, or of smelling or tasting, or of touching in the season of sleep."[37] Gregory then explains how it is that one can be asleep and awake at the same time. He mentions the beautiful objects that we see in the created world and comments:

> When vision of the truly good leads us to look beyond all such things, the bodily eye is inactive, for then the more perfect soul, which uses its understanding to look only on matters that are beyond seeing, is not drawn to any of the things to which that eye directs its attention. In the same way

---

these there be a dynamic that is proper to itself and irreconcilable with the other. For that in us which is intelligent and light has its native course upwards, but the heavy and material is ever borne, and ever flows, downwards."

34. Thus, Gregory comments in connection with interpretation that we "should not stick with the letter but, by a more deliberate and laborious way of understanding, transpose [*metalabein*] what is said to the level of spiritual comprehension, after distancing the mind from the literal sense."

35. Cf. the comment of Franz Dünzl: "Erlösung bedeutet in den *CantHom* vor allem 'Erziehung,' 'Aufstieg' und den 'Heilsweg der Liebe' . . ." (*Braut und Bräutigam: Die Auslegung des Canticum durch Gregor von Nyssa* (Beiträge zur Geschichte der biblischen Exegese 32; Tübingen: Mohr, 1993) 396.

36. *Homilies* 10, 327.

37. *Homilies* 10, 327.

> too the faculty of hearing becomes a dead thing and goes out of operation when the soul occupies itself with things beyond speech.
>
> As to the more bestial of the senses, they are hardly worth mentioning. Long since, like some graveyard stench attached to the soul, they have been put away: the sense of smell, scenting out odors; and the sense of taste, bound to the belly's service; and the sense of touch as well, the blind and servile organ that nature, we may think, created only for the sake of the blind. When all these are as it were bound in sleep by disuse, then the working of the heart is pure, and its discourse is focused on what is above it, untroubled and unaccompanied by the noise that stems from the stirrings of sense perception.[38]

Anagogical transposition implies a sharp disjunction. We now look beyond *all* perceptible things. The more perfect soul now looks *only* on matters that are beyond seeing, and the more bestial of the senses have "long since" (*porrōthen*) been put away.

In like manner, since hair lacks sensation, Gregory links the Bridegroom's comment, "Your hair is like flocks of goats" (Song 6:5) with St. Paul's comment that a woman's glory is her hair (1 Cor 11:15). The woman's hair in both texts refers to the believers' pursuit of the beautiful and the good: for the wise,

> [s]ight does not serve as their criterion of beauty, taste does not provide their assessment of goodness, their judgment of virtue does not depend on smell or touch or any other organ of perception; on the contrary, all sense perception is done to death, and it is through the agency of the soul alone that they touch the good things and yearn for them as they are manifested in an intelligible form. In this manner they bring glory to the woman, the church, being neither puffed up by the honors accorded them nor shrunken down by pusillanimity in the face of pain.[39]

The transposition from physical to spiritual senses involves bodily renunciation. The denial is of such a radical character that Gregory latches on to hair as one of the few bodily elements that are without sensation in order to describe the required attitude toward the bodily senses.

Furthermore, since myrrh is a spice used for burying the dead, Gregory looks to the Song's references to myrrh as also indicative of the denial of the passions, and

---

38. *Homilies* 10, 329.
39. *Homilies* 15, 479.

he contrasts it with frankincense, which is used to praise God. Thus, myrrh stands for mortification while frankincense implies vivification. Gregory comments that

> the person who intends to dedicate himself to the worship of God will not be frankincense burned for God unless he has first become myrrh—that is, unless he mortifies his earthly members, having been buried together with the one who submitted to death on our behalf and having received in his own flesh, through mortification of its members, that myrrh which was used to prepare the Lord for burial. When these things have come to pass, every species of the fragrances that belong to virtue—once they have been ground fine in the bowl of life as in some mortar—produces that sweet cloud of dust, and he who inhales it becomes sweet-smelling because he has become full of the fragrant Spirit.[40]

Anagogical transposition implies for Gregory a mortification of the bodily senses, so that one becomes dead to that which one perceives by means of these senses. Conversely, as we participate in the virtues of Christ, our lives begin to give off the odour of frankincense and other sweet-smelling perfumes.

In this discussion, Gregory carefully balances the otherness of God with the fact that we genuinely image him. Commenting on Song 1:12 ("My spikenard gave off his scent"), Gregory distinguishes between the spikenard itself and its scent: "[T]he words of the text are teaching us this, namely, that that Reality, whatever it is in its essence, which transcends the entire structure and order of Being, is unapproachable, impalpable, and incomprehensible but that, for us, the sweetness that is blended within us by the purity of the virtues takes its place because by its own purity it images that which is by nature the Undefiled."[41] St. Gregory also uses the sense of sight to describe this same participation by way of imitation. The eye functions as a mirror. When the Bridegroom says that the bride's eyes are doves, he refers, according to Gregory, to the fact that when a person looks at an object, its image is reflected in the eye. We do not gaze upon the divine glory itself. Nonetheless, explains Gregory, when the soul's "purified eye has received the imprint of the dove, she is also capable of beholding the beauty of the Bridegroom."[42] When in Song 5:12 the Bridegroom's

---

40. *Homilies* 6, 202–03. Cf. *Homilies* 7, 253–55; 8, 263; 12, 363–67; 14, 427–31.

41. *Homilies* 3, 99. Cf. *Homilies* 1, 39: "For whatever name we may think up, she says, to make the scent of the Godhead known, the meaning of the things we say does not refer to the perfume itself. Rather does our theological vocabulary refer to a slight remnant of the vapor of the divine fragrance. In the case of vessels from which perfumed ointment is emptied out, the ointment itself that has been emptied out is not known for what it is in its own nature."

42. *Homilies* 4, 117.

eyes are compared to doves ("doves by pools of waters, washed in milk, sitting by pools of waters") Gregory comments on the fact that, unlike water, milk does not reflect any image. This should stir in us the highest praise for the Bridegroom's eyes, that is, for the church's teachers: "[T]hey do not mistakenly image anything unreal and counterfeit and empty that is contrary to what truly is but look upon what *is* in the full and proper sense of that word. They do not take in the deceitful sights and fantasies of the present life. For this reason, the perfect soul judges that it is the bath in milk that most surely purifies the eyes."[43] As a result, in the clear mirror of the church one indirectly sees the Sun of Righteousness itself (Mal 4:2).[44] While human beings' virtuous lives genuinely mirror God, our spiritual senses do not grasp the essence of the divine glory itself.

A word of caution may be in order at this point. Gregory's focus on the spiritual senses does not mean that he regards the bodily senses as unimportant. Contemporary Gregory of Nyssa research is right to highlight the commonality between animals and human beings in terms of embodiment, and it is also true that Gregory regards the human passions positively in that they serve to draw us closer to God.[45] Nonetheless, Gregory's theology of the spiritual senses makes clear that he regards anagogical transposition as absolutely essential to the process of salvation. We do not do justice to the Cappadocian mystic by domesticating his theology. We must keep his focus on bodily renunciation as central. Embodied existence and bodily senses are important for Gregory precisely because they allow for a transposition to spiritual perception, which is to say, to a life of participation in divine virtue. Without the sensuous images of the Song of Songs, we would have no way to express the transposition that characterizes the Christian life. For Gregory, it is the body and its senses that allow for anagogical ascent. But to regard the bodily senses themselves as ultimate would be, according to St. Gregory at least, to misconstrue the nature of the good and the beautiful. Bodily passions serve bodily pleasure. For Gregory, a focus on bodily passions involves a radical misconception of the nature of salvation. Salvation means transposition of our passions from this-worldly to otherworldly

---

43. *Homilies* 13, 417-19. Cf. *Homilies* 7, 229-31. Gregory uses the language of a reflecting mirror not only for the eye but also for human nature as a whole. Thus, human nature either reflects Beauty or it reflects the image of the Serpent (*Homilies* 4, 115; 5, 163; 15, 467-69).

44. *Homilies* 8, 269-71.

45. It also appears that there is some development in Gregory's thought, with later works being more positive than earlier works with regard to human embodiment. See, for instance, Ludlow, "Gregory of Nyssa and the Body."

realities. Such a transposition from bodily to spiritual senses demands a radical reorientation of human desires and passions.

Bodily Text

The "obvious sense" (*procheiros emphasis*) of the text, as St. Gregory repeatedly calls the literal meaning,[46] functions in a manner analogous to the role played by the physical body. Like the physical body, the "obvious sense" of the text—or, as I will call it here, the "bodily text"—is indispensable.[47] Without the bodily text, Gregory does not believe it is possible for the text to serve in the useful way that it is meant to serve. At the same time, we will see that the "obvious sense"—the bodily text—is not ultimate. It is not just the physical body that must be anagogically transposed; the bodily text of Scripture too undergoes a transposition that allows us, through a redirection of the passions to move away from the straightforward meaning of the text in order to contemplate its spiritual reality. For Gregory salvation requires us to be in tune with the purpose of Scripture. Since salvation involves a redirection or transposition of the passions, our reading of Scripture should follow the same anagogical pattern. What is more, the ascent from the bodily senses enables the anagogy of the biblical text and vice versa.

Gregory is well aware of the controversial character of what is often called allegorical interpretation. He introduces his commentary with a preface in which he defends the practice over against certain church leaders (*tisi tōn ekklēsiastikōn*)—likely some of the more literalist interpreters from the Antiochian tradition—who "stand by the letter" (*paristasthai tē lexei*) of Holy Scripture rather than take into account the "enigmas and below-the-surface meanings" (*ainigmatōn te kai hyponoiōn*).[48] For Gregory, what is important is the biblical precedent for a deeper or spiritual meaning, not the terminology used to describe it. Most of the preface consists of an appeal to biblical passages that, on Gregory's understanding, support the use of anagogical transposition in the exegesis of Scripture.[49]

---

46. *Homilies* Preface, 3; Preface, 5; Preface, 7; Preface, 11; 1, 31; 1, 33; 5, 153; 12, 381.

47. Throughout this essay, my "bodily text" and Gregory's "obvious meaning" will be regarded as identical. Thus, my phrase "bodily text" does not refer to the *words* on the page; instead I mean the surface-level or literal *meaning* of the text.

48. *Homilies* Preface, 3. Cf. Cahill, "Date and Setting," 447–60; Ronald E. Heine, "Gregory of Nyssa's Apology for Allegory," *VC* 38 (1984) 360–70.

49. Gregory appeals to the following passages: Rom 7:14; Gal 4:24; 1 Cor 10:11; 9:9–10; 13:12; 2 Cor 3:16, 6. In addition, he also appeals to various OT texts that he believes do not make sense if taken literally.

With regard to terminology, Gregory shows himself clearly indifferent. The Antiochians tended to regard the term "allegory" (*allēgoria*) with suspicion because of its allegedly arbitrary and ahistorical connotations and preferred to speak of "contemplation" (*theōria*) instead. Gregory, although influenced by the allegorical tradition of Origen and the other Alexandrians, refuses to make terminology an issue. He often adopts the language of *theōria*, most famously in the twofold division of *De vita Moysis*, where the first part gives a historical rendering of Moses' life (*historia*), while the second part provides the contemplative meaning (*theōria*).[50] In the preface to his Songs commentary, Gregory reiterates his indifference regarding terminology: "One may wish to refer to the anagogical interpretation of such sayings as 'tropology' or 'allegory' or by some other name. We shall not quarrel about the name as long as a firm grasp is kept on thoughts that edify."[51]

While Gregory restricts his defence to an appeal to biblical precedent, much more is at stake. Interpretation, for Gregory, is not primarily a search for authorial intent. He reads Scripture for the sake of the usefulness that it has with regard to salvation. St. Paul is concerned, maintains Gregory in his preface, to interpret "in accordance with what gives him satisfaction [*areskon*] in his search for what edifies [*ōphelimon*]."[52] The latter aspect, the "usefulness" of Scripture, is an important category for Gregory. This "usefulness" is something we come to know "by spiritual inquiry and discernment" (*dia tēs pneumatikēs theōrias*).[53] Thus, when he discusses Song 2:3 ("As the apple among the trees of the wood, so is my kinsman among the sons"), Gregory rhetorically questions what this text could possibly be driving at: "[W]hat guidance in virtue would there be in this, unless there were some idea profitable [*ti noēma tōn ōphelountōn*] for us contained in the words?"[54] This passage makes clear that usefulness has to do, for Gregory, with growth in virtue (*aretē*). Drobner rightly comments that "Gregory's allegorizing is based on soteriology and ethics. At the beginning, the question of the utility (*ōpheleia*) for believers is asked."[55] For Gregory, right interpretation is useful interpretation.

---

50. See Gregory's *De vita Moysis* (GNO VII/1; ET: *The Life of Moses* [trans. Abraham J. Malherbe and Everett Ferguson; Classics of Western Spirituality; New York: Paulist, 1978]).

51. *Homilies* Preface, 3–5.

52. *Homilies* Preface, 5.

53. *Homilies* 15, 463.

54. *Homilies* 4, 139.

55. Hubertus R. Drobner, "Allegory," in *Brill Dictionary*, 21–26, at 24. Cf. also Manlio Simonetti, "Exegesis," in *Brill Dictionary*, 331–38.

This moral usefulness, the aim of virtue, can hardly be overestimated. Anagogical transposition means, according to Gregory, transposition into the goodness and beauty of God himself. Anagogical interpretation thus leads to participation in divine virtue. Throughout his homilies Gregory comments on the centrality of virtue, noting that virtue is the deeper meaning to which the words of the Song refer. Whether the talk is of perfumes,[56] of the vine's branches that shoot out,[57] of necklaces,[58] of cedar beams,[59] of blossoms,[60] of Solomon's crown,[61] of a pomegranate,[62] of honeycomb,[63] of a paradisal garden,[64] of the bride's teeth,[65] or of lilies,[66] in each case Gregory sees a reference to the soul's life of virtue. We store the fruit of Wisdom in our hearts as in a beehive, imitating the wise bee in the "noble work of the virtues."[67] To the modern reader, such omnipresence of virtue may well seem arbitrary.[68] To Gregory, however, the recognition of virtue in the biblical text is simply a matter of being faithful to its purpose or scope, namely, the salvific transposition of the soul into the life of God. As David Ney puts it: "When we interpret Gregory's spiritual interpretations in light of his hermeneutic of virtue, we find that they are all simply different expressions of his allegorical impulse to transform the

---

56. *Homilies* 1, 37–39; 3, 101; 4, 137; 9, 281–83; 9, 287; 10, 323; 12, 363–65.

57. *Homilies* 2, 67.

58. *Homilies* 3, 91.

59. *Homilies* 4, 121–23.

60. *Homilies* 5, 165–67.

61. *Homilies* 7, 225.

62. *Homilies* 7, 241.

63. *Homilies* 9, 285.

64. *Homilies* 9, 289–99.

65. *Homilies* 7, 239.

66. *Homilies* 15, 469.

67. *Homilies* 9, 285.

68. The question of arbitrariness often comes up by way of objection to patristic and medieval allegorizing. A full response to this objection lies beyond the scope of this paper but would have to include discussion of the following elements: (1) the wide variety of results yielded by historical critical exegesis, which opens it up to the same charge of arbitrariness; (2) the often remarkable similarities in approach and actual exegetical outcome among a broad range of pre-modern interpreters; (3) the church's liturgy and "rule of faith" as setting boundaries for what constitutes proper interpretation; (4) the Spirit's guidance of the faithful in the church in adhering faithfully to the divine intentions of the church's book; (5) the function of "usefulness" as simply being more important to the believer than arriving at the exact authorial intent; and (6) many pre-modern interpreters' openness to multiple interpretations of one particular text.

literal text into an agent of perfection in virtue."⁶⁹ In other words, for Gregory, the bodily text is simply an occasion for anagogical transposition into a life of virtue.

Not only is the life of virtue the very *purpose* of the exegetical enterprise, which justifies its allegorical approach, but virtue is also a *prerequisite* for proper interpretation. Searching for the hidden meaning of Scripture is like moving from the outside of the tabernacle into the holy of holies itself. We will only recognize its marvels after "washing off in the bath of reason all the filth of shameful thinking."⁷⁰ When he embarks on Homily 3, Gregory comments that the verses of the previous two homilies were not yet "a pure light" but "were calculated to point us to the rising of the true light."⁷¹ Gregory then announces:

> Now, however, the voice of the Bridegroom himself, like a sun's orb, rises up and eclipses with the light of its rays all the brightness both of the stars that shone earlier and of the glistening dawn.
>
> To be sure, the previous passages all have the power that belongs to means of purification and lustration. By their agency souls that have been purified are prepared for the reception of the divine. But the words of the present passage are a participation in the Godhead itself, since the divine Word in his own voice confers on the hearer a fellowship with the undefiled Power.
>
> And just as Israel, at Mount Sinai, was prepared beforehand for two days by rites of purification and then, at dawn on the third day, was judged worthy of the theophany (cf. Exod 19:10–11), being no longer busied with the cleansing of garments but openly receiving God himself, for whose sake the soul's filth had been washed away by the earlier purifications, so now, in our own case, the insight into the prefatory parts of the Song of Songs that we achieved on the preceding two days in our earlier homilies has been of profit to the extent that the sense contained in the words has been washed and scrubbed to remove the filth of the flesh.⁷²

---

69. David Ney, "Gregory of Nyssa's Hermeneutic of Virtue" (Th.M. thesis, Regent College, 2010) 159.

70. *Homilies* 2, 49. For detailed discussions of Gregory's description of the Song of Songs as holy of holies, see Martin Laird, "Under Solomon's Tutelage"; Norris, "The Soul Takes Flight." The innermost sanctuary (*adyton*) plays an important role in Gregory's theology since it symbolizes the place where the soul comes to the mystical knowledge of God. Cf. Lucas Francisco Mateo-Seco, "*Adyton*," Brill Dictionary, 6–8.

71. *Homilies* 3, 79.

72. *Homilies* 3, 79–81.

Gregory, preaching his third sermon in the Lenten period, insists that the first two sermons affected the purgation of the believers, just as the Israelites prepared themselves for two days before God would come down for them on Mount Sinai. Only after two days of extensive preparatory preaching are the people ready to enter into the divine presence itself and can take the next step in the interpretation of the Song of Songs.[73]

This spiritual preparation requires not only tremendous human effort, but it likewise means that the anagogical transposition depends on the Spirit's grace. Speaking of the custom of sailors offering up prayer before venturing on a sea journey, Gregory comments:

> Before our discourse there stretches the vast ocean of insight and inquiry into the divine words. From this venture we hope for great riches in the way of knowledge, and this animate ship of ours, the church, with its own full crew, looks expectantly forward to its voyage of explication. But no sooner does the helmsman, who is our reason, lay a hand on the tiller than a common prayer is raised to God by the whole company aboard the ship: that the power of the Holy Spirit may blow upon us and stir up the waves of our thoughts, and that by their means it may prosper the voyage of our discourse and lead it on a direct course. In this way, finding ourselves on the high seas in our search for insight, we will traffic in the riches of knowledge, always supposing that in response to your prayer the Holy Spirit comes to fill the sails of our discourse.[74]

It is only when the Holy Spirit blows into the church's sails that the readers of Scripture are equipped to understand it and so to attain to the wealth of saving knowledge, which is the purpose of the voyage.

This life of virtue, both as preparation for and as outcome of spiritual interpretation, is itself a participation in the divine life. Western readers (perhaps especially Protestants) may well be put off by Gregory's focus on virtue, especially since it is accompanied with a strong emphasis on free will.[75] We should keep in mind, however, that for Gregory the life of virtue is never something independent from God.[76]

---

73. Cf. *Homilies* 9, 277, where Gregory enjoins his hearers that they should "attend to today's passage as persons who are dead to the body and draw out no fleshly meaning from its words."

74. *Homilies* 12, 361–63.

75. For Gregory's repeated insistence on free will, see *Homilies* 2, 55; 4, 115; 5, 173; 7, 221; 10, 321; 12, 363–65; 14, 433; 15, 487–89.

76. For discussions on the relationship between grace and free will in Gregory, see Lucas Francisco Mateo-Seco, "Grace," in *Brill Dictionary*, 364–67; Daniel F. Stramara, "Jesus as Moral Exemplar and

Human goodness is a participation in divine goodness, a participation that in no way lessens the transcendence of God, since God's infinity implies that the soul's desire will never be satiated and will always continue to stretch forward in its participatory journey in the life of God. Gregory explains:

> As, therefore, the divine Nature draws human nature to participation in itself, it always surpasses that which participates in it to the same degree, in conformity with its superabundance of goodness. For the soul is always becoming better than itself on account of its participation in the transcendent. It does not stop growing, but the Good that is participated remains in unaltered degree as it is, since the being that ever more and more participates in it discovers that it is always surpassed to the same extent.[77]

The progression appears to be an orderly structured entry into God's life. The human race, says Gregory, "does not achieve its perfect state again all at once, as at its first creation. Rather does it advance toward the better along a road of sorts, in an orderly fashion [*akolouthias*], one step after another, and rids itself bit by bit of its susceptibility to that which opposes its fulfillment."[78] This never-ceasing and ordered progression in virtue constitutes Gregory's doctrine of *ekeptasis*: the soul continuously stretches forth throughout eternity.[79] Salvation, therefore, is not simply the result of moralistic striving. Instead, it is a matter of having one's desires so transposed that the virtuous life becomes a progressive participation in the virtuous life of God.[80] Salvation, for Gregory, is participation in God, a never ceasing deifying participation.

Saviour according to Gregory of Nyssa," *The Patristic and Byzantine Review* 25/1-3 (2007) 10-21; Verna E. F. Harrison, *Grace and Human Freedom according to St. Gregory of Nyssa* (Studies in the Bible and Early Christianity 30; Lewiston, N.Y.: Mellen, 1992); Gregorios, *Cosmic Man*, 199-218; Donald C. Abel, "The Doctrine of Synergism in Gregory of Nyssa's *De instituto christiano*," *The Thomist* 45 (1981) 430-48; Ekkehard Mühlenberg, "Synergism in Gregory of Nyssa," *Zeitschrift für die Neutestamentliche Wissenschaft* 68 (1977) 93-122; Adolf Martin Ritter, "Die Gnadenlehre Gregors von Nyssa nach seiner Schrift 'Über das Leben des Mose,'" in *Gregor von Nyssa und die Philosophie: Zweites internationales Kolloquium über Gregor von Nyssa; Freckenhorst bei Münster 18.-23 September 1972* (ed. Heinrich Dörrie, Margarete Altenburger, and Uta Schramm; Leiden: Brill, 1976) 195-239; A. S. Dunstone, "The Meaning of Grace in the Writings of Gregory of Nyssa," *Scottish Journal of Theology* 15 (1962) 235-44.

77. *Homilies* 5, 171. Cf. *Homilies* 5, 151.

78. *Homilies* 15, 487.

79. Cf. Everett Ferguson, "God's Infinity and Man's Mutability: Perpetual Progress according to Gregory of Nyssa," *Greek Orthodox Theological Review* 18 (1973) 59-78; Kristina Robb-Dover, "Gregory of Nyssa's 'Perpetual Progress,'" *Theology Today* 65 (2008) 213-25.

80. The notion of *epektasis* comes from Phil 3:13-14, in which Paul comments, "Brethren, I do

Since he regards the soul's salvific process and the anagogical interpretation of the Song as linked, Gregory believes that the Song is structured in such a way as to enable the soul's growth in deification. The Song follows an ordered pattern of ascending steps. We already saw that at the beginning of his third homily, Gregory explained that the first two homilies had been presented by way of purgation, so that now the reader could enter into the innermost sanctuary of the divine presence.[81] This same sense of structured progression comes to the fore when, throughout the text of his homilies, Gregory inserts brief sections that summarize the various steps of ascent that the soul has already taken.[82] Although these steps are orderly and each one allows the soul genuinely to move upward, Gregory's doctrine of *epektasis* means that every ascending step is like a new beginning. When he introduces his fifth homily, Gregory comments: "I reckoned that the soul that had been exalted through so many stages had achieved the height of blessedness. Yet it seems that what has already been accomplished is still the preliminary stage of her climb."[83] The perpetual progression of the soul matches the perpetual progression of the Song.

This orderly "epektatic" anagogy also corresponds to an anagogical transposition from OT to NT. When Song 2:9 says that the Bridegroom "stands behind our wall, leaning through the windows, peering through the lattices," Gregory comments:

> The anagogical sense [*hē de kata anagōgēn theōria*] of the words, however, adheres closely to the line of thought we have already uncovered, for the Word follows a certain path and a certain sequence [*hodō gar kai akolouthia*] in adapting human nature to God. First of all he shines upon it by means of the prophets and the law's injunctions. (This is our interpretation: the windows are the prophets, who bring in the light, while the lattices are the network of the law's injunctions. Through both of them the beam of the true Light steals into the interior.) After that, however, comes the Light's perfect illumination, when, by its mingling with our nature, the true Light shows itself to those who are in darkness and the shadow of death. At an earlier stage, then, the beams of the prophetic and legal ideas,

---

not consider that I have made it my own; but one thing I do, forgetting what lies behind and straining forward [*epekteinomenos*] to what lies ahead, I press on toward the goal for the prize of the upward call of God in Christ Jesus." Gregory often refers to this verse, both in these homilies and elsewhere. Cf. Catherine LeBlanc, "Naked and Unashamed: Epektasis in Gregory of Nyssa's Commentary on the Song of Songs" (M.A. thesis, University of St. Michael's College, 2007); Daniélou, *Platoni et théologie mystique*, 291–307.

81. *Homilies* 3, 79–81. Cf. Norris, "Introduction," xxxii–xxxiii.

82. See, for example, *Homilies* 4, 129; 5, 151; 6, 189–91.

83. *Homilies* 5, 151.

which illumine the soul by way of its windows and lattices, as we have understood, induce a desire to see the sun in the open air, and then, in the way indicated, the Desired steps forward to do his work.[84]

The windows and the lattices, i.e., the prophets and the law, allowed only some of the light to enter. The gospel, by contrast, allows the fullness of the light to shine in on us.[85] The progress of anagogical salvation takes place only in and through the newness of the gospel, that is to say, in and through Christ, the true Solomon.[86]

The bodily text of the Song, its "obvious sense," is not unimportant to Gregory. Nonetheless, Gregory's approach clearly hinges on an anagogical transposition away from the bodily text to a spiritual participation in divine goodness and beauty. The words of the text are important for Gregory precisely because of the veiled character of the truth.[87] The "obvious sense" must be taken into account because it is precisely the references to bodily senses and bodily passions that allow the spiritual transposition to take place. The ultimate concern though for Gregory as a preacher is that his hearers move *through* the bodily text in order to attain salvation, the spiritual reality of progressive participation in the life of God.

Bodily Garments

So far we have seen that salvation for Gregory means anagogical transposition into deifying participation in virtue and in the goodness of God. We have, however, not yet sufficiently asked the question of the role of Christ in this saving process. One way in which to address Christ's role in saving human beings is by discussing the imagery of a change in clothing, a metaphor that Gregory often uses to describe the saving transposition. Gregory's soteriology is predicated on a contrast between "tunics of hide" and the "holy garb" of the Lord Jesus Christ. The very opening words of the first homily illustrate the contrast:

> You who in accordance with the counsel of Paul have "taken off" the old humanity with its deeds and lusts like a filthy garment [*peribolaion*] (Col

---

84. *Homilies* 5, 158–59.

85. Cf. *Homilies* 5, 173–75; 9, 281–83; 10, 319.

86. *Homilies* 7, 215–19.

87. Witness, for example, the opening words of Homily 10: "The task now set us of probing these divine words taken from the Song of Songs involves thoughts that are difficult to understand and, because of their obscurity, hidden and ineffable. We have need, therefore, of greater diligence—or better, of greater assistance through prayer and of guidance on the part of the Holy Spirit" (*Homilies* 10, 311).

3:9) and have clothed yourselves by purity of life in the lightsome raiment [*himatia*] of the Lord, raiment such as he revealed in his transfiguration on the mountain (cf. Mark 9:2–3 and par.), or, rather, you who have "put on" our Lord Jesus Christ himself (Gal 3:27) together with his holy garb [*stolēs*] and with him have been transfigured for impassibility and the life divine: hear the mysteries of the Song of Songs.[88]

St. Paul's mixed metaphor of an "old man" that he encouraged believers to "take off" so they could "put on" the "new man" (Eph 4:22; Col 3:9) was for the Alexandrian tradition reason to interpret the "garments of skin" or "tunics of hide" that God gave to Adam and Eve after the fall (Gen 3:21, *chitōnas dermatinous*) as the human body in its fallen condition. In line with this, the "putting on" of the "new man" became the reversal of the effects of the fall resulting from an identification with Jesus Christ and a renewal of the image of God (cf. Eph 4:24; Col 3:11). Gregory is no exception in this regard, though he is careful how he expresses himself: the human body itself is not a result of the fall but a good gift of the creator God.[89]

The believer's identification with Christ in the "putting on" of the "new man" is evident not only in the passage already quoted, but also in Gregory's reflections in Homily 11 on the bride's words, "I have removed my tunic [*chitōna*]. How shall I put it on?" (Song 5:3). Not surprisingly, Gregory immediately spots here a reference to paradise and sees here a reversal of the effects of the fall. The bride "put off that 'tunic of skin' [*ton dermatinon ekeinon chitōna*] that she had put on after the sin (cf. Gen 3:21)."[90] This stripping off of the tunic of hide is, at the same time, one's identification with Christ. Gregory comments:

---

88. *Homilies* 1, 15.

89. While Origen identifies the tunics of hide with the body as such, Gregory is much more circumspect, regarding the tunics of hide as the fallen condition of the mortal body. Cf. Lucas Francisco Mateo-Seco, "Tunics of Hide," in *Brill Dictionary*, 768–70. In what follows, I analyze Gregory's discussions of garments in his Songs commentary. He gives more systematic treatments in *De hominis opificio* (PG 44, 124–256; ET: *On the Making of Man*, in *Nicene and Post-Nicene Fathers*, Second Series, vol. 5, *Gregory of Nyssa: Dogmatic Treastises, Etc.* [ed. Philip Schaff and Henry Wace; trans. H. A. Wilson; 1893, reprint, Peabody, Mass.: Hendrickson, 1994] 387–427) and in *De anima et resurrectione* (PG 46, 12–160; ET: *On the Soul and the Resurrection*, in *Saint Gregory of Nyssa: Ascetical Works* [trans. Virginia Woods Callahan; The Fathers of the Church 58; 1967, reprint, Washington, D. C.: Catholic University of America Press, 1999] 193–272).

90. *Homilies* 11, 347. Elsewhere, Gregory sees a reference to the fall in the parable of the Good Samaritan (Luke 10) in which Jesus "relates the downward journey of the human being, the thieves' ambush, the stripping off of the incorruptible garment [*aphthartou endymatos*], the wounds of sin, death's occupation of the half of human nature (the soul remains immortal)" (*Homilies* 14, 453).

> So whoever has taken off the old humanity and rent the veil of the heart has opened an entrance for the Word. And when the Word has entered her, the soul makes him her garment [*endyma*] in accordance with the instruction of the apostle; for he commands the person who has taken off the rags [*rakōdē*] of the old humanity "to put on the new" tunic [*chitōna*] that "has been created after the likeness of God in holiness and righteousness" (Eph 4:24); and he says that this garment [*endyma*] is Jesus (cf. Rom 13:14).[91]

For Gregory, Jesus is the new tunic that the believer puts on when removing the old tunic of skin. Put differently, Gregory describes the anagogical transposition in such a way that our very bodily existence changes when in and through Christ we regain the immortality lost through the fall.

This identification with Christ in the putting on of bodily garments (a "new man" or "new tunic") is of great importance for our understanding of Gregory's doctrine of salvation. He closely aligns salvation with identification with Christ, to the point of insisting that an "exchange" takes place between Christ and the person who puts him on as a new tunic. Thus, when reflecting on the bride's well-known comment that she is "dark and beautiful" (Song 1:5),[92] Gregory explains the first term as referring to the result of the fall and the second term as a reversal that takes place through the Bridegroom's identification with his bride:

> For she says: "Do not marvel that Righteousness has loved me. Marvel rather that when I was dark with sin and at home in the dark because of my deeds, he by his love made me beautiful, exchanging [*antallaxomenos*] his own beauty for my ugliness. For having transferred to himself the filth of my sins, he shared his own purity with me and constituted me a participant in his own beauty—he who first made something desirable out of one who had been repulsive and in this way acted lovingly."[93]

Later Gregory has the bride exclaim, "For how shall I not love you, who so loved me—even when I was dark—as to lay down your life for the sheep that you shep-

---

91. *Homilies* 11, 347.

92. For extended discussion of Gregory's reflections on this passage (along with racial implications) see Mark S. M. Scott, "Shades of Grace: Origen and Gregory of Nyssa's Soteriological Exegesis of the 'Black and Beautiful' Bride in Song of Songs 1:5," *HTR* 99 (2006) 65–83.

93. *Homilies* 2, 51.

herd? It is not possible to conceive a love greater than this: to give up the well-being of your life in exchange [*antallaxasthai*] for mine."[94]

Gregory's strong christological focus, along with the notion of "exchange," should not be read through the lens of later Protestant-Catholic debates. Gregory does not have in mind a forensic exchange.[95] Rather, the removal of the tunic of hide is an ontological transposition that allows us to identify with Christ in and through the life of virtue. The growth of virtue is what constitutes our transposition into Christ. Thus, Gregory reminds us in his first homily on Moses' decree that "no one should dare the ascent of the spiritual mountain until the garments [*himatia*] of our hearts are washed clean and our souls are purified by the appropriate sprinklings of reasoned thoughts (cf. Exod 19:10, 14)."[96] He makes the identification of a "new tunic" with new virtues even more explicit when in Homily 9 he reflects on Song 4:11 ("the fragrance of your garments [*himatiōn*] is as the fragrance of frankincense"). The combination of the mentioning of garments and of frankincense proves irresistible to Gregory. "This statement," he maintains, "indicates what the goal of the life of virtue is for human beings. For the limit that the virtuous life approaches is likeness to the Divine."[97] Gregory then goes on to speak about the weaving of a garment of virtues:

> Now the virtuous manner of life is not uniform or marked by a single style, but just as in the making of a fabric [*hyphasmatōn*] the weaver's art creates the garment by using many threads, some of which are stretched vertically and others are carried horizontally, so too, in the case of the virtuous life, many things must twine together if a noble life is to be woven. Just so the divine apostle enumerates threads of this sort, threads by means of which pure works are woven together; he mentions love and joy and peace, patience and kindness (cf. Gal 5:22) and all the sorts of thing that adorn the person who is putting on the garment of heavenly incorruptibility in place of [*metendyomenos*] a corruptible and earthly life (1 Cor 15:53). This is why the Bridegroom acknowledges that the adornment of the Bride's garment [*esthēti*] is, as far as its fragrance goes, like frankincense.[98]

---

94. *Homilies* 2, 69. Cf. *Homilies* 15, 471: Paul renounced "his life so as to exchange [*antallaxētai*] his own suffering for the salvation of Israel."

95. A. S. Dunstone misreads Gregory when he states that for Gregory, Christ's sinlessness meant "that Christ was able to impute to others His own righteousness" (*Atonement in Gregory of Nyssa*, 26).

96. *Homilies* 1, 27.

97. *Homilies* 9, 287.

98. *Homilies* 9, 287.

For Gregory, there is no difference whatsoever between putting on Christ as a garment, on the one hand, and weaving for oneself a garment of virtue, on the other hand.

The result is that Gregory can apply the doctrine of *epektasis* also to the removal of the tunic of hide and to one's putting on the garment of Christ. We already saw that in Homily 9, Gregory reflects on the bride's comment, "I have removed my tunic [*chitōna*]. How shall I put it on?" (Song 5:3). He refers back to this statement when he notes the bride's comment that "the watchmen of the walls took my veil [*theristron*] away from me" (Song 5:7). Gregory begins by noting an apparent incongruity: "How, then, does one who has been stripped of all covering [*periblēmatos*] still wear the *veil* [*theristron*] that the *guards* now remove from her?"[99] Gregory explains this by referring to the soul's continuous (epektatic) ascent in virtue:

> But is it not the case that these words show how much progress upward she has made from that previous state? She who had removed that old tunic [*chitōna*] and been freed of all covering [*peribolēs*] becomes so much purer than herself that by comparison with the purity that now becomes hers she does not seem to have taken off that clothing [*peribolaion*] but again, even after that former stripping, finds something on her to be taken off.[100]

The stripping of the garment and the removal of the veil become simply two stages of the continuous growth in virtue, a growth that Gregory regards identical to the putting on of Christ. For Gregory, it appears, it is impossible to separate the saving exchange between Christ and the soul, on the one hand, and the continuous growth in virtue, on the other hand.[101]

---

99. *Homilies* 12, 381.

100. *Homilies* 12, 381.

101. Shifting images somewhat, Gregory also adopts the Platonic imagery of "wings" that we have lost in the fall and that we regain through God's grace. The Song comments: "Turn your eyes away from that which is opposed to me, for they give me wings" (Song 6:5). Gregory connects Scripture's attribution of wings to God (Ps 17:8; 91:4; Deut 32:11; Matt 23:37) with our being made in God's image and likeness, and then proceeds to explain that the fall "robbed us of such wings as these" (*Homilies* 15, 475). When, however, God looked on his bride in love, he furnished her with new wings, so that the bride takes up the wings of a dove (*Homilies* 15, 475). Cf. Marguerite Harl, "Références philosophiques et références bibliques du langage de Grégoire de Nysse dans ses Orationes in Canticum canticorum," in *Hermēneumata: Festschrift für Hadwig Hörner zum sechzigsten Geburtstag* (ed. Herbert Eisenberger, Bibliothek der klassischen Altertumswissenschaften NS 2/7; Heidelberg: Carl Winter Universitätsverlag, 1990) 117–31, at 120–21; Gregorios, *Cosmic Man*, 180–84; Jean Daniélou, "The Dove and the Darkness in Ancient Byzantine Mysticism," in *Man and Transformation: Papers from the Eranos Yearbooks* (ed. Joseph Campbell; trans. Olga Froebe-Kapteyn; Bollingen Series 30/5; Princeton: Princeton University Press, 1964) 270–96, at 276–79.

While this putting on of new bodily garments is clearly something for the individual soul to concern herself with, Gregory's theology of the body is not a purely individual matter. Anagogical transposition of salvation requires the church. Throughout his homilies Gregory moves effortlessly back and forth between an identification of the bride as the individual soul and as the church. The connection with Christ begins in the mystical water of baptism through which one enters into the church.[102] It is through belonging to the church that anagogical transposition takes place and that the individual soul finds salvation from sin and renewal in Christ.

The underlying rationale for this ecclesial focus in Gregory has to do with the incarnation. Christ identifies not just with individual people, but as the good shepherd he takes our entire human nature (*pasa hē anthrōpinē physis*) upon himself.[103] Brian Daley captures it well when he comments:

> Gregory assumes ... that the saving process begins in the revelation of the glory of God, and that the Son has achieved this in a new and unparalleled way in his life, death and resurrection, by the moral and physical transformation of weak human flesh. The real news of the Gospel, Gregory suggests here, is that the Word, who remains transcendent and unchanging, has taken on human nature in the man Jesus and made it his own, so

---

102. For Gregory, the "laver of rebirth" washes away the bride's "dark appearance" (*Homilies* 2, 53). Similarly, speaking of the Gentiles as represented by the Ethiopian queen, Gregory comments: "Those of the Gentiles who approach by way of faith and who once were far off draw near, having washed off their darkness in the mystical water" (*Homilies* 7, 217). The crossing of the Red Sea is liberation from servitude to the enemy through the "mystical water," from which one must rise up "purified, bringing along in one's subsequent life nothing of the Egyptian self-awareness" (*Homilies* 3, 87). The Jordan River, which springs from the peak of Sanir and Hermon (Song 4:8) "is for us the beginning of our being remodeled for existence at the level of the divine" (*Homilies* 8, 263). When the bride washes her feet (Song 5:3) this means "that she who has once and for all, through baptism, taken off her sandals (for it is the proper business of a baptizer to loose the thongs of those who are wearing sandals, just as John testified that he was unable to do this in the sole case of the Lord, for how could he loose one who had never been bound by the thong of sin?) she has had her feet washed and has shed, with her sandals, all earthy filth" (*Homilies* 11, 351). The Song describes the bride's hands dropping myrrh as she rises up to open the door to her beloved, the Word (Song 5:5) "For by these words she states the way in which the door is opened to the Bridegroom: 'I have risen up by being "buried with him through baptism into his death" (cf. Rom 6:4) for the resurrection does not become actual if it is not preceded by voluntary death'" (*Homilies* 12, 363; cf. *Homilies* 8, 263; 14, 429–31).

103. *Homilies* 2, 69. Gregory uses the same imagery in *Antirrheticus adversus Apollinarium* 16 (GNO III/1, 152–53) and in *Oratio catechetica* 32 (GNO III/4, 78). Cf. the comment of Lucas Francisco Mateo-Seco: "According to Gregory, the Word, in incarnating, unites Himself to his humanity through which He unites Himself to all human beings, taking all of humanity, the lost sheep, on his shoulders" ("Mystical Body," in *Brill Dictionary*, 515–18, at 515).

that "everything that was weak and perishable in our nature mingled with the Godhead, has become that which the Godhead is."[104]

Christ, for Gregory, is the one in whom humanity and divinity come together so that we can become divine by participating in the deified humanity of Christ.

Gregory beautifully illustrates this significance of the incarnation at several points of his exegesis of the Song. First, the Song's reference to an apple (2:3) must be a reference to Christ taking on human nature: "He who for love of humanity [*tēs physeōs hēmōn*] grew up in the woods of our nature became an apple by sharing flesh and blood. For in the coloring of this fruit one can see a likeness to each of these. By its whiteness it copies a characteristic of flesh, while its reddish tinge by its appearance attests its kinship with the nature of blood."[105] Second, when the bride says to the Bridegroom, "Behold, you are fair, my beloved and beautiful, overshadowing [*syskios*] our bed" (1:16), the mentioning of the "bed" is, according to Gregory, a reference to the "blending" (*anakrasis*) or the "union" (*henōsis*) of the divine and human natures. Gregory's exposition is worth quoting at length:

> Then she adds: *thickly shaded* [*syskios*] *at our bed*. That is, "Human nature [*hē anthrōpinē physis*] knows you, or will know you, as the One who became shaded [*syskios*] by the divine Economy. For you came," she says, "as the beautiful *kinsman*, the glorious one, who became present at our couch thickly shaded [*syskios*]. For if you yourself had not shaded yourself [*syneskiasas*], concealing the pure ray of your Deity by the 'form of a slave' (Phil 2:7), who could have borne your appearing? For no one shall see 'the face' of the Lord 'and live' (Exod 33:20). Therefore you, the glorious one, came, but you came in such wise as we are able to receive you. You came with the radiance of Divinity shaded [*syskiasas*] by the garment [*tē peribolē*] of a body." For how could a mortal and perishable nature be adapted to live together with the imperishable and inaccessible, unless the shadow [*skia*] of the body had mediated between the Light and us who live in darkness (cf. Isa 9:1)?
>
> In a figurative turn of speech the Bride uses the word *bed* to mean the mingling [*anakrasin*] of the human race with the Divine.[106]

---

104. Brian E. Daley, "Divine Transcendence and Human Transformation: Gregory of Nyssa's Anti-Apollinarian Christology," in *Re-Thinking Gregory of Nyssa* (ed. Sarah Coakley; Malden, Mass.: Blackwell, 2003) 67–76, at 69. Daley's quotation from Gregory is taken from his letter *Ad Theophilum* (GNO III/1, 126).

105. *Homilies* 4, 139.

106. *Homilies* 4, 119–21.

Gregory here describes the human nature of Christ as a bodily garment (*peribolē*) that overshadows his divinity, so that the incarnation not only permits the divine nature to be present in and with the human nature but also allows us to see the very Son of God.

One of the characteristic elements of Gregory's doctrine of salvation is that he immediately links this union of the two natures to the ecclesial union between Christ and the church. Thus, the homily continues by saying that "the great apostle has the virgin—us—'betrothed' to Christ (2 Cor 11:2), and leads the soul in a bridal procession, and declares that the joining of the two in the communion [*koinōnian*] of one body is the great mystery of the union [*henōseōs*] of Christ with the church (cf. Eph 5:32)."[107] For Gregory the union of the two natures is almost the same as the union between Christ and the church. Christ's taking up of our human nature means, at the same time, that he nourishes his body, the church:

> And since he once for all, through its firstfruits, drew to himself the mortal nature of flesh, which he took on by means of an uncorrupted virginity, he ever sanctifies the common dough of that nature through its firstfruits, nourishing his body, the church, in the persons of those who are united to him in the fellowship of the mystery; and those members that are grafted into him through faith he fits into the common body, and he fashions a comely whole by fitly and appropriately assigning believers to roles as eyes and mouth and hands and the other members.[108]

St. Gregory focuses on the union between the two natures of Christ to ground the salvation of the church and of humanity.[109]

Gregory regards, therefore, the ecclesial body as central to Christ's work of restoring human beings to salvation.[110] First Corinthians 12, with its reference to the

---

107. *Homilies* 4, 121.

108. *Homilies* 13, 403. For a similar move from human nature to the church, see *Homilies* 14, 449. Here Gregory speaks of Ps 92:12 [LXX 91:13], where the just man is described as a "cedar in Lebanon." Gregory comments: "For the truly righteous one (and the Lord is the righteous one who rose from the earth for our sake) the towering palm tree that rose up in the stuff of our nature, became a mountain abounding in the cedars that are people rooted in him by faith; and when these have been planted 'in the house' of God, 'they shall bloom in the courts of . . . God' ([LXX] Ps 91:14)" (*Homilies* 14, 449).

109. Cf. Joseph Munitz's comment: "With surprising facility he [i.e., Gregory] can turn from the individual 'body of Christ' to the whole of mankind" ("The Church at Prayer: Ecclesiological Aspects of St Gregory of Nyssa's In Cantica Canticorum," *Eastern Churches Review* 3 [1970/71] 385–95, at 393).

110. This is not the place to enter into a discussion of Gregory's doctrine of *apokatastasis* or restoration, which in most places he regards as universal in character. Cf. Ilaria L. E. Ramelli, "Christian Soteriology and Christian Platonism: Origen, Gregory of Nyssa, and the Biblical and Philosophical

church as Christ's body, is one of Gregory's favourite biblical passages as he reflects on the bride's identity. Gregory fastens on a reference to the Bridegroom's eyes being as doves (Song 5:12) as an occasion to comment on the need for a combination of the contemplative life (eyes) and the active life (hands), since St. Paul maintains that the eyes cannot dismiss the hands as unnecessary (1 Cor 12:21).[111] Repeatedly, Gregory focuses on the leaders of the church as being the "eyes" of the body.[112] The church as the body of Christ is of obvious importance to Gregory for the believers' growth in virtue and so for their participatory journey of salvation in God.[113] It is in and through the church as the body of Christ that the soul exchanges her tunic of hide for the new bodily garment of Christ himself. Or, to put it differently, the new tunic of Christ and the fellowship of the church are essential and closely linked bodily means of salvation.

Gregory thus regards bodily garments (the "new tunic" of Christ) and the body of the church as indispensable means for the anagogical transposition of all humanity. The new tunic and the church are, indeed, saving bodies, though, of course, the church's saving role is entirely dependent on and subservient to that of Christ. Gregory focuses on these bodies, the body of Christ in the incarnation as the "new tunic" for believers and the body of the church, in order to effect a salvific transposition. This transposition means that the life of virtue and bodily renunciation are integral to Gregory's understanding of salvation. A twofold anagogical transposition—of the bodily senses and of the bodily text—lies at the heart of Gregory's understanding of the soul's saving participation in the life of God. The undue focus of some contemporary Gregory of Nyssa scholarship on the physical body, human sexuality, and passions such as human grief misinterpret him at a key point. They underestimate the centrality of anagogical transposition in his theology. In so doing they deprive him of a much needed voice in a cultural context in which it has become

---

Basis of the Doctrine of Apokatastasis," *VC* 61 (2007) 313–56. It seems to me that Gregory does not neatly resolve the tension between the universal reach of Christ's salvation through his human nature and the requirement of the soul and of the church to conform to Christ.

111. *Homilies* 13, 415. Cf. *Homilies* 14, 431 for a similar reference.

112. *Homilies* 7, 227–29; 13, 417.

113. See also *Homilies* 13, 403; 14, 445–47; 14, 449. The significance of the church is such that Gregory, rather like St. Augustine, can describe the church as Christ himself. Thus, in *In illud: Tunc et ipse filius*, Gregory explains the reference to Christ's submission in 1 Cor 15:28 as the eschatological submission of the body of Christ (which he interprets as all of humanity). See GNO III/2, 2–28; ET: Casimir McCambley, "When (the Father) Will Subject All Things to (the Son) Then (the Son) Himself Will Be Subjected to Him (the Father) Who Subjects All Things to Him (the Son) A Treatise on First Corinthians 15:28 by Saint Gregory of Nyssa," *Greek Orthodox Theological Review* 28 (1983) 1–25.

difficult to look beyond this-worldly bodies, both in terms of the physical body and its passions and in terms of the body of the biblical text. Gregory's theology offers a salutary reminder that Christ and the church are the saving bodies that graciously lead us upward through the bodily senses and the bodily text into the life of God.

RANSOMED, HEALED, RESTORED, FORGIVEN (JOHN 5:1-16)

Carol M. Norén

During the years that I have taught preaching here at North Park, I have become aware of some fairly predictable patterns in biblical interpretation. By predictable patterns I mean that if I set a particular passage of Scripture in front of the introductory class—people who probably have not worked substantively with the text before—they will gravitate toward engaging the Word in certain ways. No one tells them to do this. North Park does not have a doctrinal statement that students must sign in order to graduate or get a letter of reference. Yet the majority follows just a few well-worn paths into a pericope.

For example, when dealing with a narrative such as today's Gospel reading, women students will nearly always identify with the least powerful person in the text, especially if the character is female. They are more prone to focus on relational dynamics and impute motives that cannot be established in the text. So in the story of healing the lame man on the Sabbath, I would anticipate an amplification of the text, having the lame man's sufferings made more vivid, and imagining what was going on in Jesus' mind when he saw a person who had been disabled for thirty-eight years. On the other hand, men students in general will stand a little bit outside the scene, identify the good guys vs. the bad guys, and direct the action, perhaps reminiscent of playing with toy soldiers or trucks. That means in this passage the conflict between Jesus and the Jewish authorities will take center stage, and the power and rightness of Jesus will be highlighted.

But lest you think I am reducing biblical interpretation to a question of gender, let me identify a few other well-worn paths. A student with a passion for social justice will always be quick to see the socio-political dynamics of the gospel. Such a student will zero in on the location where Jesus encountered the lame man: an area northeast of the Temple where sheep were brought into town for sacrifice. It was a very public place in the Holy City, where over the years thousands of religious people would have walked by the lame man and his comrades in affliction. But not one of those pious people helped him into the pool when the water was troubled. How many of us today are guilty of the same blithe pococurantism towards "the least of these, Christ's brothers and sisters?" Then there will be the student who has been reading Tertullian or already had a sacramental orientation, who will liken the pool by which the man lay to the waters of baptism, Jesus' question and the answer to catechesis, and rising and taking up one's bed to resurrection. Still another pattern or orientation will be expressed by an international student or someone lucky enough to have studied abroad. This preacher will use Powerpoint slides showing the layout of the Temple precincts, use a laser pointer to identify the Sheep Gate, and compare the intermittent spring that caused the water to bubble with other interesting and often beautiful pools in the ancient Middle East that were reputed to have healing power. Such a sermon fills my mind with thoughts of redemption—redemption of my frequent flyer miles, that is!

There is one last predictable way of engaging the text that I want to note: a route I know well, because I so often take it myself. The path is taken by many Kern scholars who are anxious to maintain the grade point average necessary for their scholarships, by seniors and graduates who are candidating for a pastoral call, by faculty members intimidated by the prospect of preaching to a community of scholars. Rather than developing a message with a single focus, a preacher on this path tries to look everywhere at once, to read just six more commentaries and consult five on-line resources before trying to proclaim everything a passage could possibly have to say. You can imagine the sort of sermon on today's text that would result. We would start off with some general observations about the authorship, date, and theological emphases of John's Gospel as compared to the Synoptics, note that this is the second healing miracle in John, and compare it to the healing of another paralytic recorded in Mark 2. We would spend some time asking why, unlike other stories of healing, this account includes no confession of faith on the part of the afflicted or a person seeking help for the afflicted, no thanksgiving or doxology afterward, and no words of challenge from onlookers. The sermon would include discussion of whether the Sabbath motif is a secondary addition to the healing narrative or part of the original story. Perhaps there would be speculation on possible underlying anti-Semitism in the Fourth Gospel. At its extreme, such a sermon would take refuge behind exegetical minutiae and information overload and keep the Word a safe distance from addressing us.

Indeed, it does address us, as we conclude a symposium on atonement, God reconciling the world to himself in Christ. The predictable paths of engagement with the text that I have outlined all have varying degrees of homiletical merit, but one aspect of this story that sets it apart from other healings, that connects with the atonement and gives us hope is in v. 6. It says Jesus saw the man, he knew about him, and he said to him, "Do you want to be healed?" Our Lord took the initiative toward him. Even though the lame man grumbled and did not give a straight answer, God made the first move. Even while he placed his trust in animistic folklore, grace was extended. Even as he was oblivious to the identity of Love Incarnate, wholeness and new life were offered. He did not have to get his act together before God's Son could restore him. The same is true for us. While we were still weak, at the right time Christ died for the ungodly. While we were yet sinners, Christ died for us (Rom 8:6, 8).

Jesus approached someone who did not know enough to ask him for help. Our Savior put a question to him: "Do you want to be healed?" It may impress us as a strange query with an obvious answer, but the obvious answer was not what the man gave. He replied, "I have no one to put me into the pool." Did he expect Jesus to hang around until the next time the water was troubled? It sounds to me more like a *defensive* answer from someone who could not imagine life being any different or better. We should keep in mind that this was not a private conversation. At least some of the disciples were present, and also present were invalids, blind, lame, or paralyzed people. Some Jewish authorities who took a dim view of healing on the Sabbath were listening in. This exchange was *meant* to be overheard, and the Gospel writer makes sure we hear it too. Lameness was not the only affliction the Messiah witnessed that day. He saw prejudice, apathy, malice, pride, self-satisfaction, and all manner of sin needing to be forgiven and healed. Jesus manifested grace and ultimately shed his blood as ransom for them too—for the sins of the whole world. God knows what needs to be redeemed and restored in each of us today. You may be able to describe some of the brokenness in your life, but you cannot name it all as God can, because he knows you better than you know yourself. Do you want to be healed? Are you ready for life to change beyond what you can hope or imagine by the power of Christ's Holy Spirit at work within you? Will you receive this gift, this grace, or will you erect barricades of debate about the identity of the One who offers it?

The story does not end there. After the healing, Jesus disappeared into the crowd, but later in the temple he sought out and found the man he had healed and spoke to him again. Now the man learns who made him whole, and he is advised how to live as one who has been delivered. John's Gospel shows us that grace continues to abound even after healing; we live into the redemption wrought by Christ who never fails us nor forsakes us (Heb 13:5). The Triune God still seeks us out and shows us the way forward. The Gospel reveals the nature of Christ, bears witness to

Jesus' relationship to the Father, and testifies that the Spirit is working still. In Christ we are a new creation, but a creation in process. God is not finished with us yet. As the Apostle Paul put it, now we know in part; then we shall understand fully, even as we have been fully understood (1 Cor 13:12).

There is a future promised for the lame man who was healed, and not just to him. The same promise held for the disciples, for the Jewish authorities, for people of every time and place. Further on in this chapter Jesus declared, "as the Father raises the dead and gives them life, so also the Son gives life to whom he will . . . . Truly, truly I say to you, whoever hears my word and believes him who sent me has *eternal* life; he does not come into judgment, but has passed from death to life" (John 5:21, 24). This is the fulfillment we await, the "future all sublime" we await, the good news we are entrusted to share with others: "the grace that's brought us safe thus far, is the grace that will lead us home." Thanks be to God for his inexpressible gift (2 Cor 9:15).

BIBLIOGRAPHY

Anderson, Gary A. *Sin: A History.* New Haven, CT: Yale University Press, 2009. A compelling presentation on the biblical and Jewish roots of the Anselmian perspective of the atonement, specifically from the economic angle.

Andersson, Axel. *The Christian Doctrine of the Atonement according to P. P. Waldenström.* Chicago: Covenant, 1937. Andersson provides access for English readers to Waldenström's view of the atonement. Waldenström sought to be as scripturally based as possible and insisted on biblical backing for any argument being made. The issue with atonement is not that God needed to be reconciled to us but rather that we needed to be reconciled to God.

Anselm of Canterbury, "Why God Became Man [Cur Deus Homo]." Pages 260–356 in *Anselm of Canterbury: The Major Works.* Edited by Brian Davies and Gillian Evans. New York: Oxford University Press, 1998. Anselm's systematic treatment of "Why God Became Man" is the primary example of what has come to be known as the "satisfaction" model of atonement. However, in reading this treatment of God's necessary action in paying for humanity's sins, there is more than a mere transactional model. Anselm's discussion is not merely about righteousness but must be considered in respect to his discussions on prayer and the nature of human life which are also parts of this collection.

Augustine. *The Trinity.* Translated by E. Hill. Brooklyn: New City, 1991. In this sweeping and demanding treatise, Augustine searches for his God—the Father, Son, and Holy Spirit. In books four and thirteen he discusses in some depth the saving ministry of Jesus.

Aulén, Gustaf. *Christus Victor.* Translated by A. G. Hebert. London: Society for Promoting Christian Knowledge, 1931. Many Christians, not content with the satisfaction theory of atonement, find a focus on Christ's triumph over evil to be more fitting. Aulén argues this model is the "classic" interpretation of atonement and takes his reader through history in order to prove it.

Averbeck, Richard E. "כָּפַר (*kāpar* II)." Pages 689–710 in vol. 2 of *New International Dictionary of Old Testament Theology and Exegesis.* Edited by William A. VanGemeren. Grand Rapids: Zondervan, 1997. This entry in the excellent *NIDOTTE* presents ancient Near Eastern data, discusses various theories of meaning for *KPR*, and covers biblical texts using this root. The author sees three main results of atonement: consecration, purification, and forgiveness.

Balthasar, Hans Urs von. *Mysterium Paschale: The Mystery of Easter.* San Francisco: Ignatius, 1990. Balthasar's work considers the mystery of Easter and shows the importance not only of the cross as an atoning work but also of Christ's death bound to both his incarnation and his resurrection. This work is both deeply theological and pastoral.

Banks, Robert, ed. *Reconciliation and Hope: New Testament Essays on Atonement and Eschatology.* Grand Rapids: Eerdmans, 1974. This collection of essays puts an eschatalogical focus on atonement, justification, and reconciliation. Part I (reconciliation) especially deals with Christ's death, resurrection, and atonement.

Bantum, Brian. *Redeeming Mulatto: A Theology of Race and Christian Hybridity*. Waco, TX: Baylor University Press, 2010. This text describes the significance of Christ's being human and divine but also places Christ's death in relationship to the contemporary reality of modern "interracial" existence and the bodily and social death that so often accompanies those victimized by racism. Bantum understands Jesus as a radical unity of flesh and Spirit that can be mirrored through the modern phenomenon of the "interracial" or mulatto person.

Barth, Karl. *The Doctrine of Reconciliation*. Edited by G. W. Bromily. London: Continuum, 2004. This synthesis of volume 4 of Karl Barth's *Church Dogmatics* provides some of the essential aspects of Barth's discussion of God's reconciling work, especially the importance of considering Christ as Immanuel or "God with us."

———. *The Great Promise*. Eugene, OR: Wipf and Stock, 2004. In considering the atoning work of Christ it is crucial to understand the child that was born to die. Reflecting on the events related to the incarnation, *The Great Promise* is an exegesis of Luke 1 that opens up an interpretive framework through which the reader can understand the possibility of life and death already present in Christ's conception.

Baxter, Christina A. "The Cursed Beloved: A Reconsideration of Penal Substitution." Pages 54–72 in *Atonement Today*. Edited by John Goldingay. London: Society for Promoting Christian Knowledge, 1995. Baxter offers a refined view of the penal substitution model of the atonement and seeks to reintegrate the rehabilitated model into mainstream soteriology.

Beilby, James and Paul R. Eddy, eds. *The Nature of the Atonement: Four Views, With Contributions by Gregory A. Boyd, Joel B. Green, Bruce R. Reichenbach, and Thomas R. Schreiner*. Downer's Grove, IL: InterVarsity, 2006. This compilation of essays offers an overview of atonement and major models attempting to explain it. The respective authors present the Christus victor, penal substitution, healing, and kaleidoscopic (multivalent) interpretations of the atonement and critique the models other authors present.

Boersma, Hans. *Violence, Hospitality, and the Cross: Reappropriating the Atonement Tradition*. Grand Rapids: Baker Academic, 2004. This book provides a reappropriation of traditional atonement theories in light of contemporary criticisms related to violence and retributive punishment. Drawing on the Reformed tradition, along with an appreciation of the ecumenical conversation, the author links the paradox of redemptive violence to the unconditional nature of God's eschatological hospitality.

Bonhoeffer, Dietrich. *Christ the Center*. New York: Harper & Row, 1960. Bonhoeffer's lectures on Christology emphasize the importance of maintaining a deep connection between Christ's person and work. He explains that to understand Christ's atoning work on the cross as the "humiliated one" we must also understand his person as fully God.

Brondos, David. *Fortress Introduction to Salvation and the Cross*. Minneapolis: Fortress, 2007. Brondos surveys ten soteriological models and the role of the cross in each. He includes material from the NT, early theologians, and contemporary contributions.

Brown, Raymond E. *The Death of the Messiah: From Gethsemane to the Grave: A Commentary on the Passion Narratives in the Four Gospels*. Vol 1. New York: Doubleday, 1994. Brown follows the story of the four canonical gospel passion narratives, scene by scene, as the evangelists recorded them. The aim of the work is to "explain what the evangelists intended and conveyed to their audiences by their narratives." This is accomplished through analysis of the text, history, and theology in each narrative.

Brueggeman, Walter. *In Reverberations of Faith: A Theological Handbook of Old Testament Themes*. Louisville: Westminster John Knox, 2002. Brueggeman provides a helpful overview of key themes in the OT. His treatment of atonement is especially helpful in framing how atonement was understood in the early practice of Israel.

Carroll, John T., and Joel B. Green. *The Death of Jesus in Early Christianity*. Peabody, MA: Hendrickson, 1995. A scholarly treatment of the death of Jesus in the various NT writings. There are also additional essays on related historical and theological issues.

Clifton-Soderstrom, Michelle A. "Where is it Written? Understanding the Cross and the Church's Ministry of Love." *Covenant Companion* (April, 2008) 13–15. This article revisits Paul Peter Waldenström's view of the doctrine of the atonement and addresses what Scripture says about forgiveness and repayment. This is joined with an application of how reconciliation and "at-onement" are important for the church.

Daley, Brian E. "'He Himself is Our Peace' (Eph 2:14): Early Christian Views of Redemption in Christ." Pages 149–176 in *The Redemption: An Interdisciplinary Symposium on Christ as Redeemer*. Edited by Stephen T. Davis, Daniel Kendall and Gerald O'Collins. Oxford: Oxford University Press, 2004. This article emphases that early Christians focused less on "what Jesus did" to promote salvation, and more on "who Jesus is."

Daly, Robert J. *The Origins of the Christian Doctrine of Sacrifice*. Philadelphia: Fortress, 1973. This brief history follows the progression of the Christian doctrine from the OT practice of burnt offerings to NT and early Church Father's writings on sacrifice. Atonement is viewed in both its OT sin-offering context and through a crucifixion lens.

Deane-Drummond, Celia. *Christ and Evolution: Wonder and Wisdom*. Theology and the Sciences. Minneapolis: Fortress, 2009. A fresh and powerful reading of the atonement in the light of the cross and evolutionary biology.

Denney, James. *The Christian Doctrine of Reconciliation: The Cunningham Lectures for 1917*. New York: George H. Doran Company, 1918. This collection of lectures deals with the scholarly and practical voices on reconciliation as found in the NT and in early Christian thought. Chapter five deals specifically with reconciliation as achieved by Christ.

———. *The Death of Christ*. Edited by R. V. G. Tasker. London: Tyndale, 1956. Denney focuses on Christ's death as a central subject of NT writings, following the theme through the

Gospels, Letters, early Christian preaching, and theology. He then deals with several "modern" problems with the atonement.

Dillistone, F. W. *The Christian Understanding of Atonement.* Philadelphia: Westminster, 1968. Through "analogues" and "parables" Dillistone covers several expressions of the atonement including sacrifice, redemption, tragedy, judgement, compassion, forgiveness, integration, and reconciliation.

Dodd, C. H. *The Bible and the Greeks.* 2nd ed. London: Hodder and Stoughton, 1954. This is a classic study of the influence of Hellenistic culture on Judaism. Chapter five is devoted to atonement. The author concluded that the Greek translators of the OT understood *KPR* as *expiation* rather than *propitiation*.

Driver, John. *Understanding the Atonement for the Mission of the Church.* Scottdale, Pa: Herald, 1986. After a brief survey and critique of principle atonement theories, Driver covers the primary biblical images of atonement. All of this is then worked into the implications of these images for the church with a focus on restoration and community.

Duff, Nancy J. "Atonement and the Christian Life: Reformed Doctrine from a Feminist Perspective," *Interpretation* 53 (January 1999) 21-33. This is a balanced and nuanced presentation of the atonement from a feminist perspective. This whole issue of *Interpretation* is devoted to treatment of atonement.

Ek, Henry E. *Dr P. P. Waldenström's Theory of the Atonement.* Chicago: Henry E. Ek, 1925. Ek provides another explanation in English of Waldenström's theory of atonement. Waldentröm believed strongly that the atonement was about humanity's reconciliation with God and rejected the idea that God needed to be reconciled to humanity since God's character is defined by love. Waldentröm focused on biblical evidence and argued against misconceptions of atonement.

Fiddes, Paul S. *Past Event and Present Salvation.* London: Darton, Longman & Todd, 1989. This book addresses the question of how the atonement relates to the human situation, particularly how the crucifixion as an historical event relates to the ongoing process and experience of salvation in the present. Atonement images drawn from biblical texts and theological interpretation are considered and drawn into conversation with social and political issues facing contemporary human existence.

Fortin, John R., ed. *Saint Anselm—His Origins and Influence.* Texts and Studies in Religion. Vol 91. Lewiston, NY: Edwin Mellen, 2001. This work is comprised of essays which seek to give a holistic portrayal of Anselm of Canterbury. His influence in the subject of the atonement is unparalleled, and this background information on his identity allows the reader better to understand his theology.

Frisk, Donald C. *Covenant Affirmations: This We Believe.* Chicago: Covenant, 1981. This book is an attempt to present in a relatively small volume the basic theological affirmations of the Evangelical Covenant Church, including images and implications of atonement.

Girard, René. *Things Hidden since the Foundation of the World.* Translated by Stephen Bann and Michael Metteer. Palo Alto, CA: Stanford University Press, 1987. Originally written in French, this is a more theory-driven look at sacrifice and atonement through anthropological, psychological, and scriptural lenses. Girard seeks an escape from the violence of the world.

Goldingay, John, ed. *Atonement Today*. London: Society for Promoting Christian Knowledge, 1995. This is an examination of the biblical teaching and the church's doctrinal tradition of atonement, especially the Evangelical tradition. Issues such as feminism, interfaith dialogue, and pastoral theology are covered.

———. *Israel's Faith*. Vol. 2 of *Old Testament Theology*. Downers Grove, IL: InterVarsity, 2006. This work looks at the OT portrayal of the character of God. By treating scriptural passages that speak of God, one is better able to understand the Bible and its relevance for our lives.

Gorman, Michael J. *Cruciformity: Paul's Narrative Spirituality of the Cross*. Grand Rapids: Eerdmans, 2001. Gorman argues the cross is the shape as well as the source of salvation, and he shows how the cross is connected to ethics, spirituality, and ecclesiology.

———. *Inhabiting the Cruciform God: Kenosis, Justification, and Theosis in Paul's Narrative Soteriology*. Grand Rapids: Eerdmans, 2009. Gorman provides an argument for theosis—becoming like God by participation in the life of God—as the fundamental effect of Christ's death, the meaning of justification, and the center of Paul's theology.

Gorringe, Timothy. *God's Just Vengeance*. Cambridge Studies in Ideology. Vol 9. Cambridge: Cambridge University Press, 1996. There has always been a tension between church and state, law and religion. Gorringe sees this relationship as one that relates to atonement; in order fully to understand the atonement one must see the relationship between atonement and penalty.

Grant, Jacquelyn. *White Women's Christ and Black Women's Jesus: Feminist Christology and Womanist Response*. Atlanta: Scholar's, 1989. This book offers a critique of feminist theologians' articulation of christological issues and the method of feminist theology, arguing that they reflect the experience of white women predominantly and fail to speak to the concerns of non-white women. It sets forth a womanist theology and Christology that emerge from and are adequate to the reality of contemporary black women.

Grayston, Kenneth. *Dying, We Live: A New Enquiry into the Death of Christ in the New Testament*. New York: Oxford University Press, 1990. This is a text-by-text exegetical look at scriptural references dealing with death and resurrection in the NT.

Green, Joel B., and Mark D. Baker. *Recovering the Scandal of the Cross: Atonement in New Testament & Contemporary Contexts*. Downers Grove, IL: InterVarsity, 2000. The authors explore how the atonement has been understood within a variety of contemporary contexts, both Western and non-Western, and show how we can enter into the thoroughly Christian mission of restating the saving scandal of the cross in our multicultural world of the twenty-first century.

Greene-McCreight, Kathryn. *Feminist Reconstructions of Christian Doctrine: Narrative Analysis and Appraisal*. New York: Oxford University Press, 2000. Holding to a narrative view of Scripture, the author examines the relationship between feminist theology and classical Christian theology. The book provides an evaluation of a wide range of mainline feminist theologians and how they use the Bible to undergird their theological reconstructions of various Christian doctrines such as sin, Christology, and the Trinity.

Gregorios, Paulos Mar. *Cosmic Man: The Divine Presence: The Theology of St. Gregory of Nyssa (ca 330 to 395 A.D.)*. 1980; reprint, New York: Paragon, 1988. This book gives an excellent and readable introduction to Gregory's thought. The anti-Western attitude of the Orthodox author may be somewhat bothersome at times, but the author has a very good sense of where Gregory is coming from.

Gregory of Nyssa. *Address on Religious Instruction*. Pages 268–325 in *Christology of the Later Fathers*. Edited by E. R. Hardy. Philadelphia: Westminster, 1954. This important Cappadocian treatise offers one of the earliest, extended accounts of the "Christus Victor" theory that Gustaf Aulén championed. Perhaps more interesting in this treatise is Gregory's clear insistence that an account of Jesus' crucifixion needs to portray God's role in this death fittingly. Note the many attributes of God he finds confirmed in Jesus' death.

Grieb, A. Katherine. "'So That in Him We Might Become the Righteousness of God' (2 Cor 5:21): Some Theological Reflections on the Church Becoming Justice." *Ex Auditu* 22 (2006) 58–80. An important interpretation of atonement in Paul that integrates the apostle's understanding of atonement, justification, and justice.

Gunton, Colin E. *The Actuality of Atonement: A Study of Metaphor, Rationality and the Christian Tradition*. London: T. & T. Clark, 2003. This is a reissue of Gunton's 1988 examination of the doctrine of atonement and the nature of theological language that expresses it. He considers traditional metaphors drawn from the battlefield, the altar, and the law courts, examining their meaning for contemporary Christianity.

Harrisville, Roy A. *Fracture: The Cross as Irreconcilable in the Language and Thought of the Biblical Writers*. Grand Rapids: Eerdmans, 2006. A creative exploration of the continuities and discontinuities between NT interpretations of the cross and the cultural environments (Jewish and non-Jewish) in which they were formulated.

Hayes, John H. "Atonement in the Book of Leviticus," *Interpretation* 52 (January, 1998) 5–15. This article is an accessible primer to the biblical view of sacrifice and atonement according to Leviticus, with a particular focus on ch. 16.

Heim, S. Mark. *Saved from Sacrifice: A Theology of the Cross*. Grand Rapids: Eerdmans, 2006. Heim addresses the paradox of the Jesus' crucifixion, an event that is filled with saving power and profound tragedy. Working from the foundation laid by René Girard, he develops his theology of the atonement in light of the history of violence resulting from human scapegoating. The crucifixion is presented as both a saving act of God and a sinful act of humanity.

Hengel, Martin. *The Atonement: The Origins of the Doctrine in the New Testament*. Philadelphia: Fortress, 1981. As the title suggests, this work attends to the shaping of atonement theology in the first-century, Graeco-Roman world. Despite being short, this is a valuable work. Hengel deals with the context from which atonement theology arose as well as the soteriological interpretation of Jesus' death by Paul and other NT sources.

Heyer, C. J. den. *Jesus and the Doctrine of the Atonement: Biblical Notes on a Controversial Topic.* Translated by J. Bowden. Harrisburg, PA: Trinity Press International, 1998. Heyer investigates every NT passage relating to the death of Jesus in an attempt to understand what Jesus' intentions were and to compare those intentions with later Christian doctrine on atonement. Working solely from the NT text, Heyer sees a substantial gap between what the Gospels and Epistles say about Jesus' death and what has been said in Christian doctrine.

Hooker, Morna D. "Did the Use of Isaiah 53 to Interpret His Mission Begin with Jesus?" Pages 88–103 in *Jesus and the Suffering Servant: Isaiah 53 and Christian Origins.* Edited by William H. Bellinger Jr. and William R. Farmer. Harrisburg, PA: Trinity Press International, 1998. This volume is a collection of views on how Isaiah 53 (the Suffering Servant) is interpreted through a Christian lens. This specific chapter focuses on Jesus' use of the text and whether it was Jesus or Paul who first connected Isaiah's teaching with atoning sacrifice.

———. "Interchange and Suffering." Pages 70–83 in *Suffering and Martyrdom in the New Testament.* Edited by William Horbury and Brian McNeil. Cambridge: Cambridge University Press, 1981. This is one of four articles in which Hooker advocates for "interchange" as a helpful metaphor for understanding atonement. She focuses on Pauline teaching on identification with Christ and its relation to atonement, participation theories, substitution, and suffering.

———. *From Adam to Christ: Essays on Paul.* Cambridge: Cambridge University Press, 1990; reprint, Eugene, OR: Wipf and Stock, 2008. A collection of essays that includes classic treatments of Paul's interpretations of Christ's death as "interchange," holding together incarnation, atonement, and ethics.

———. *Not Ashamed of the Gospel: New Testament Interpretations of the Death of Christ.* Grand Rapids: Eerdmans, 1994. A succinct yet comprehensive overview of the significance of Jesus' death in the various NT writings.

Janowski, Bernd. *Sühne als Heilsgeschehen.* WMANT 55. Neukirchen-Vluyn: Neukirchener Verlag, 1982. An exhaustive study of the root *KPR* in Semitic languages and in the OT.

Jones, Serene. *Feminist Theory and Christian Theology: Cartographies of Grace.* Minneapolis: Fortress, 2000. This book presents two sets of "maps," one from feminist theory and the other from Christian theology, and explores the debates within each to suggest new approaches to Christian doctrine. This is complemented by specific narratives from women's lives which provide the context for theological analysis. Theological anthropology, the doctrine of God, Christology, and pneumatology are all considered.

Jüngel, Eberhard. *Justification: The Heart of the Christian Faith.* Translated by Jeffrey F. Cayzer. Edinburgh: T. & T. Clark, 2001. Precipitated by the Lutheran-Roman Catholic Joint Declaration on the Doctrine of Justification and intended for pastors and thoughtful laypersons, this book examines the role of justification in Christian faith, emphasizing its central importance. The author develops the subject from within a Trinitarian framework to establish justification as a relational concept. It also provides valuable systematic presentations of the doctrines of sin, evil, and grace.

Käsemann, Ernest. "The Saving Significance of the Death of Jesus in Paul." Pages 32–59 in Ernest Käsemann. *Perspectives on Paul.* Translated by M. Kohl. Philadelphia: Fortress, 1971. This is a classic treatment of Paul's understanding of atonement with emphasis on the fact that the gift cannot be separated from the Giver.

Kiuchi, N. *The Purification Offering in the Priestly Literature.* JSOT Supplement Series 56. Sheffield: Sheffield Academic, 1987. This is a valuable and well-organized study of ḥaṭṭāʾt (purification or sin offering) in the OT. Because of the close connection of the offering with *KPR*, it is a great contribution to the study of "atonement texts" as well. Regarding *KPR* the author concludes, that it is a hypernym of expressions like "purify," "sanctify" and "de-sin."

Lawson, Todd. *The Crucifixion and the Qur'an: A Study in the History of Muslim Thought.* Oxford: Oneworld, 2009. This book, along with Zahniser's *The Mission and Death of Jesus in Islam and Christianity* (below), offers an able orientation to Jesus' death as seen from Muslim perspectives.

Louth, Andrew. *Discerning the Mystery: An Essay on the Nature of Theology.* 1983; reprint, Oxford: Clarendon, 2003. This may be the best introduction to allegorical exegesis available today. Louth places the topic in the context of Western cultural and philosophical developments that have rendered contemplative exegesis suspect and have allowed modern exegesis to become subject to the search for a "method" of interpretation.

Love, Gregory. *Love, Violence and the Cross: How the Nonviolent God Saves Us Through the Cross of Christ.* Eugene, OR: Cascade, 2010. Love provides a discussion of support, problems, and alternatives to the penal substitution model of the atonement. Ultimately the author points toward a "salvific death effected by a nonviolent God."

Lubac, Henri de. *Scripture in the Tradition.* Translated by Luke O'Neill, 1968. New York: Crossroad, 2000. De Lubac was a Catholic theologian who did a great deal in the mid-twentieth century to recover patristic and medieval exegesis. This book is an excellent and readable introduction that treats many of the common objections to allegory.

Maimela, S. S. "The Atonement in the Context of Liberation Theology." *International Review of Mission* 75 (1986) 261–69. A survey of traditional understandings of atonement with a more specific look at how liberation theology has led to a broader understanding of the significance of Jesus' life and death, especially as it applies to oppressed peoples.

Martens, Peter. "The Quest for the Anabaptist Atonement: Violence and Nonviolence in J. Denny Weaver's *The Nonviolent Atonement.*" *The Mennonite Quarterly Review* 82 (April 2008) 281–327. Martens critiques Weaver's Anabaptist model of a nonviolent atonement, claiming that the model does not do justice to the kind of nonviolence displayed by Jesus in the Gospels. The article includes Weaver's response to Martens.

Bibliography

McDonald, H. D. *The Atonement of the Death of Christ in Faith, Revelation, and History.* Grand Rapids: Baker, 1985. This book provides a broad overview of atonement from the early church and the NT to Gustavo Gutiérrez. The number of scholars treated is surprising.

———. *Forgiveness and Atonement.* Grand Rapids: Baker, 1984. In this shorter work McDonald looks at forgiveness and revelation, Christ, grace, justification, guilt, experience, and atonement. The last chapter looks specifically at atonement as sacrifice and as substitution.

McKnight, Scot. *A Community Called Atonement.* Nashville: Abingdon, 2007. This is an insightful exploration of the various dimensions of the atonement and their implications for the life of the church as an alternative to narrow, monolithic views.

———. *Jesus and His Death: Historiography, the Historical Jesus, and Atonement Theory.* Waco, TX: Baylor University Press, 2005. McKnight provides a study of Jesus' own understanding of his death. He contends that Jesus anticipated his death as an atoning sacrifice, something that stood at the heart of his mission.

McKnight, Scot, Jason Clark, Kevin Corcoran, and Peter Rollins. *Church in the Present Tense: A Candid Look at What's Emerging.* Grand Rapids: Brazos, 2011. This work is a collection of views on the emerging church, including its view of philosophy, theology, worship, Bible, and doctrine. Scot McKnight deals specifically with the atonement in his chapter, "Atonement and Gospel" (chapter 8).

Melito of Sardis. *On Pascha.* Translated by A. Stewart-Sykes. Crestwood, NY: St. Vladimir's Seminary Press, 2001. This short, accessible work provides a figurative interpretation of the Passover in the book of Exodus, seeing in it an anticipatory type or model of Jesus' later crucifixion. Alongside the Day of Atonement outlined in the book of Leviticus, Passover was instrumental in early Christian attempts to see Jesus' saving death foreshadowed in the law and prophets.

Milgrom, Jacob. "Sin-Offering or Purification-Offering?" *Vetus Testamentum* 21 (1971) 237-39. Milgrom explores the theological understanding of the Hebrew *ḥaṭṭāʾt* (an offering for ritual purification).

Morris, Leon. *The Apostolic Preaching of the Cross.* Grand Rapids: Eerdmans, 1965. In this classic work on penal substitution Morris' purpose is to define the major biblical terms involved in theological discussions about the atonement. Through understanding the meaning of words like "propitiation" or "justification," one can understand what is at stake in the discussion of atonement.

———. *The Atonement: Its Meaning & Significance.* Downers Grove, IL: InterVarsity, 1983. Here Morris explores covenant, sacrifice, the Jewish Day of Atonement, Passover, redemption, reconciliation, propitiation, and justification as a means to understand the broad biblical dimensions of salvation by atonement.

———. *The Cross in the New Testament.* Grand Rapids: Eerdmans, 1977. For Morris the subject of atonement is synonymous with the cross. He traces this theme through the NT to gain a holistic view of the cross within Christianity. He finds and argues that Christ's death on the cross substitutes for the death we, as sinners, should have had; this then is the true meaning of atonement.

Moule, C. F. D. *Forgiveness and Reconciliation and Other New Testament Themes.* London: Society for Promoting Christian Knowledge, 1998. These collected works of Moule, a sterling scholar and Christian of a previous generation, blend history, language, and literature to address crucial theological topics. These essays treat the theology of forgiveness, Christology, the Holy Spirit, the Eucharist, Jesus-Traditions, and the authority of Scripture. A few of the essays deal explicitly with atonement theology, including "Preaching the Atonement" and "Retribution or Restoration?"

Mozley, John Kenneth. *The Doctrine of the Atonement.* London: Duckworth & Co., 1915; reprint, 1953. This older, well-known study gives a historical and descriptive study of the formation of atonement doctrine from both Testaments and historical theologies down through the Reformation.

Nestorius. *First Sermon Against the "Theotokos."* Pages 123–31 in *The Christological Controversy.* Edited and translated by R. A. Norris, Jr. Philadelphia: Fortress, 1980. This short text offers a lucid Antiochene account of how Jesus' death "paid our debts." Here is a notable early use of the sort of financial language Anselm would utilize much later, though not in dependence upon Nestorius.

Noel, James A., and Matthew V. Johnson, eds. *The Passion of the Lord: African American Reflections.* Minneapolis: Fortress, 2005. These reflections on the passion of Christ by black theologians offers crucial insight about how the power of the cross not only speaks of a spiritual cleansing but how Christ's suffering reverberates within the lives of those who suffer presently.

O'Keefe, John J., and R. R. Reno. *Sanctified Vision: An Introduction to Early Christian Interpretation of the Bible.* Baltimore: Johns Hopkins University Press, 2005. O'Keefe and Reno provide numerous exegetical examples to show what motivated the early Fathers in their exegesis of Scripture. This book is quite readable while at the same time giving significant information.

Origen. *The Commentaries of Origen and Jerome on St. Paul's Epistle to the Ephesians.* Oxford Early Christian Studies. Translated and edited by Ronald E. Heine. Oxford: Oxford University Press, 2002. This text provides helpful insight into interpretations of the book of Ephesians offered by two of the most important scholars in the early church. Of importance is the way Christ's atoning work was interpreted in light of the creation of a "new humanity."

Packer, J. I. "What Did the Cross Achieve? The Logic of Penal Substitution." Lecture presented at the Tyndale Bible Theology Lecture. Cambridge, July 17, 1973. Packer seeks to clarify misconceptions about the model of penal substitution and to rehabilitate the understanding of Christ as substitution.

Parsons, Susan Frank, ed. *The Cambridge Companion to Feminist Theology.* Cambridge: Cambridge University Press, 2002. This book is a helpful introduction to the discipline of feminist theology and offers critique and reconstruction. The book is divided into two sections, the first considering the overall shape of feminist theology and the second exploring subjects of specific doctrinal importance such as the Trinity, Christology, and eschatology.

Paul, Robert S. *The Atonement and the Sacraments: The Relation of the Atonement to the Sacraments of Baptism and the Lord's Supper.* Nashville: Abingdon, 1960. This is an influential discussion of the relation of atonement to the sacraments. It includes among other things a historical treatment of the meaning of the word "atonement" and a theology of atonement starting with the early church fathers.

Peacore, Linda D. *The Role of Women's Experience in Feminist Theologies of Atonement.* Eugene, OR: Pickwick, 2010. This book analyzes the category of women's experience, including its definition and use in feminist theology broadly, and its role in feminist atonement theologies specifically. Peacore surveys a wide range of feminist theologians and evaluates the strengths and limitations of feminist approaches to soteriology.

Pelikan, Jaroslav. *Jesus through the Centuries: His Place in the History of Culture.* New Haven, CT: Yale University Press, 1999. Pelikan's work is an immensely helpful discussion of how Jesus' person and work has been interpreted in the church's history. The historical record of how Jesus was received or his work interpreted highlights the varying weight that has been given to his divinity or his humanity, his weakness or his power, his commands or his obedience, or to his ministry and his work upon the cross. This work demonstrates how the atonement is always central to these conceptions but also how atonement is used in varied ways throughout Christian history.

Peterson, David, ed. *Where Wrath and Mercy Meet: Proclaiming the Atonement Today.* Carlisle, UK: Paternoster, 2001. This compilation of essays strives to reexamine the issue of penal substitution and other issues important within the atonement dialogue by examining different biblical perspectives and themes.

Phelan, John E., Jr. "René Girard and Paul Peter Waldenström: Reconsidering the Atonement." Pages 84–97 in *In Spirit and In Truth: Essays in Theology, Spirituality, and Embodiment in Honor of C. John Weborg.* Edited by Philip Anderson and Michelle Clifton-Soderstrom. Chicago: Covenant, 2006. This essay revisits the popular penal substitution view of the atonement. After a survey of criticisms, including a critique of Anselm's satisfaction model, Phelan offers aspects of Waldenström's view (against God as the one being reconciled) and of Girard's (concerning mimetic rivalry and scapegoats), pointing out that both emphasize the reconciling, community-creating effect of the cross.

Placher, William C. "Christ Takes Our Place: Rethinking Atonement," *Interpretation* 53 (January 1999) 5–20. Placher provides a well-argued reworking of atonement theory that affirms substitutionary atonement without falling into the penal perspective. This issue of *Interpretation* includes several different articles on atonement; including feminist, postmodern, and church-focused perspectives.

Rashdall, Hastings. *The Idea of Atonement in Christian Theology: Being the Bampton Lectures for 1915.* London: MacMillan, 1920. This older but quite influential work focuses on the actions of Jesus through his crucifixion and how this atoning event has been portrayed throughout Christianity. This work seeks to understand how the church viewed our atonement and Christ's participation in our atonement throughout different periods of history.

Robinson, H. Wheeler. *Redemption and Revelation in the Actuality of History*. London: Nisbet, 1947. This is another older but influential work. Robinson argues that Christ's death and resurrection are victorious, sacrificial, and representative in dealing with human sin.

———. *The Cross in the Old Testament*. Philadelphia: Westminster, 1955. This book combines three of Robinson's influential works: T*he Cross of Job, The Cross of the Servant,* and *The Cross of Jeremiah*. Robinson looks into the suffering of each biblical character in order to understand a biblical view of suffering.

Sanders, John, ed. *Atonement and Violence: A Theological Conversation*. Nashville: Abingdon, 2006. Through the articles and responses of Hans Boersma, T. Scott Daniels, Thomas Finger and J. Denny Weaver, this book wrestles with Christ's crucifixion and the suffering through violence he endured. The question raised is what role specifically God had in the crucifixion event. Was God tolerating or even promoting violence through this horrific death, or is he rather not involved in the actual physical event?

Schäfer, Peter. *Jesus in the Talmud*. Princeton: Princeton University Press, 2007. This insightful book explores the rabbinic assessment of Jesus in the Talmud. It offers important chapters on Jesus' sinful ministry and why, from a later Jewish perspective, he died.

Schwager, Raymund. *Must There Be Scapegoats? Violence and Redemption in the Bible*. Translated by Maria L. Assad. San Francisco: Harper & Row, 1987. Schwager argues that Jesus' sacrifice is not an act of appeasement of the Father and that the suffering and death is not compensation for an infinite offense against God. This study argues that God is not a God of violence and the atonement is evidence of this.

Shaw, Ian J., and Brian H. Edwards. *The Divine Substitute: The Atonement in the Bible and History*. St. Louis: Buswell Library, 2006. This book argues that the understanding of the death of Christ as a work of penal substitution is the principal way, though not the only way, in which the Bible views the death of Christ, and that far from being a recent teaching, it has been taught at every period in the history of the church.

Shelton, R. Larry. *Cross and Covenant: Interpreting the Atonement for 21st Century Mission*. Milton Keynes, UK: Paternoster, 2006. Shelton offers an incarnational and participatory interpretation of atonement similar to the work of Hooker and Gorman. In some contrast to traditional models, he argues that Christ's loving, sacrificial death restores the divine covenant with human communities and individuals.

Shepherd, Massey H., Jr., ed. and trans. *The Martyrdom of Polycarp*. Pages 141–58 in *Early Christian Fathers*. Edited and translated by C. C. Richardson. New York: Touchstone, 1996. For many Christians in the first three centuries of the church, the most obvious implication of Jesus' saving death for their lives was martyrdom. It is worth keeping in mind the ramifications of Jesus' death for Christian living, especially when we recall the persecutions that many Christians still endure around the globe today.

Smith, J. Warren. *Passion and Paradise: Human and Divine Emotion in the Thought of Gregory of Nyssa*. New York: Herder & Herder, 2004. This is a balanced and solid introduction to Gregory's understanding of the passions, of emotion, and of sexuality. Smith does not go along with some of the contemporary rereadings of Gregory, and the result is a fine (though fairly difficult) book.

Stevenson, Peter K., and Stephen I. Wright. *Preaching the Atonement*. Louisville: Westminster John Knox, 2009. Given that the atonement is not an easy topic for preaching, this book offers significant and informed help for those who have the task of doing justice to the biblical treatment of atonement and need insight into ways it can be communicated to people in the pew. The authors analyze ten specific texts and offer a sample sermon of each.

Stott, John R. W. *The Cross of Christ*. Downers Grove, IL: InterVarsity, 1986. With his typical clarity Stott focuses on the centrality of the cross, why Christ died, the self-substitution of God, and other topics on salvation, including living under the cross.

Stuhlmacher, Peter. *Reconciliation, Law, & Righteousness: Essays in Biblical Theology*. Philadelphia: Fortress, 1986. Stuhlmacher believes that reconciliation, law, and righteousness are prevalent themes in the NT because they were important to first-century Israel. In his essays he traces these themes throughout the Bible in order to provide a frame of reference for interpretation. His article on reconciliation is particularly important.

Sykes, Stephen. *The Story of Atonement. Trinity and Truth*. London: Darton, Longman & Todd, 1997. Sykes writes about the theological issues and themes related to atonement that often go misunderstood or unaddressed. This creatively written work stresses that by seeking to understand these other things one is able to understand the complexity of the atonement.

———, ed. *Sacrifice and Redemption: Durham Essays in Theology*. Cambridge: Cambridge University Press, 1991. In this collection of essays Sykes compiles a variety of opinions on the meaning of sacrifice and its significance within Christianity. By offering the reader different theological perspectives he allows one to form his or her own opinion.

Tannehill, Robert C. *Dying and Rising with Christ: A Study in Pauline Theology*. Berlin: Alfred Töpelmann, 1967; reprint, Eugene, OR: Wipf and Stock, 2006. This is a wonderful, short exegetical study of a neglected but crucial theme in Paul's letters. Tannehill also treats the concepts of "old being" and "new being" and views them as primarily corporate.

Taylor, Vincent. *Jesus and His Sacrifice: A Study of the Passion-Sayings in the Gospels*. 1937. Reprint, London: Macmillan, 1955. Through examination of OT material and the passion sayings in the Gospels, Taylor discusses the true meaning of "sacrifice." It is through this that the meaning of atonement is best understood.

———. *The Atonement in New Testament Teaching*. London: Epworth, 1941. Reprint, Eugene, OR: Wipf and Stock, 2009. This is a didactic and text-based look at NT thought about atonement, followed by a discussion of the implications and problems associated with the doctrine of atonement in light of NT teaching.

Torrance, Thomas F. *Atonement: The Person and Work of Christ*. Edited by Robert T. Walker. Downers Grove, IL: InterVarsity, 2009. This work looks at a variety of facets within the topic of the atonement. Torrance understood the complexity of this issue and addresses at length the incarnation, death, resurrection, and ascension of Jesus in order to comprehend what the atonement meant for Jesus' life and for our lives.

Trelstad, Marit, ed. *Cross Examinations: Readings on the Meaning of the Cross Today*. Minneapolis: Augsburg Fortress, 2006. This collection of essays examines both positive and negative views of the cross. Through exploring the suffering of the cross and the peace and atonement it brought one is able to gain better understanding of its importance.

Tull, James E. *The Atoning Gospel*. Macon, GA: Mercer University Press, 1982. A topical, practical discussion of the doctrine of atonement as it relates to Christian life; specifically to other doctrines, to the character of Christ, and to the life of the church. The author is a Southern Baptist theologian.

Turner, H. E. W. *The Patristic Doctrine of Redemption: A Study of the Development of Doctrine During the First Five Centuries*. London: Mowbray, 1952. Reprint, Eugene, OR: Wipf & Stock, 2004. Turner summarizes different views of the atonement during the Patristic period. Christ was viewed variously as illuminator, victor, giver, and victim. This is a helpful historical analysis of atonement options.

Tuttle, Gary A., ed. *Biblical and Near Eastern Studies: Essays in Honor of William Sanford LaSor*. Grand Rapids: Eerdmans, 1978. This collection covers a variety of New and Old Testament topics as well as Ancient Near Eastern subjects, giving a broad background to ancient Jewish understandings of sin, judgment, and Messiah.

Volf, Miroslav. *The End of Memory: Remembering Rightly in a Violent World*. Grand Rapids: Eerdmans, 2006. Memory is a powerful tool that can allow one reconciliation or generate anger. Volf writes about the importance of truthfully remembering events, but also the blessing of forgetting other aspects in order to move on.

———. "Forgiveness, Reconciliation and Justice." Pages 268–87 in *Stricken by God? Nonviolent Identification and the Victory of Christ*. Grand Rapids: Eerdmans, 2007. Volf believes that at the heart of Christianity is peaceful living, and in this essay he argues why this is the case.

Waldenström, Paul Peter. *The Reconciliation. Who Was to Be Reconciled? God or Man? Or God and Man? Some Chapters on the Biblical View of the Atonement*. Translated with notes and introduction by J. G. Princell. Chicago: John Martenson, 1888. Waldenström's view on atonement challenged the reader to rethink the basis of reconciliation. God did not need reconciliation as he is perfect; rather, sinful humans needed to be reconciled with God in order to live.

Weaver, J. Denny. *The Nonviolent Atonement*. Grand Rapids: Eerdmans, 2001. Weaver writes a thought-provoking book that deals with modern day issues such as black theology, feminist theology, and womanist theology in the context of the atonement.

West, Angela. *Deadly Innocence: Feminist Theology and the Mythology of Sin*. London: Cassell, 1990. This book challenges assumptions within feminist theology that are related to women's responsibility for sin. The author invites feminists to reconsider aspects of the Christian tradition that many feminist theologians have determined to be a stumbling block, including the acknowledgement of women's capacity for sin and biblical authority.

Wheeler, David L. *A Relational View of the Atonement: Prolegomenon to a Reconstruction of the Doctrine*. New York: Peter Lang, 1989. Wheeler discusses the components of and influences on the theology of atonement. By setting the background of the atonement, he is able to create an environment in which to discuss the nature of the atonement and how it relates to us as well as to God.

Wright, Christopher J. H. "Atonement in the Old Testament." Pages 69–82 in *The Atonement Debate: Papers from the London Symposium on the Theology of Atonement*. Edited by D. Tidball, D. Hilborn, and J. Thacker. Grand Rapids: Zondervan, 2008. The book is a collection of papers from a symposium on atonement in 2005, and the subjects treated include biblical foundations, theological contributions, historical perspectives, and contemporary perspectives. Wright's contribution gives a broad portrayal of an OT understanding of the human predicament and what it means for people and situations to be "put right." Understanding atonement language gets one partway to understanding a problem that includes guilt, shame, rebellion, disturbed shalom, broken relationships, uncleanness and death.

Young, Frances M. *The Use of Sacrificial Ideas in Greek Christian Writers from the NT to John Chrysostom*. Patristic Monograph Series 5. Cambridge: Philadelphia Patristic Foundation, 1979. Separating *sacrifice* language from *atonement* language, this work emphasizes the importance and diversity of sacrificial concepts in the theology and life of the early Eastern Church. Also important to this study is the treatment of Christ's atoning death and the sacrifice of the Eucharist.

Zahniser, A. H. Mathias. *The Mission and Death of Jesus in Islam and Christianity*. Maryknoll, NY: Orbis, 2008. This book, along with T. Lawson's *The Crucifixion and the Qur'an* (above), offers a worthwhile orientation to Jesus' death as seen from Muslim perspectives.

NORTH PARK THEOLOGICAL SEMINARY
SYMPOSIUM ON THEOLOGICAL INTERPRETATION OF SCRIPTURE

SEPTEMBER 23–25, 2010

ATONEMENT

PRESENTERS

BRIAN BANTUM
Seattle Pacific University, Assistant Professor of Theology

VIKTOR BER
Evangelikální teologický seminář, Czech Republic, Lecturer in Old Testament

HANS BOERSMA
Regent College, J. I. Packer Professor of Theology

WILLIAM P. BROWN
Columbia Theological Seminary, Professor of Old Testament

MICHELLE A. CLIFTON-SODERSTROM
North Park Theological Seminary, Associate Professor of Theology and Ethics

MICHAEL J. GORMAN
St. Mary's Seminary and University, Professor of Sacred Scripture and Dean of the Ecumenical Institute of Theology

PETER W. MARTENS
Saint Louis University, Assistant Professor of Greek Patristics

CAROL NORÉN
North Park Theological Seminary, Professor of Homiletics

LINDA D. PEACORE
Fuller Theological Seminary, Adjunct Professor of Theology

RESPONDENTS

JO ANN DEASY
    Sojourner Covenant Church, Interim Pastor

MICHAEL HARDIN
    Preaching Peace, Executive Director

MARK HUSBANDS
    Hope College, Associate Professor of Reformed Theology

TIMOTHY J. JOHNSON
    North Park Theological Seminary, Associate Professor of Ministry/Director of Field Education

MICHAEL LeFEBVRE
    Pastor, Christ Church Reformed Presbyterian Church

TROY MARTIN
    Saint Xavier University, Professor of New Testament

BRADLEY NASSIF
    North Park University, Professor of Biblical and Theological Studies

JEREMY J. WYNNE
    Whitworth University, Adjunct Professor of Theology

EX AUDITU

Volumes Available

Vol. 1 (1985) consists of selected articles presenting the issues inherent in the theological interpretation of Scripture.

Vol. 2 (1986) discusses the theme: "Church and State Relationship." In addition, there are two lead articles: one by Peter Stuhlmacher on "EX AUDITU and the Theological Interpretation of Holy Scripture," and the second by Ben F. Meyer on "The Primacy of Consent and the Uses of Suspicion."

Vol. 3 (1987) "Creation."
Vol. 4 (1988) "The Church and Israel (Romans 9–11)."
Vol. 5 (1989) "What is Salvation?"
Vol. 6 (1990) "Prophetic and/or Apocalyptic Eschatology."
Vol. 7 (1991) "Christology and Incarnation."
Vol. 8 (1992) "Worship."
Vol. 9 (1993) "Resurrection."
Vol. 10 (1994) "The Church."
Vol. 11 (1995) "Biblical Law and Liberty."
Vol. 12 (1996) "Holy Spirit."
Vol. 13 (1997) "What is a Human?"
Vol. 14 (1998) "The Theological Significance of the Earthly Jesus."
Vol. 15 (1999) "Idolatry and the Understanding of God."
Vol. 16 (2000) "The Task of Interpreting Scripture Theologically."
Vol. 17 (2001) "Biblical Ethics."
Vol. 18 (2002) "Spiritual Formation."
Vol. 19 (2003) "The Authority and Function of Scripture."
Vol. 20 (2004) "Judgment."
Vol. 21 (2005) "Health and Healing."
Vol. 22 (2006) "Justice."
Vol. 23 (2007) "Christianity's Engagement with Culture."
Vol. 24 (2008) "The Idolatry of Security."
Vol. 25 (2009) "Conversion."
Vol. 26 (2010) "Atonement."

Pickwick Publications
An Imprint of Wipf & Stock Publishers
199 West 8th Avenue, Ste. 3
Eugene OR 97401

www.ingramcontent.com/pod-product-compliance
Lightning Source LLC
Chambersburg PA
CBHW081350230426
43667CB00017B/2786